AF510410

Women Prisoners in Custody

JAYASREE LAKKARAJU

2008
Kaveri Books
New Delhi - 110 002

First Published in 2008

ISBN-10: 81-7479- 091-8
ISBN-13: 978-81-7479- 091-0

Published by
Kaveri Books
4697/ 5-21 A, Ansari Road,
New Delhi - 110 002 (India).
Ph.: 011-2328 8140, 2324 5799
E-mail: kaveribooks@vsnl.com

Laser Typesetting by
Aarati Computers, Delhi - 110 009

PRINTED IN INDIA

Dedicated

To

My Beloved Father

LAKKARAJU VENKATA LAKSHMI NARASIMHA RAO

Acknowledgment

First of all, I wish to express my profound sense of gratitude to my Research Director, **Prof. N. Rangaiah,** *LL.M., Ph.D.,* Professor of Law, P.G. Department of Legal Studies and Research, Acharya Nagarjuna University a for his supervision and able guidance. But for his encouragement and constructive criticism, I am sure, this work would not have been completed.

During the field study officers of the Jail Department, Government of Andhra Pradesh, helped me with all their co-operation and support. **Sri M.A. Basith,** *I.P.S.,* Director General and Inspector General of Prisons and Correctional services at that time gladly welcomed the study on women prisoners and promptly issued the letter of permission to visit all the Central Jails in the State of Andhra Pradesh. I express my sincere thanks to Sri M.A. Basith.

Special thanks are due to **Sri M.R. Ahmed**, D.I.G. of Prisons, Hyderabad for sharing his experiences in the Jail Administration and for providing information on the proposed jail reforms in the State of Andhra Pradesh. He is a resourceful person on the Prison Administration and a discussion with him on the subject before visiting the jails helped me a lot in preparing myself for the empirical part of the study.

I also thank **Sri B. Mahendar Reddy**, D.I.G., Central Prison, Rajahmundry, **Sri B. Samuel Johnson**, D.I.G.

Central Prison, Cuddapah, **Sri A.G. Sainatha Reddy**, Superintendent of Central Prison, Visakhapatnam for helping me by providing the necessary data on the women prisoners under their custody.

I express my sincere thanks to **Ms. R. Sarada**, Superintendent of State Jail for Women, Hyderabad, **Ms. T.V. Lakshmi**, Jailor in the State Jail for Women, Rajahmundry who went out of the way in helping me in all aspects during my visits to jails. But for their soft-spoken nature and compassion towards women prisoners my task of interviewing the prisoners couldn't have been completed.

My thanks are due to **Sri P.G. Sai Ram Prakash**, Jailor, State Institute for Correctional Administration (SICA) without whose support, I couldn't have access to the Jail Administration in Andhra Pradesh.

I am thankful to **Dr. K. Krishna Murthy**, Medical Superintendent, Mental Health Hospital, Hyderabad and to **Dr. G. Bhagya Rao**, Medical Officer, Mental Health Hospital, Visakhapatnam for permitting me to visit mentally ill-prisoners. **Dr. Krishna Murthy** spent considerable time in discussing the Mental Health Act and made several suggestions which formed part of my study.

I also express my thanks to the officer-in-charge of State Rescue Home, Hyderabad for providing the data on the women held in the Home.

I fail in my duty if I do not express my thanks to all the women prisoners in Andhra Pradesh for their willingness to share their custodial experiences which formed the basis for my study.

— L. Jayasree

Preface

Crime and criminality are terms of neutral gender. Any one can commit a crime. Women are no exception. The State has the authority to apprehend, prosecute, sentence and keep in custody any person committing a crime. The police can arrest any one irrespective of sex and keep him/her in their custody as authorised by law. When such an arrested person is produced before the Magistrate he/she may be remanded to police/judicial custody. On conviction a sentence may be imposed and he/she may be sent to prison custody.

Whatever may be the type of custody, the International Conventions demand a dignified treatment of the prisoners. Except the freedom of movement, it is agreed, every aspect of life should be fair to the persons in custody. There are several safety provisions in the law. Guidelines by the judiciary and administrative instructions also exist in order to protect the dignity of the prisoners.

Despite all the good intentions of the State, custodial violence is often reported. Incidents of unlawful detentions, use of abusive and threatening language against people in custody, not caring for the prisoners' rights, torture, custodial deaths, etc., are normal occurrences. This scenario is common for both the sexes in custody.

The condition of women in custody is further aggravated by the gender syndrome. By their very sex, the women are susceptible to many sexual aggressions, more so when the custodians are male. Touching private parts, threat of rape or even rape, molestation and sexual harassment are some of the custodial violations recorded against women. Thus the condition of women prisoners became a hot topic for debate and discussion among the Human Rights activists and academicians.

The Expert Committee which studied the conditions of women prisoners recommended compassionate and dignified handling of women in custody. In order to protect the women in various custodies effective safeguards against possible violations and victimisation are essential in a sound criminal justice system.

The Indian Constitution sanctioned positive discrimination towards the socially disadvantaged section of the people. Women and children are part of such people who needed special privileges and Art. 15(3) of the Constitution permitted the State to make special laws including the laws to protect the women in custody. However, the existing laws to protect women in custody under various statutes like I.P.C., Cr.P.C. and Prison Acts are not many. This is the state of affairs in the 60th year of Independent India. In the absence of adequate protective provisions and ubiquitous unbecoming attitude of the custodians, violence against women in custody is on the increase.

For some reasons both sociologists and criminologists have not paid much attention to the subject of 'women criminals'. The conditions of women in penal and non-penal custodies, the statutory protections that are available to them, the judicial directions issued, the recommendations of various committees and commissions and their implementation is not studied in their totality.

It is in this backdrop that the entire subject of custodial justice to women deserves a comprehensive and critical study. The present work is an attempt to understand the custodial justice meted out to women under police, jail, social welfare and mental health custodies in Andhra Pradesh besides discussing the legal provisions available for the protection of women in custody and to identify the shortcomings in the substantive law and procedures followed, and to offer appropriate suggestions to make the life of women in custody more humane.

Contents

List of Cases

A.R. Antulay v. R.S. Nayak, (1992) 1 SCC 225: AIR 1992 SC 1701: 1992 CriLJ 2717.

Agarwal v. Smt. Ram kali, AIR 1968 SC 1: 1968 CriLJ 82 AC.

Anganmal (Mrs.) v. State of Tamil Nadu, 2003 CriLJ 806.

Anguri (Smt.) v. State, 2001, CriLJ 3697 (Del) (DB).

Arvinder Singh Bagga v. State of U.P., AIR 1995 SC 117: (1994) 6 SCC 565.

B.R.Shah v. D.K.Guha, AIR 1973 SC 1196.

Bharawada Bhoginbhai Hirjibhai v. State of Gujarat, AIR 1983 SC 753: (1983) 3 SCC 217: 1983 CriLJ 1096.

Bheemamma v. Station House Officer, Hyderabad, 2002 CriLJ 694.

Bhim Singh v. State of Jammu & Kashmir, AIR 1986 SC 494: (1985) 4 SCC 677: 1986 CriLJ 192.

Bijoe Emmanuel v. State of Kerala, AIR 1987 SC 748: (1986) 3 SCC 615.

Cf. Raja v. State of Haryana, (1971) 3 SCC 945.

Challa Ram Konda Reddy v. State of A.P., AIR 1989 AP 235.

Chandania v. State of U.P., 2001 CriLJ 2090 (All) (DB).

Chandrabai Yadav v. State of M.P., 1997 CriLJ 3844.

Chandrakala (Smt.) v. State of Rajasthan, 1991 Raj Cri C 426.

Chandravati v. State of U.P., 1992 CriLJ 3634.

Charles Sobhraj v. Superintendent, Central Jail, Tihar, AIR 1978 SC 1514: (1978) 4 SCC 104: 1978 CriLJ 1534.

Chinnama Sivadas v. State of Delhi Administration, Writ Petition No.2526 of 1981 order dt. 14-9-1981.

Choki v. State of Rajasthan, AIR 1971 Raj 10.

Citizens for Democracy through its President v. State of Assam, AIR 1996 SC 2193: (1995) 3 SCC 743: 1996 CriLJ 3247.

Collector of Monghyr v. Keshav Prasad Goenka, AIR 1962 SC 1614.

Common Cause, a Registered Society v. Union of India, (1999) 6 SCC 667: AIR 1999 SC 2979.

"Common Cause", a Registered Society through its Director v. Union of India, AIR 1996 SC 1619: (1996) 4 SCC 33: 1996 CriLJ 2380 (SC).

Common Cause Welfare Council of India v. Government of Maharashtra, 1995 CriLJ 4223.

D.B.M. Patnaik v. State of A.P., AIR 1974 SC 2092: (1975) 3 SCC 185: 1975 CriLJ 556.

D.K. Basu v. State of West Bengal, AIR 1997 SC 610: 1997 CriLJ 743: (1997) 1 SCC 416.

Dhanno (Smt.) v. Union of India, 2001 CriLJ 4119 (Del) (DB).

Dharambir v. State of U.P., (1979) 3 SCC 645: 1979. SCC (Cri) 862: AIR 1979 SC 1595.

Dharmishtaben Narendrasinh Zala v. State of Gujarat, 1997 CriLJ 3866.

Durga (Smt.) v. State of Rajasthan, 1981 Raj Cri C 100.

Fattuji v. Superintendent of Police, Akola, 2002 CriLJ 914.

Francis Coralie Mullin v. Administrator, Union of Territory of Delhi, AIR 1981SC 746: (1981) 1 SCC 608: 1981 CriLJ 306 (SC).

Gaurav Jain v. Union of India, (1997) 8 SCC 114: AIR 1997 SC 3021.

Geeta (Smt.) v. Lt. Governor, 1999 CriLJ 1099 (Del).

Gurcharan Singh v. State (Delhi Administration), AIR 1978 SC 179: 1978 CriLJ 129.

Hiraman S/ o. Sakharam Borkar v. State of Maharashtra, 2000 CriLJ 4185 (Bom).

Harbans Kaur v. Union of India, (1995) 1 SCC 623.

Hussainara Khatoon v. Home Secretary, State of Bihar, AIR 1979 SC 1360: 1979 CriLJ 1036: (1980) 1 SCC 81.

Hussainara Khatoon II v. Home Secretary, State of Bihar, AIR 1979 SC 1369: 1979 CriLJ 1045: (1980) 1 SCC 98.

Inder Singh v. State of Punjab, AIR 1995 SC 1949: (1995) 3 SCC 702: 1995 CriLJ 3235.

Jacob George (Dr.) v. State of Kerala, (1994) 3 SCC 430: 1994 CriLJ 3851.

Jagadguru Sachidananda Shankarabharati Swami of Sri Kudli Sringeri Mutt v. State of Mysore, AIR 1969 Mys 96: 1969 CriLJ 423.

Jagruti v. S.G. Chaudhari, 1998 CriLJ 3251 (Guj).

Joginder Kumar v. State of U.P. and Others, AIR 1994 SC 1349: (1994) 4 SCC 260: 1994 CriLJ 1981.

K. Narayana Patra v. Gopinath Sahu, 1991 CriLJ 3219: (1991) 2 Orissa LR 301.

Kadra Pahadiya v. State of Bihar, AIR 1981 SC 939: (1981) 3 SCC 671: 1981 CriLJ 481.

Kalaben Kalabhai Desai v. Alabhai Karamshibhai Desai, AIR 2000 Guj 232.

Kamalabai v. State of Maharashtra, AIR 1962 SC 1189.

Kamini Bala Talukdav (Smt.) v. State of Assam, 1987 CriLJ 874 (Guj).

Kamla Devi (Smt.) v. Govt. of National Capital Territory of Delhi, 2000 CriLJ 4867 (Del) (DB).

Kane, W/ o. Manguram v. State, 1987 CriLR (Raj) 312.

Kashmira Singh v. State of Punjab, AIR 1977 SC 2147: (1977) 4 SCC 291: 1977 CriLJ 1746.

Kaveri v. State, 1995 CriLJ 224.

Kewal Pati v. State of U.P., 1995 CriLJ 2920: (1995) 3 SCC 600: (1995) 2 SCJ 540.

Khatri v. State of Bihar, AIR 1981 SC 928: (1981) 1 SCC 635.

Khedat Mazdoor Chetna Sangathan v. State of Madhya Pradesh, (1994) 6 SCC 260: AIR 1995 SC 31: 1995 CriLJ 508.

Kishore Singh Ravinder Dev v. State of Rajasthan, AIR 1981 SC 625: (1981) 1 SCC 503: 1981 CriLJ 17.

Krishan Lal v. State of Haryana, (1980) 3 SCC 150: AIR 1980 SC 1252.

Kulwanti v. M.P. State, AIR 1953 SC 131.

Lahari Bai (Smt.) v. State of Rajasthan, 1996 CriLJ 682 (Raj).

Lawyers' Forum for Human Rights, Calcutta v. State of West Bengal, 1997 CriLJ 1762 (Cal).

M.H. Hoskot v. State of Maharashtra, 1978 CriLJ 1678: AIR 1978 SC 1548: (1978) 3 SCC 544.

M.J. Marjina Begum and others v. Matakhal Ali, 1978 CriLJ NOC 292 (Gau).

M.P. Sharma v. Satish Chandra, District Magistrate, Delhi, AIR 1954 SC 300: 1954 CriLJ 865.

Madani (Smt.) v. State of Rajsthan, 1980 CriLR (Raj) 499.

Madhu Kishwar v. State of Bihar, (1996) 5 SCC 125: AIR 1996 SC 1864.

Madina (Mst) v. State of Rajasthan, 2000 CriLJ 4484 (Raj).

Manju Bhatia (Mrs.) v. New Delhi Municipal Corporation, AIR 1998 SC 223: (1997) 6 SCC 370.

Miranda v. Arizona, (1996) 384 U.S. 436.

Mohammad Giasuddin v. State of Andhra Pradesh, AIR 1977 SC 1926: (1977) 3 SCC 287: 1977 CriLJ 1557.

Motilal v. State, (1958) 24 CutLJ 445.

Moti Ram v. State of M.P., AIR 1978 SC 1594: (1978) 4 SCC 47: 1978 CriLJ 1703.

Muktaram Sitaram Shinde v. State of Maharashtra, 1997 CriLJ 3458.

Murti Devi v. State of Delhi, (1998) 9 SCC 604.

Nandhini Satpathy (Smt.) v. P.L.Dani, AIR 1978 SC 1025: 1978 CriLJ 968: (1978) 2 SCC 424.

Nilabati Behere (Smt.) alias Lalitha Behera v. State of Orissa, AIR 1993 SC 1960: 1993 CriLJ 2899: (1993) 2 SCC 746.

P. Viswanathan v. A.K. Burman, 2003 CriLJ 949.

Paschim Banga Khet Mazdoor Samity v. State of West Bengal, AIR 1996 SC 2426: 1996(4) SCC 37.

People's Union for Civil Liberties v. Union of India, AIR 1997 SC 1203: (1997) 3 SCC 433.

Prabha Datt v. Union of India, AIR 1982 SC 6: (1982) 1 SCC 1: 1982 CriLJ 148.

Praful Kumar Sinha v. State of Bihar, 1994 SCC (Cri) 1666: (1994) Supp 3 SCC 100.

Pramod Kumar v. Smt. Sadhana Rani, 1989 CriLJ 1772.

Prem Shankar Shukla v. Delhi Administration, AIR 1980 SC 1535: 1980 CriLJ 930: (1980) 3 SCC 526.

Puppala Seetaramaiah v. Superintendent, Sub-jail, Bapatla, 2003 CriLJ 2978.

R. Raj Gopal v. State of Tamil Nadu, AIR 1995 SC 264: (1995) 2 SCJ 86; (1994) 6 SCC 632.

Raghunath Das v. Hari Mohan Pani, 1988 CriLJ 1573.

Raj Deo Sharma v. State of Bihar, AIR 1998 SC 3281: (1998) 7 SCC 507: 1998 CriLJ 4596.

Rajyalakshmi v. State, (1956) C.W.N. 221.

Rakesh Chandra Narain v. State of Bihar, (1986) Scale 739.

Rameshwari Devi (Smt.) v. State of Rajasthan, 1979 CriLR (Raj) 601.

Rudul Shah v. State of Bihar, AIR 1983 SC 1086: (1983) 4 SCC 141: 1983 CriLJ 1644.

SAHELI v. Commission of Police, Delhi, AIR 1990 SC 513: (1990) 1 SCC 422.

Samata Vedika v. State of Karnataka, 2003 CriLJ 1003.

Samji Ladha v. State of Gujarat, 1998 CriLJ 2746 (Guj).

Sangeeta v. State, 1995 CriLJ 3923.

Sanjay Suri v. Delhi Administration, AIR 1988 SC 414: 1988 CriLJ 705.

Savitri Behra v. State of Orissa, 1998 CriLJ 4716 (Ori).

Shakuntala v. Viruppanna S., 2001 CriLJ 1129 (Kant).

Shakuntala Devi v. State of U.P., 1986 CriLJ 365 (All).

Sheela Barse v. State of Maharashtra, 1983 CriLJ 642: AIR 1983 SC 378: (1983) 2 SCC 96.

Sheela Barse v. State of Maharashtra, 1988 (1) Bom CR 58.

Sheela Barse v. Union of India, AIR 1986 SC 1773: (1986) 3 SCC 632: 1986 CriLJ 1736.

Shyama Devi v. National Capital of Delhi, AIR 1999 Del 264.

Sidheswar Ganguly v. State of West Bengal, AIR 1958 SC 143: 1958 CriLJ 273.

Solgabai Sunil Pawar v. State of Maharashtra, 1998 CriLJ 1505 (Bom).

Soubhagya (Smt.) v. Chief Secretary, State of Karnataka, 2001 CriLJ 238 (Kant).

State v. Charulata Joshi, 1999 CriLJ 2273.

State v. Ravi alias Munna, 2000 CriLJ 1125.

State of Andhra Pradesh v. Challa Ramakrishna Reddy, AIR 2000 SC 2083: (2000) 5 SCC 712.

State of Gujarat v. Hon'ble High Court of Gujarat, AIR 1998 SC 3164: 1998 CriLJ 4561: (1998) 7 SCC 392.

State of Himachal Pradesh v. Sheelan Devi, 1986 CriLJ 245.

State of Madhya Pradesh v. Shyam Sunder Trivedi, (1995) 4 SCC 262.

State of Madhya Pradesh v. Veereshwar Rao Agnihotri, 1957 SCJ 515: AIR 1957 SC 592: 1957 CriLJ 892.

State of Maharashtra v. Chandra Prakash K. Jain, AIR 1990 SC 658: 1990 CriLJ 889: (1990) 1 SCC 550.

State of Maharashtra v. Common Cause Welfare Council of India, 2004 CriLJ 14.

State of Maharashtra v. Madhukar Narain Mardikar, 1991 CriLR (SC) 187: AIR 1991 SC 207: (1991) 1 SCC 57.

State of Maharashtra v. Manubhai Pragaji Vashi, AIR 1996 SC 1: (1995) 5 SCC 730.

State of Maharashtra v. Prabhakar Panduranga Sanzgiri, AIR 1966 SC 424: 1966 CriLJ 311.

State of Maharashtra v. Ravikant S. Patil, (1991) 2 SCC 373.

State of Punjab v. Gurmit Singh, AIR 1996 SC 1393: 1996 CriLJ 1728: (1996) 1 SCJ 566: (1996) 2 SCC 384.

State of Tamil Nadu v. Nalini, AIR 1999 SC 2640.

State of U.P. v. Jogendra Singh, AIR 1963 SC 1618: 1963 CriLJ 529.

State of U.P. v. Ram Sagar Yadav, AIR 1985 SC 416: (1985) 1 SCC 552: 1986 CriLJ 836.

Suguna (Smt.) v. State of Karnataka, 2000 CriLJ 4408 (Kant).

Suk Das v. Union Territory of Arunachal Pradesh, AIR 1986 SC 991: (1986) 2 SCC 401: 1986 CriLJ 1084.

Sunil Batra v. Delhi Administration, AIR 1978 SC 1675: 1978 CriLJ 1741: (1978) 4 SCC 494.

Sunil Gupta v. State of M.P., (1990) 3 SCC 119.

Supreme Court Legal Aid Committee v. State of Bihar, (1991) 3 SCC 482.

Suresh Kumari v. State of Haryana, 1995 (4) Crimes 643. CPS 14.

Sushila Devi v. Sharada Devi, 1961 CriLJ 819 (M.P.).

T. Joicy (Smt.). v. Union of India, 2000 CriLJ 764 (Gau) (DB).

Tilotama Kar v. Ranjitarani Satpathy, (1992) 1 Orissa LR 437.

Triveniben v. State of Gujarat, AIR 1989 SC 142: (1988) 4 SCC 574: 1989 CriLJ 870.

Tukaram and another v. State of Maharashtra, AIR 1979 SC 185: 1978 CriLJ 1864: (1979) 2 SCC 143.

Uchhab Kanwar (Smt.) v. L.R. of Ram Swaroop, AIR 1995 Raj 209.

Upendra Baxi v. State of U.P., (1986) 3 SCJ 291: 1986 SCC (Cri) 381: AIR 1987 SC 191: (1986) 4 SCC 106.

Vishal Jeet v. Union of India, AIR 1990 SC 1412: 1990 CriLJ 1469: (1990) 3 SCC 318.

Wasim Beg v. State of U.P., AIR 1998 SC 1291.

Zain Yar Jung v. Raghotam, AIR 1957 Andhra 468: 1957 CriLJ 935.

Abbreviations

A.C.	-	Appeal Cases
A.I.R.	-	All India Reporter
A.P.	-	Andhra Pradesh
All.	-	Allahabad
All.L.J.	-	Allahabad Law Journal
Art.	-	Article
Bom.	-	Bombay
Bom.C.R.	-	Bombay Crime Reporter
C.W.N.	-	Calcutta Weekly Notes
Cal.	-	Calcutta
Cr.P.C.	-	Criminal Procedure Code
Cri.L.J.	-	Criminal Law Journal
Cri.L.R.	-	Criminal Law Reporter
Cut.L.J.	-	Cuttack Law Journal
D.B.	-	Division Bench
Del.	-	Delhi
F.B.	-	Full Bench
Gau.	-	Gauhati
Guj.	-	Gujarat

H.C.	-	High Court
H.P.	-	Himachal Pradesh
I.P.C.	-	Indian Penal Code
I.T.P.A.	-	Immoral Traffic (Prevention) Act
Kant.	-	Karnataka
M.P.	-	Madhya Pradesh
Mys.	-	Mysore
N.C.W.	-	National Commission for Women
N.E.C.	-	National Expert Committee
N.G.Os.	-	Non-Governmental Organisations
N.H.R.C.	-	National Human Rights Commission
N.O.C.	-	Notes of Cases
Ori.	-	Orissa
Orissa L.R.	-	Orissa Law Reports
Raj.	-	Rajasthan
Raj. Cri.C.	-	Rajasthan Criminal Cases
S.C.	-	Supreme Court
S.C.C.	-	Supreme Court Cases
S.C.J.	-	Supreme Court Journal
Sec.	-	Section
S.I.C.A.	-	State Institute of Correctional Administration
S.P.O.	-	Special Police Officer
U.P.	-	Uttar Pradesh
U.S.	-	United States

1

Introduction

The criminality of women as a subject has long been neglected by both criminologists and sociologists because of their traditional belief that women are relatively less crime prone. This belief is reflected in the penal thinking as well as legal literature. Only a fraction of the attention was paid to women criminals by the scholars and reformers of the criminal justice system. Hence, the interests and needs of women criminals remained unprotected.

Various reasons can be identified for this indifference towards women criminals. The main reason is the unequal status given to women, particularly in the tradition bound Indian society. The freedom of women remained curtailed, historically. They were neither treated as independent entities nor offered economic or social freedom for thought or action. Their productivity was exploited under the manipulative feudal system in the society and patriarchal oppression within the family. So, there was no separate study on women criminals or prisoners for a long time in India.

The other reason is the involvement of low percentage of women in crime. Their statistically insignificant numbers have become a basis for continued neglect and discrimination against them at all stages of the criminal – correctional process. As per the Mulla Committee[1] report, the women in jail population hardly formed 3%. The field study conducted by the scholar on the conditions of women prisoners in Andhra Pradesh in May 2003 indicates that the percentage of women prisoners in Andhra Pradesh is as low as 4.82%. As observed by Justice J.S. Verma, former Chief Justice of India, the low numbers is partially responsible for the lack of adequate concern for the women prisoners.[2]

The third reason is the lack of interest among sociologists, psychologists and criminologists in India on research issues relating to women. They collectively failed to appreciate, understand and analyse the psychology of women and their special and separate needs. Since their interaction with women is limited both in scope and field study, whatever little work they have done suffered from bias and they stereotyped about women. This is true of the studies made on the 'Crime by Women' in different parts of the world.[3]

This lack of concern for women prisoners can also be noticed in various legislations relating to women in custody. The Indian Constitution provided safeguards to the accused in general but there are no specific provisions for protecting the women accused. The Indian Penal Code, 1860, the Criminal Procedure Code, 1973, collectively contain a negligible number of special protective provisions to women in custody. Those statutes which are exclusively applicable to prisoners viz., the Prisons Act, 1894, the Prisoners Act, 1900, the Transfer of Prisoners Act, 1950, the Prisoners (Attendance in Courts) Act, 1955 have also failed in taking into account the vulnerability of women and their special needs.

Need for the Study

The social and economic position of a section of women has changed more drastically in 20th century. Growing urbanisation and industrialisation have changed the status of women within the family. The economic independence, coupled with the social and political freedom of women have changed their status in the society. The concept of emancipation has matured women personality-wise but at the same time that attainment has brought its own perils. While the women's liberation paved the way for better social status, it also has its negative impact through the increased female criminality.[4] The growing participation of women in various fields may be one contributing factor for the increase of crime among them.[5] A report of the United Nations Secretariat's survey on female criminality, however, revealed that in developed as well as in developing countries, the crime rate among women shows a tendency either to approach nearer to, or exceed that of, their opposite sex.[6] The increase of arrest of female criminals as compared to males is also supported by Sutherland and Cressey.[7]

India is no exception. In the last decade the proportion of female arrests in total number of persons arrested has increased rapidly.[8] The crime-pattern among women varied from place to place and time to time. Female crime is higher in the states of Andhra Pradesh, Assam, Kerala, Maharashtra, West Bengal, Himachal Pradesh, and Jammu and Kashmir.[9] The increase in some of these States can perhaps be partly explained by the growing participation of women in economic activities. Studies conducted on female criminality showed that an increase in women's employment results in higher rates of female criminality.[10] According to India's nodal crime documentation body – National Crime Records Bureau (NCRB)-in 2001, 144,608 women were arrested for cognizable crimes under the Indian Penal Code. According to their data, women constituted 5.4 per cent of the total arrests in Himachal Pradesh, Maharashtra and Tamilnadu, recording the highest numbers.[11] This factor brings to the fore the need to work on the subject of women in custody and the matters relating to custodial justice. The reported custodial offences against women make it all the more necessary to undertake a critical study of the existing legal provisions, their systematic violation and the ways and means, legally and practically, to plug the loopholes in the treatment of women prisoners at various stages of accusation, conviction and confinement.

Survey of Literature

The study of female criminality was started in the nineteenth century by a French mathematician and astronomer Quetelet.[12] He compared the physical strength of males and females and postulated that since female physical strength was half that of male, the criminality in females was also half of the male violent criminality. This was followed by Lombrozo, who found that women criminals have certain abnormalities on the basis of measurements of bones of human skeletons of female criminals.[13]

Bonger[14] a Dutchman and a disciple of Karl Marx argued that socio-economic factors should form the basis for analysing the criminality of females.

Keller (1900)[15], Weidensall (1916)[16], Fernald (1920)[17], Thomas (1967)[18] opined that women may commit crime out of a sense of deficiency. Glueeks (1934)[19] examined the female offenders by studying the biological and environmental conditions to which these offenders were exposed.

Pollack (1950)[20] tried to analyse the female offenders in the light of their total integration in society and maintained that crimes were limited by the psychological and physiological characteristics in female anatomy.

Mannheim (1973)[21] tried to examine female deviance in relation to penal legislations in their historical and comparative perspective. He focussed on the discriminatory nature of the penal legislation prevalent in the U.S.A. and many parts of Europe.

Klein and Kress (1976)[22] emphasised that increase in the arrest of women may reflect the politics of law enforcement, the changing perceptions of female offenders by the criminal justice system and the changing realities of women's economic position. Thus in subsequent years, it is the socio-economic and environmental factors which have been given importance in explaining women's criminality.

The following research works of the authors given below have contributed to the study of female criminality in western countries.

Weiden Sall, J. (1916),[23] Fernald M.R. and A. Dawley (1920)[24], Glueek, S. and Gleeck, E.T. (1934),[25] Monahan Florence (1941),[26] Pollack, O. (1950)[27] & (1961),[28] Lombroso Ceasare and Ferrere W. (1958),[29] Smith Ann D. (1962),[30] Morris Rutu (1964),[31] Giallombardo, R. (1966),[32] Anderson, C.M. (1967),[33] Heidensohn, R. (1969),[34] Bertrand (1969),[35] Francis, K. (1970),[36] Cowie, J., *Cowie, V. and Slater E.* (1971),[37] Burkhart (1973),[38] Hoffman Bustamonle D. (1973),[39] Brodsky, A.M. (1975),[40] Simon, R.J. (1975),[41] & (1976),[42] Alder F. (1975)[43] & (1977),[44] Smart C. (1976),[45] (1977),[46] (1979),[47] Leventhal G. (1977),[48] Bowker Lee, H. (1978),[49] Widom C. (1978),[50] Adler and Simon (1979),[51] Jones Ann. (1980),[52] Datesman and Scarpitti (1980),[53] Marguerite Q. Warren (1981),[54] Martin R.L.Cloninger, C.R. and Guze, S.B. (1982),[55] Leonard, E. (1982),[56] Kolarczk, J. (1983),[57] Carlen P. (1983),[58] Hart J. (1985),[59] Heidensohn, F. (1985),[60] Chesney Lind (1986),[61] B. Brown (1986),[62] J.Messerschanidi (1987),[63] K. Carrington (1990),[64] A. Howe (1990),[65] M.Coin (1990),[66] P.Carlen & Warall (eds.) (1990),[67] Worrall, A. (1990),[68] Gwyhn (1993),[69] Ealton, M. (1993),[70] Carol Smart (1998),[71] Hahn Rafter N. and Heidensohn, F. (eds.) (1995),[72] Meda Chesney Lind (1997),[73] Naffine N. (1997),[74] Joy Celyn M. Pallock (1998),[75] Susan L. Miller (1998),[76] Meda Chesney-Lind and Lisa Pasko (2003).[77]

In India, professional interest in female criminality has greatly increased during the last four decades. Though the number of researchers and publications are not many, their contribution to the study is significant. Some such research works are: Sharma R.K. (Mrs.) (1963),[78] Ahuja (1969)[79] and (1970),[80] Patel, N. (1974),[81] Sivanandam, M.C. (1974),[82] Sahoni Neera K. (1975)[83], Devi Shakuntala (1975),[84] Shastri, Tara (1975),[85] Sharma, S. (1975),[86] Rani, B.M. (1977),[87] Bhanot and Misra (1978),[88] Ran B. (1981),[89] Singh, A. (1981),[90] Prasad, Krishna, S.K. (1981),[91] Nagla, B.K. (1982),[92] Misra and Gautam (1982),[93] Prasad, S.K. and Krishna, K.P. (1982),[94] Mohan and Singh (1982),[95] Singh, S. (1982),[96] Sanyal and Agarwal (1982),[97] Kawale, K.G. (1982),[98] Rao S. Venugopal (1982),[99] Trivedi and Krishna (1983),[100] Rani Bilmoria (1983),[101] Paramguru, P. (1984),[102] Sharma, R.K. (1985),[103] Sohoni, Neera, K. (1985),[104] Srivasthava, P.K. (1985),[105] Krishna K.P. and Trivedi, B.V. (1985),[106] Nagla B.K. (1985),[107] Sanyal, S. (1986),[108] Sharma M. and Dang, R. (1987),[109] Bilmoria Rani (1987),[110] Bhattacharya (1989),[111] Bose and Mukherji (1989),[112] Mohanty (1989),[113] Sharma and Madhu (1989),[114] Srivasthava, S.P. (1989),[115] Nagla, B.K. (1989),[116] Ram Ahuja (1989),[117] Jogan Shankar (1990),[118] Ghosh, S.K. (1993),[119] Nagla, B.K. (1993),[120] M.Sundara Raj (1993),[121] Chikarmane, Poornima (1999),[122] Anju Bajpai & P.K. Bajpai (2000),[123] Sonali Patnaik (2000),[124] A. Thomas William and A.I. Christopher (2004).[125]

The Survey of Literature reveals that the empirical studies in India on women criminality were made mainly under four basic categories:

(i) Nature and extent of women criminality;

(ii) Social background of female offenders;

(iii) Causes and consequences of women criminality, and

(iv) Social roles of women

But there are inadequate research studies regarding various legal rights of the women while in penal and non-penal custodies and their observance. As already pointed out by Sutherland and Cressey (1970), Rani (1987), Nagla (1991), the female criminality is on the increase. Women continue to be in jails for long periods, sometimes for very minor violations of law, unable to defend themselves and totally ignorant of the ways and means of securing legal aid or help, even to file a writ petition for quick disposal of their cases. They are not aware of the rules of remission or premature release and live a life of resignation at the mercy of the officials who seldom have any understanding of their problems. The kind of illiterate, shy, inhibited village women that usually land in jails have no courage to communicate their needs to the male staff posted to their jails and they maintain a 'purdah' as such on their sufferings as on their faces. They have no means of communicating their needs to the higher officials as there is hardly any women officers at the headquarters of the prison department who would appreciate their needs and requirements.[126]

Some of the committees appointed by the Government of India, from time to time, to study the conditions of women prisoners have also contributed to enrich the knowledge on women criminality. Some important committees include All India Jail Reforms Committee (1980-83) under the chairmanship of Justice Mulla, which studied the condition of women criminals in prisons. The National Expert Committee (1986-87) headed by the former Supreme Court Judge, Justice V.R. Krishna Iyer, studied the handling of women detainees and reviewed their treatment. The National Commission for Women, a statutory body,[127] makes periodic review of the issues concerning women, including women criminals.

It is clear from the literature that women are also crime-prone and are held in both penal and non-penal custodies and their number is increasing day by day. That the women in custody are vulnerable is evident from many reported violations of custodial justice.

Women in detention is a subject which has led to a spectrum of feelings - feelings that emanate both from the mind and the heart. It also at the same time raises a broad range of issues from ensuring gender justice to upholding the rights of the women. Human rights institutions and organizations all over the world have accorded importance to the amelioration of the conditions of women who have to undergo detention. Custodial justice to women in India is one of those areas about which the Governments have always remained very much concerned.[128]

Despite the vulnerable position of women in custody, other than the committee reports there is no systematic academic study on the conditions of women in custody in India. It is to fill this gap, an investigation into the conditions of women in custody in Andhra Pradesh is attempted through this study.

Research Problem

In the light of the above, the Researcher has formulated the following Research Problems:

1. Whether the existing constitutional and legal provisions are adequate to protect the interests of the women in custody.
2. Whether the women are safe in custody.
3. Whether the physical conditions of the custodies are in accordance with the Rules.
4. Whether the directions issued by the Supreme Court from time to time are implemented by the concerned authorities.
5. Whether the recommendations made by the National Expert Committee are implemented.
6. Whether the recommendations made by the National Commission for women are implemented.

7. Whether there are any reformative and rehabilitative programmes relating to women in custody.
8. Whether the State is implementing any after-care programmes to women prisoners.

Scope of the Study

The study is broadly aimed at understanding the legal rights of women in custody in various statutes and the practical implementation of those rights by various authorities.

The study includes both penal and non-penal custodies. Thus it consists of three principal types of custodies viz., criminal and correctional, social welfare and medical. With this orientation, the canvass of custodial institutions to be studied include:

- Police custody
- Judicial custody
- Prison custody
- Social welfare custody
- Mental health custody

Women reach these custodial centres in several ways as:

1. Accused of crime
2. Convicted of crime
3. Informants, witnesses (aiding the criminal process)
4. Detainees (detained for preventive purpose)
5. Victims of crime and those taken into protective custody
6. Lunatics
7. Prostitutes or those subjected to immoral traffic
8. Destitutes

Since the study is related to women prisoners and their legal rights in various custodies, the study is restricted to women as accused, convicted, etc., as stated above. Their interaction with the criminal justice process at every stage, from pre-arrest to arrest, remand, conviction, custodialization for correction and release as well as rehabilitation, has to be dictated by constitutional and judicial directives aimed at social and gender justice.

The study also involves the principal operation of the criminal justice system at various stages viz., the police, the magistrate, the prison and other custodial staff and the protection and after-care officers.

Objectives of the Study

The specific objectives of the study are:

a) to make a critical review of the legal status of women in custody in the Indian context through various legislations and relevant orders, recommendations, guidelines, etc.,

b) to study the various procedures and practices in handling women in various custodies,

c) to discuss the conditions governing the treatment of women in penal and non-penal institutions as existed in the statutes,

d) to review the aspects of implementation or otherwise of the legal rights of women in the custody and document any wrong treatment meted out to some of the women while in custody through the recorded cases,

e) to examine the present situation of women prisoners in the jails of Andhra Pradesh and also in some non-penal custodies,

f) to examine the efficiency of institutional and other services for the reformation and rehabilitation of women in custody,

g) to find out the reasons for the failures, if any, in implementing the legal provisions intended to protect women in custody,

h) to study the suggested measures for improving the legal, administrative and organisational efficiency in ensuring fair, humane and effective handling of women offenders at various stages of the criminal justice system, and

i) to list out and discuss the various innovative methods proposed as an alternative to the existing provisions in law and the treatment of prisoners in general and women prisoners in particular.

Hypotheses

Taking into account the research problem and the objectives of the study, as stated above, the following hypotheses are formulated for this research study.

1. At present, the conditions and treatment of women in custody are not satisfactory.

   Women are:

   (a) arrested with scant regard to norms,

   (b) ill-treated in lock-ups,

   (c) not produced before magistrate within the stipulated time,

   (d) not offered bail,

   (e) not given legal aid facility,

   (f) not treated fairly while in detention.

(2) There are no reformative and rehabilitative programmes in penal as well as non-penal custodies.

(3) The custodial authorities pay scant regard to the important directions of the Supreme Court with regard to the treatment of prisoners.

(4) The bad situation of the women in custody, both penal and non-penal, is because of the following factors:

(a) the women prisoners are mostly uneducated and ignorant of their rights,

(b) the police are authoritative and insensitive to the dignity of the women in custody,

(c) there are very few women on police and jail staff,

(d) non-observance of proper procedure in treating women in custody,

(e) non-implementation of the recommendations made by various committees and also the judicial directions,

(f) failure of the lower level judiciary in protecting women prisoners as per the legal provisions, and

(g) attitude of the custodial staff towards the conditions in custody and the treatment of women prisoners.

(5) Removal of some of the obstructive procedures in treating women in custody, effective implementation of the existing legal provisions, implementing the judicial directives and recommendations made by various committees and finally securing the sensitivity of the staff involved through appropriate orientation programmes will go a long way towards ameliorating the bad situation in which women criminals are placed and improving the conditions of custodial institutions in which they are lodged.

Methodology

The present study includes both theoretical and empirical investigation to find answers to the questions posed in the research problem and to verify the hypotheses formulated.

The theoretical study includes a critical analysis of the provisions in the Cr.P.C. and I.P.C. meant for the safety and security of the women in custody – starting from the stage of questioning of the women suspect and the time of arrest to the various stages of judicial processes. These statutory provisions concerning the women in custody are discussed in detail. The procedures, practices, jurisdiction, the powers of various authorities and the safety provisions as interpreted by the courts also formed an important part of the present study. The recommendations made by various committees and the existing provisions in A.P. Jail Manual exclusively meant for women prisoners are thoroughly reviewed. Besides, the review of statutory provisions relating to women prisoners under the Immoral Traffic (Prevention) Act, 1956 and Mental Health Act, 1987 and the directions of the Supreme Court and the recommendations made by the National Expert Committee also formed part of the present study.

The empirical part of the study deals with the assessment of actual situations which women in custody are experiencing in Andhra Pradesh (A.P.). There are in all two State Jails for Women in Andhra Pradesh situated at Rajahmundry and Hyderabad, where all women convicted for more than one month are lodged. Besides, there are separate women enclosures in other seven central jails in different parts of the State where undertrial women prisoners are confined. These jails do have a defined territorial jurisdiction. However, there is a provision for transfer of a woman prisoner from one central jail to another, based on the prisoner's request and satisfaction of the concerned jail authorities for such a need for transfer.

The two State Jails have been visited by the researcher on two different occasions for the following purposes:

A. In order to assess the prevailing conditions in jails, observations are made on the barracks, the lock-up cells, the jail kitchen, jail school, hospital inside the jail with regard to the sanitary conditions and the way they are run.

B. To find out the actual procedure followed at the time of admission of undertrials / convicts into the jail and their release from jail, the mode of physical verification, health check, handing-over to the escort police for court appearance and the acceptance of undertrial prisoners from escort police.

C. To obtain the personal details of the women lodged in State Jails, the jail records are accessed and all the data available on the women undertrials and convicts are recorded.

D. To interview women prisoners in order to have first hand information on their experience while in custody – police and judicial - during the trial and in jail.

E. To solicit the views of the jail staff on the administrative and practical difficulties faced by them and also the rehabilitative programmes implemented, innovative methods devised for the efficient functioning of the jail, the officials concerned are interviewed.

There is only one rescue home in the State of Andhra Pradesh located at Hyderabad and two mental health hospitals-one at Hyderabad and the other at Visakhapatnam. All these three institutes were visited –

(a) to assess the physical conditions in which the women prisoners are lodged,

(b) to interview the women prisoners to obtain their version, and

(c) to interact with the custodial staff to find out the rehabilitative programmes under implementation and the proposed ones.

The data collected with the help of the above research tools are analysed, discussed and related to the hypotheses to find out whether the hypotheses formulated are proved or not.

References

1. All India Jail Reforms Committee (1980-83) – Chairman Justice Mulla.
2. Justice J.S. Verma. Key note Address, Seminar Report on 'Women in Detention', National Commission for Women, 2001, p.19.
3. Datesman and Scarpitti - Women, Crime and Justice (1980), Oxford University Press, New York, pp.6-7.
4. Nagla, B.K. - Women, Crime and Law (1991) Rawat Publications, New Delhi, pp.31-32.
5. *Ibid*., p.18.
6. Quoted in M.B. Rani, "Female Criminality – An empirical study in Andhra Pradesh" (1987), Eastern Book Company, p.2.
7. Sutherland E.H. and D.R. Cressey – Criminology (1970), J.P. Lippincott Task Force Report, New York.
8. Nagla, B.K. - *op. cit*,. p.37.
9. *Ibid*., p.38.
10. Rao, S. Venugopal – Female Criminality – Readings in Criminology (1982) Souvenir Volume, Calcutta. Cited in Nagla, B.K. *op. cit.*, p.38.
11. 'You Can't do that to her' – The Telegraph – Wednesday 21, January 2004, p.15.
12. Sur E' Momme etle development de ses faculties, sa de physique sociale, Bachelier, Paris.
13. "The Female Offender" (1958): Philosophical Library, New York.
14. Criminality and Economic Conditions, Little Brown, Boston, p.478.
15. Psychological and Environmental Study of Women Criminals. The American Journal of Sociology, pp.527-543, 671-682.

16. The Mentality of the Criminal Women, Warwick & York, Baltimore.
17. "A Study of Women Deliquencies in New York State" Century, New York.
18. The Unadjusted Girl, Harper and Rant, New York.
19. Five Hundred Delinquent Women, Knopf, New York.
20. "The Criminality of Women", University of Pennsylvania Press, Philadelphia.
21. "Comparative Criminology", Routledge and Kegan Paul, London.
22. "Any Women's Blues", Crime and Social Justice, Spring-Summer.
23. "The Mentality of the Criminal Women", Warwick & York, Baltimore.
24. "A Study of Women Delinquencies in New York State", Century, New York.
25. "Five hundred Delinquent Women", Knopf, New York.
26. "Women in Crime", Ives Washburn, Inc., New York.
27. "The Criminality of Women", University of Philadelphia Press, Philadelphia.
28. "The Criminality of Women", A.S. Barnes Company, New York.
29. "The Female Offender", Philosophical Library, New York.
30. "Women in Prison: A Study in Penal Methods", Stevens and Sons, London.
31. "Female Delinquency and Relational Problems", Social Forces 43, p.83.
32. "Society of Women : A Study of a Women's Prison", (Ed.) 1976, John Wiley & Sons, Inc., New York, Juvenile Delinquency, John Wiley & Sons, Inc., New York.
33. "The Female Offender". American Journal of Correction. 29(6), 7-9.
34. "Prison for Women". Howard Journal of Penology and Crime Prevention, 12: 281-288.
35. "Self Image and Delinquency: A contribution to the study of Female criminality and women's image", Acts Criminologica, p.71.

36. Psychological and Environmental Study of Women Criminals committing Major and Minor Crimes, The American Journal of Sociology, 527, 671-682.
37. "Delinquency in Girls", Heinemann Educational Book Ltd., London.
38. "Women in Prison", Double day, New York.
39. "The Nature of Female Criminality". Issues in Criminology, 8 No.2, (Fall): pp.117-37.
40. "The Female Offender", Sage Publications, Inc., Beverley Hills, London.
41. "Women and Crime", Mass D.C. Heath. Lexington, M.A.
42. "American Women and Crime". Annals of the American Academy of Political and Social Science 423 (January) 31-46.
43. "Sisters in Crime: The Rise of the New Female Criminal", McGraw-Hill, New York.
44. The Interaction between Women's Emancipation and Female Criminality", IJPC, May.
45. "Women, Crime and Criminology: A Feminist Critique", Routledge and Kegan Paul, London.
46. "Criminological Theory: Its ideology and Implication concerning women". The British Journal of Sociology, Vol. XXVIII, No.1, March.
47. The New Female Criminal: Reality or Myth? The British Journal of Criminology, Vol.19, No.1, January.
48. Female Criminality. Psychological Reports, 41: 1179-1182.
49. "Women, Crime and the Criminal Justice System", Mass DC, Heath, Lexington.
50. "Toward an Understanding of Female Criminality", Research, 8: 245-308.
51. "The Criminality of Deviant Women", Houghton Mifflin Company, Boston.
52. "Women Who Kill", Holf Reinchart & Winston, New York.
53. "Women, Crime and Justice". Oxford University Press, New York.
54. "Comparing Female and Male Offenders", Sage Publications, New Delhi.

55. "The Natural History of Somatization and Substance Abuse in Women Criminals; A Six Years Follow-up"; Comprehensive Psychiatry, 23(2): 528-537.
56. "Women, Crime and Society; A Critique of Theoretical Criminology", Longman, London.
57. "Psychometric Characteristics of Women Prisoners", Prezeglad Psychologiczncy 26(2): 343-351.
58. "Women's Imprisonment", Routledge and Kegan Paul, London.
59. "Why do Women Commit less Crime? New Society", 70 (1183) 298-300.
60. "Women and Crime", MacMillian Edn. Ltd., London.
61. "Women and Crime: the female offender" (1986) ed. by (Ngaire Naffine) Gender, Crime and Feminism: University of Adelaide, Australia.
62. "Women and Crime: The dark figures of criminology"; *Ibid*.
63. "Feminism, Criminology and the rise of the female sex delinquent, 1880-1930" (1987); *Ibid*.
64. Feminist readings in female delinquency (1990); *Ibid*.
65. "Prologue to a history of Women's Imprisonment in search of a feminist perspective" (1990); *Ibid*.
66. Towards Transgression: New Directions in Feminist Criminology (1990); *Ibid*.
67. Women, Crime, Feminism and Realism (1990); *Ibid*.
68. "Offending Women: Female Law Breakers and the criminal justice system", Routledge, London.
69. "Women and Crime. The Failure of Traditional Theories and the Rise of Feminist Criminology". Monash University Law Review 19(1): 92-103.
70. "Women after Prison". Milton Keyney: Open University Press.
71. Laws, Crime and Sexuality; Essays in Feminism, Sage, London.
72. International Feminist Perspectives in Criminology: Engendering a Discipline, Open University Press, Buckingham.
73. "The Female Offender – Girls, Women and Crime", Ed. by N. Naffins, Manoa: Sage Publications, New Delhi.

74. "Feminism and Criminology", Polity Press, Cambridge.
75. "Counselling Women in Prison", Texas, Sage Pub., New Delhi.
76. "Crime Control and Women", New York, Sage Publications, New Delhi.
77. "Girls, Women and Crime", University of Hawain, Sage Publications, New Delhi.
78. "Women Offenders of U.P.: A Psychological Social Study of Women Convicts and Undertrial Prisoners in U.P. Jails", Unpublished Thesis, Lucknow University.
79. "Female Offendes in India", Meenakshi Prakashan, Meerut.
80. "Female Murderers in India – A Sociological Study", The Indian Journal of Social Work, Vol. VLIII, No.20.
81. "Women and Crime", Eve's Weekly of India and "Women and Crime" Indian Journal of Criminology, Vol.12, No.2, July.
82. "A Comparative Study of the Intelligence of the normal delinquent and criminal female subjects", Indian Journal of Criminology.
83 "Women Prisoners in India", International Social Work, 18.
84. "Will Liberation Make Crime a Female Stronghold", Eve's Weekly, June 21.
85. "A Socio-economic Survey of Women Prisoners in Maharashtra State", National Institute of Social Defence, New Delhi.
86. "An Analysis of Crime Among Women in Punjab", Unpublished M.Litt. Thesis, Patiala: Punjab University.
87. "A Report of Female Criminality in India", Yojana, August 15.
88. "Criminality Amongst Women", Bureau of Police Research and Development, New Delhi.
89. "The Pattern and Nature of Female Criminality in Andhra Pradesh", Indian Journal of Social Work, Vol. XLI, No.4, pp.393-401.
90. "Personality of Female Murderers", Indian Journal of Criminology, 9.2, pp.156-160.
91. "A Study of Women Prisoners in Tamil Nadu", Paper presented at the X Annual Conference of Indian Society of Criminology, Aurangabad.

92. "Women and Crime, A Sociological Analysis of Women Criminality in India", The Indian Journal of Social Work, Vol. XLIII, No.3 (October) pp.273-282.
93. "Female Criminality – Causes and Consequences", Readings in Criminology, Souvenir Vol., Calcutta.
94. "A Study of Women Murderers in Tamil Nadu", *Ibid*.
95. "Sex Differences in the Adjustment of Murderers", Indian Journal of Criminology, Vol.10, No.1, pp.53-55.
96. "The Relationship between Menstruation and Crime", Indian Journal of Criminology, Vol. 10, No.2, pp.129-131.
97. "Self Esteem of Female Convicts", Readings in Criminology, Souvenir Vol., Calcutta.
98. "Nature of Crimes Committed by Women in Nanded", News Bulletin, ISC, Calcutta.
99. "Female Criminality", *Ibid*. Readings in Criminology, Souvenir Vol., Calcutta.
100. "Murderer and her Victim", Indian Journal of Criminology, Vol. II, No.2, pp.115-118.
101. "Homicides by Females", Indian Journal of Criminology, No.1, Jan.
102. "Women and Crime", Indian Journal of Criminology, Vol.12, No.2, July.
103. "Mass Murder by Women", Indian Journal of Criminology, Vol.13, No.1, January.
104. A Socio-Demographic Study of Women Convicts in Maharashtra, Pune University.
105. "Female Offenders", Unpublished Ph.D. Thesis, Gorakhpur University.
106. "Personal and Familial Antecedents of Female Offenders", Social Change 15(2), pp.37-42.
107. "Women and Crime: A Sociological Analysis of Women Criminality in India", Indian Journal of Criminology and Criminolistics 3 & 4, 148-157.
108. "Female Criminals in India", Uppal Publishing House, New Delhi.
109. "Crime and Women: A Psychological Perspective", Indian Journal of Criminology 15(2), pp.126-130.

110. "Female Criminality - An Empirical Study in Andhra Pradesh", Eastern Book Co., Lucknow.
111. "Female Convicts and Social Defence", in Leelamma Devasia and V.V. Devasia (eds.). "Female Criminals and Female Victims", Nagpur, Dattsons.
112. "Female Criminality: A Psychological Analysis with special emphasis on West Bengal Incidents", *Ibid*.
113. "Female Prisoners and Vocational Training", *Ibid*.
114. "Women and Crime: Psychological Implications", *Ibid*.
115. "Explaining Female Criminality and Victimization", *Ibid*.
116. "Women and Crime – A Sociological Analysis of Women Criminality in India", *Ibid*.
117. "Female Crime : A New Theoretical Perspective", *Ibid*.
118. "Devadasi Cult: A Sociological analysis", Ashish Publishing House, New Delhi.
119. "Women and Crime" – Ashish Publishing House, New Delhi.
120. "Women as Victim of Crime – A Sociological Analysis. In Dimension of Indian Womenhood" ed. by C.M. Agarwal, Almora : Shri Almora Book V.3, pp.285-305.
121. "Prostitution in Madras : A Study in Historical Perspective", Konark Publishers Pvt. Ltd., Delhi.
122. "Too Big For Their Boots? Women and the Policing of Violence against Women", pp.312-336. In Institution, Relations and outcomes : A Framework and case studies for Gender-Aware Planning, ed. by Naila Kabeer and Ramya Subrahmanian, New Delhi, Kali for women.
123. "Female Criminality in India", Rawat Publication, Jaipur.
124. "Women Criminals in India : An Approach to Crime and Rehabilitation", Anmol Publishers, New Delhi.
125. "Women Criminals in India: Sociological and Social Work Perspectives", Anmol Publishers, New Delhi.
126. Jail Reforms Committee (JRC) 1980-83, p.186: 13.6. Ref. in Report of National Expert Committee on Women Prisoners (1986-87), Vol. I, p.116.
127. Constituted by an Act of 1990.
128. Seminar Report on "Women in Detention", National Commission for Women 2001, p.15.

2

Rights of Prisoners under International Law and the Indian Constitution

There are various Conventions, Declarations and other instruments dealing with the rights of the accused in the international legal regime. Likewise, there are the Constitution of India and other laws, regulations and directions of the Government at the national level dealing with these matters. In this chapter, an attempt is made to present and analyse the international and national legal regimes concerning the rights of the accused and the prisoners. However, the scope of this survey of the rights is limited to only those rights that concern women in custody either generally or in particular.

It should be borne in mind that historically women were treated as chattel in all legal systems and as such all rights discourse consisted of only 'his' rights, and not 'his' and 'her' rights. In the immediate aftermath of the Second World War, with the advent of the new era of human rights jurisprudence, women found some space in the rights discourse, though not a proper place. The fact that the Chairperson of the drafting committee of Universal Declaration of Human Rights (UDHR) was a woman helped in drafting UDHR without much gender discrimination. However, the movement for recognition of women's rights as human rights and a woman as a fullfledged person in her own right is of recent origin. This historical backdrop is reflected in all international human rights instruments which fail to specially take care or recognise women's position. It is only in the very recent past that one finds some instruments that specifically deal with women's rights.[1] The international instruments concerning custodial justice to women are briefly discussed below, firstly the Conventions dealing with the rights of prisoners in general and secondly the specific provisions dealing with women in custody.

(i) International Legal Regime Regarding Persons in Custody

United Nations and Custodial Justice

The primary source of authority for the promulgation of human rights standards by the United Nations bodies may be found in the UN Charter itself. One of the principal aims of the organization is stated in the second preambular paragraph of the Charter.

> " ... to reaffirm faith in fundamental human rights, in the dignity and worth of the human person, in the equal rights of men and women and of nations large and small ..."

This preambulary assertion of the UN's aims recognised women as equal partners of men in the conferment of human rights.

Article 1, paragraph 3, of the Charter establishes the principle that international co-operation is to be sought in promoting and encouraging respect for human rights and for fundamental freedoms for all without distinction as to race, sex, language or religion ...

The quasi-legislative activity of the United Nations has since produced several instruments, each building on and adding more detail to its predecessors. Most importantly, for the present purpose of analysing custodial justice the important instruments are: The Universal Declaration of Human Rights (UDHR), 1948 and the two Covenants of 1966 viz. The International Covenant on Economic, Social and Cultural Rights, and the International Covenant on Civil and Political Rights. Together, these three instruments constitute the International Bill of Human Rights.[2]

Universal Declaration of Human Rights (UDHR), 1948

The Universal Declaration represents a great step forward taken by the International Community in 1948. Its persuasive moral character derives from the fact that it is agreed to be a statement of generally accepted international norms. This outline of human rights objectives is drafted in broad and general terms, and was the source - the substantive frame work - for the two other instruments making up the International Bill of Human Rights. Moreover, the Universal Declaration enumerated and defined the fundamental rights proclaimed in the Charter of the United Nations. Of particular importance for the administration of justice are Articles 3, 5, 9, 10 and 11 of the Universal Declaration. These Articles address, respectively, the right to life, liberty and security of person, the prohibition of torture and of cruel, inhuman and degrading treatment or punishment, the prohibition of arbitrary arrest, the right to a fair trial; the right to be presumed innocent until proved guilty, and the prohibition of retroactive penal measures. Thus these Articles are most directly relevant to law enforcement.

Important provisions of this Declaration are:

1) All human beings are born free and equal in dignity and rights. They are endowed with reason and conscience and should act towards one another in the spirit of brotherhood.[3]

2) Every one has a right to life, liberty and security of person.[4]

3) No one shall be subjected to torture or to cruel, inhuman or degrading treatment or punishment.[5]

4) Every one has a right to recognition everywhere as a person before the law.[6]

5) No one shall be subjected to arbitrary arrest, detention or exile.[7]

6) Everyone is entitled in full equality to a fair and public hearing by independent and impartial trial at which he has all the guarantee necessary for his defence.[8]

7) Every one charged with a penal offence has the right to be presumed innocent until proved guilty according to law in a public trial at which he has had all the guarantees necessary for his defence. No one shall be held guilty of any penal offence on account of any act or omission which did not constitute a penal offence, under national or international law, at the time when it was committed. Nor shall a heavier penalty be imposed than the one that was applicable at the time the penal offence was committed.[9]

Apart from this, Art. 7 reads, "All are equal before law and are entitled without any discrimination to equal protection of the law. All are entitled to equal protection against any discrimination in violation of this Declaration and against any incitement to such discrimination."

The International Covenant on Civil and Political Rights (ICCPR) contains similar provisions and requires the law to prohibit discrimination on any of the usual grounds such as race, colour, sex, language and religion.[10]

The European Convention on Human Rights, 1950[11]

The European Convention not only gave specific legal content to human rights in an international agreement but also provided for the establishment of a machinery for supervision and enforcement. The important provisions of this Convention are:

1) Everyone who is arrested shall be informed promptly in a language which he understands of the reasons for his arrest and of any charge against him.[12]

2) No one shall be subjected to torture or inhuman or degrading treatment or punishment.[13]

3) Every one has a right to liberty and security of person. No one shall be deprived of his liberty save in the following cases and in accordance with the procedure prescribed by the law:

   (a) The lawful detention of a person after conviction by a competent court.

   (b) The lawful arrest or detention of a person for non-compliance with the lawful order of a court or in order to secure the fulfilment of any obligation prescribed by the law.

   (c) The lawful arrest or detention of a person effected for the purpose of bringing him before the competent legal authority on reasonable suspicion of having committed an offence or when it is reasonably considered necessary to prevent him from committing an offence or fleeing after having done so.

   (d) The detention of a minor by lawful order for the purpose of educational supervision or his lawful detention for the purpose of bringing him before the competent legal authority.

   (e) The lawful detention of a person for the prevention of spreading of infectious disease; of persons of unsound mind, alcoholics or drugs-addicts or vagrants.[14]

4) Where the interest of juveniles or protection of the private life of the parties so require or to the extent strictly necessary in the opinion of a court in such circumstances where the publicity would prejudice the interest of justice, the Press may be excluded from hearing.[15]

Standard Minimum Rules for the Treatment of Prisoners, 1955[16]

The Standard Minimum Rules were adopted by the First United Nations Congress on the prevention of crime and treatment of offender held in Geneva in 1955 and later approved by the Economic and Social Council.

(1) General rules

The important rule in this part has incorporated the principle of equality, that there shall be no discrimination on ground of race, sex, colour, religion, political, or other opinion, national or social origin, property, birth or other status among prisoners. Prison authorities are supposed to respect the religious beliefs and moral precepts of the community to which a prisoner belongs.[17]

Another important rule states that the different categories of prisoners shall be kept in separate institutions or parts of the institutions on the basis of their sex, age, criminal record and other circumstances. Many of the countries like the U.K., U.S.A., India, Australia, Japan, etc., have given recognition to this rule.[18]

(2) Rules regarding separation of prisoners

The Standard rules give due consideration to the separation of the different categories of prisoners.[19] The rule states that the men and women shall so far as possible and practicable be detained in separate institutions and in the institution which requires both, the whole of the premises allocated to women shall be entirely separate.[20]

The undertrial prisoners should be kept separate from tried and convicted prisoners. There must be complete separation between the civil prisoners detained for debt, etc., and persons imprisoned by reason of a criminal offence. Young prisoners should be kept separate from adult prisoners.[21]

(3) Prohibition of corporal punishment

So far as jail offences are concerned, no punishment can be given except through proper trial. The punishments like closed confinement or reduction in diet shall never be inflicted unless the medical officer has examined the prisoner and certified in writing that the prisoner is fit to sustain such punishments. Instruments of restraint such as handcuffs, chains, irons and strait jackets shall never be applied as a punishment. Corporal punishment by placing in dark cell and all cruel, inhuman, degrading punishment shall be completely prohibited.[22]

(4) Rules for providing minimum facilities

Separate accommodation for different types of prisoners should be provided. Separate bedding and clothing giving due consideration to the hygienic conditions for living should be provided. The food served must be of nutritional value, adequate for health and strength. The services of qualified medical officers having some knowledge of psychiatry should also be made available. Facilities of T.V., radio, newspaper and magazines should also be provided. Prisoners should be allowed to communicate with their family members and friends at regular intervals.[23]

(5) Rules for under-trials

Provisions should be made for separation of under-trials on the basis of age. Young untried prisoners should be kept separate from adults and shall be detained in separate institutions. They may have their own food at their own expenses through their family and friends. They may also be allowed to wear their own clothings.[24]

(6) Social relations and after-care

These rules also provide reformative aspects of the punishment. The purpose of punishment should not be to torture but to reform the prisoner and to make him or her a good citizen. Rule 60(2) states that before the completion of the sentence, it is desirable that necessary steps should be taken to ensure for the prisoner a gradual return to normal life in society. This aim may be achieved depending on the case by a pre-release regime organised in the same institution or any other appropriate institution or by release on trial under some kind of supervision which must not be entrusted to the police but should be combined with effective social aid.

International Covenant on Civil and Political Rights, 1966

The content of the rights in the Universal Declaration received further elaboration when, in March 1976, the International Covenant on Civil and Political Rights came into force. The Covenant, in Articles 6, 7, 9, 11, 14 and 15, details the right to life; the prohibition of torture; the prohibition of arbitrary arrest or detention; the prohibition of imprisonment for failure to fulfil a contractual obligation; the right to a fair trial; and the prohibition of retroactive criminal measures. With more than 100 State parties, the Covenant is a binding instrument which must be respected by Governments and their institutions, including the police.

Its implementation is monitored by the Human Rights Committee which was established under the terms of the Covenant itself.[25]

Art. 6 (Paragraphs 1, 2, 5) states that every human being has the inherent right to life. This right shall be protected by law. No one shall be arbitrarily deprived of his life.

In countries which have not abolished the death penalty, sentence of death may be imposed only for the most serious cases in accordance with the law in force. ... ... Sentence of death shall not be imposed for crimes committed by persons below 18 years and shall not be carried out on pregnant women. Art. 7 specially deals with torture and slavery. No one shall be subjected to torture, or to cruel, inhuman or degrading treatment or punishment. In particular, no one shall be subjected, without his free consent, to medical or scientific experimentation.

Art. 9 prohibits arbitrary arrest or detention. Every one has the right to liberty and security of person. No one shall be subject to arbitrary arrest or detention. No one shall be deprived of his liberty except on such grounds and such procedures as are established by law.

Anyone who is arrested shall be informed, at the time of arrest, of the reasons for his arrest and shall be promptly informed of any charges against him.[26] Any one arrested or detained on a criminal charge shall be brought promptly before a judge or other officer authorized by law to exercise judicial power and shall be entitled to a trial within a reasonable time or to release. It shall not be the general rule that persons awaiting trial shall be detained in custody, but release may be subject to guarantees to appear for trial, at any other stage of the judicial proceedings, and should occasion arise, for execution of the judgment.[27] Anyone who is deprived of his liberty by arrest or detention shall be entitled to have proceedings before a court, in order that the court may decide without delay on the lawfulness of his detention and order his release if the detention is not lawful.[28]

Any one who has been the victim of unlawful arrest or detention shall have an enforceable right to compensation.[29]

The Covenant further mandates that all persons deprived of their liberty shall be treated with humanity and with respect for the inherent dignity of the human person.[30]

No one shall be imprisoned merely on the ground of inability to fulfil a contractual obligation, under Art. 11.

As per Art.14, all persons shall be equal before the courts and tribunals. In the determination of any criminal charge against him or of his rights and obligations in a suit at law, every one shall be entitled to a fair and public hearing by a competent, independent and impartial tribunal established by law.[31] Every one charged with a criminal offence shall have the right to be presumed innocent until proved guilty according to law.[32] In the determination of any criminal charge against him, every one shall be entitled to the following minimum guarantees, in full equality:[33]

(a) To be informed promptly and in detail in a language which he understands of the nature and cause of the charge against him;

(b) To have adequate time and facilities for the preparation of his defence and to communicate with the counsel of his own choosing;

(c) To be tried without undue delay;

(d) To be tried in his presence, and to defend himself in person or through legal assistance of his own choosing; to be informed, if he does not have legal assistance, of this right; and to have legal assistance assigned to him, in any case where the interests of justice so require and without payment by him in any such case, if he does not have sufficient means to pay for it;

(e) To examine, or have examined, the witnesses against him and to obtain the attendance and examination of the witnesses on his behalf under the same conditions as those of the witnesses against him;

(f) To have the free assistance of an interpreter if he cannot understand or speak the language used in court.

(g) Not to be compelled to testify against himself or to confess guilt.

No one shall be liable to be tried or punished again for an offence for which he has already been finally convicted or acquitted in accordance with law.[34]

Declaration on Protection from Torture, 1975

On 9th December, 1975 the United Nations by consensus adopted the Declaration on Protection from Torture, 1975. The important provisions of this Declaration are:

(1) Any act of torture or other cruel, inhuman or degrading treatment or punishment is an offence to human dignity and shall be condemned as a denial of the purposes of the Charter of the United Nations and as a violation of the human rights and fundamental freedoms proclaimed in the Universal Declaration on Human Rights.[35]

(2) No State may permit or tolerate torture or other cruel, inhuman, degrading treatment or punishment. Exceptional circumstances such as a state of war or threat of war, internal political instability or any other public emergency may not be invoked as a justification for torture or other cruel, inhuman or degrading treatment or punishment.[36]

Declaration of Medical Ethics for Protection of Prisoners and Detainees against Torture, 1982

In December 1982, the United Nations General Assembly adopted a Declaration containing six principles of medical ethics for the protection of prisoners and detainees against torture and other cruel, inhuman or degrading treatment or punishment. They are as follows:[37]

(1) Health personnel, particularly physicians, charged with the medical care of prisoners and detainees have a duty to provide them with protection of their physical and mental health and treatment of disease of the same quality and standard as is afforded to those who are not imprisoned or detained.[38]

(2) It is a gross contravention of medical ethics as well as an offence under applicable international instruments, for health personnel to engage, actively or passively, in acts which constitute participation, and complicity in incitement to commit torture or other cruel, inhuman or degrading treatment or punishment.[39]

(3) It is a contravention of medical ethics for health personnel to be involved in any professional relationship with prisoners or detainees the purpose of which is not solely to evaluate, protect or improve their physical and mental health.[40]

(4) It is a contravention of medical ethics for health personnel, (a) to apply their knowledge and skills in order to assist in the interrogation of prisoners and detainees in a manner that may adversely affect the physical or mental health or condition of such prisoners or detainees and which is not in accordance with the relevant international instruments, (b) to certify, or to participate in the certification of the fitness of prisoners or detainees for any form of treatment or punishment that may adversely affect their physical or mental

health or to participate in any way in the infliction of any such punishment or treatment which is not in accordance with the relevant international instruments.[41]

(5) It is a contravention of medical ethics for health personnel to participate in any procedure for restraining a prisoner or detainee unless such a procedure is determined in accordance with purely medical criteria as being necessary for the protection of the physical or mental health or the safety of the prisoner or detainee himself, or his fellow prisoners or detainees or of his guardians and it presents no hazards to his physical or mental health.[42]

(6) There may be no derogation from the foregoing principles on any ground whatsoever, including public emergency.[43]

Convention against Torture, 1984

The Convention against Torture and other cruel, inhuman or degrading treatment or punishment entered into force in June 1984. The Convention goes considerably further than the International Covenant on Civil and Political Rights in protecting persons against international crime and torture. Under the Convention, State parties are obliged to take effective legislative, administrative or other measures to prevent acts of torture: to commit to the principle of non-refoulement when there are grounds to suspect that a returned person would be tortured; to guarantee victims of torture a right to complain and to have their case promptly and impartially examined by competent authorities; to protect complainants and witnesses; to exclude evidence or statements obtained through torture; and to compensate victims and their dependants.[44]

The Convention is based on the Declaration, but it enlarges upon many of its provisions. For example, the definition of torture is extended under Art. 1 of the Convention to include severe pain or suffering, whether physical or mental, inflicted by or at the instigation of or with the consent or acquiescence of a public official or other person acting in an official capacity.This means that the responsibility of public officials is widened to include officials at all levels who may be held responsible if they knowingly fail to prevent torture.

Art.2 reads:

1. "Each State party shall take effective legislative, administrative, judicial or other measures to prevent acts of torture in any territory under its jurisdiction.

2. No exceptional circumstances whatsoever, whether a state of war or a threat of war, internal political instability or any other public emergency, may be invoked as a justification of torture.

3. An order from superior officer or a public authority may not be invoked as a justification of torture."

The Convention includes provisions for bringing persons accused of torture to justice, regardless of their nationality or of where the crime is alleged to have been committed. It also established the Committee against Torture to assist in the implementation of the Convention. Torture is never justified under any circumstances, and no public official has any defence available to him or her for committing torture.[45]

Further, Articles 10 and 11 of the Convention ensure that education and information regarding the prohibition against torture are included in the training of law enforcement personnel and other persons involved in the custody, interrogation or treatment of detainees and to keep under a systematic review of interrogation rules, instructions and practices with a view to preventing torture.[46]

Body of Principles for the Protection of All Persons under Any Form of Detention or Imprisonment, 1988[47]

These principles were adopted by the General Assembly in December 1988.

The Body of Principles contains 39 principles and the first principle sets out the basic requirement to treat detained or imprisoned persons in a humane manner. Some important principles are -

(i) prohibition against torture (p.6)

(ii) judicial supervision of detainees (p.4, 11 & 37).

(iii) detainees to have the right to consult legal counsel (p.11, 15,17, 18).

(iv) detainees to have the right to communicate with and retain contact with their families (p.15, 16, 19, 20).

(v) adequate medical supervision of detainees (p.24 & 26).

(vi) records to be kept of the circumstances of arrest and custody (p.12)

(vii) details of the circumstances of any interrogation to be recorded (p.23).

The question of individual responsibility of law enforcement officials is addressed in principle 7, paragraph 2. This requires the officials who believe that a violation of the Body of Principles has occurred or is about to occur to report the matter to superior authorities and where necessary, to other appropriate authorities or organs vested with reviewing or remedial powers.

The Body of Principles is more relevant to police supervision of detainees than the Standard Minimum Rule for the Treatment of Prisoners.

Basic Principles for the Treatment of Prisoners, 1990

The Basic Principles adopted by the General Assembly in December 1990, complete the regime with 11 point form standards. The Basic Principles for the Treatment of Prisoners are as follows:

(1) All prisoners shall be treated with the respect due to their inherent dignity and value as human beings.

(2) There shall be no discrimination on the grounds of race, colour, sex, language, religion, political or other opinion, national or social origin, property, birth or other status.

(3) It is, however, desirable to respect the religious beliefs and cultural precepts of the group to which prisoners belong, whenever local conditions so require.

(4) The responsibility of prisons for the custody of prisoners and for the protection of society against crime shall be discharged in keeping with a State's other social objectives and its fundamental responsibilities for promoting the well-being and development of all members of society.

(5) Except for those limitations that are demonstrably necessitated by the fact of incarceration, all prisoners shall retain the human rights and fundamental freedoms set out in the Universal Declaration of Human Rights, and, where the State concerned is a party, the International Covenant on Economic, Social and Cultural Rights, and the International Covenant on Civil and Political Rights and the Optional Protocol thereto, as well as such other rights as are set out in other United Nations Covenants.

(6) All prisoners shall have the right to take part in cultural activities and education aimed at the full development of the human personality.

(7) Efforts addressed to the abolition of solitary confinement as a punishment, or to the restriction of its use, should be undertaken and encouraged.

(8) Conditions shall be created enabling prisoners to undertake meaningful remunerated employment which will facilitate their reintegration into the country's labour market and permit them to contribute to their own financial support and to that of their families.

(9) Prisoners shall have access to the health services available in the country without discrimination on the grounds of their legal situation.

(10) With the participation and help of the community and social institutions, and with due regard to the interests of victims, favourable conditions shall be created for the reintegration of the ex-prisoner into society under the best possible conditions.

(11) The above principles shall be applied impartially.[48]

Thus these three instruments i.e., Body of Principles, Standard Minimum Rules and Basic Principles provide a comprehensive regime for the protection of rights of the persons who are detained or imprisoned.

In sum, they provide that all prisoners and detainees must be treated with respect and human dignity, with regard to the conditions of their detention; treatment and discipline; contact with the outside world; health; classification and separation; complaints; records; work and recreation and religion and culture.[49]

Standard Minimum Rules for Non-Custodial Measures, 1990

In December 1990, the General Assembly adopted the United Nations Standard Minimum Rules for Non-

Custodial Measures (Tokyo Rules) in order to encourage the provision by States of a wide range of non-custodial measures. Such measures increase community involvement in the management of criminal justice and serve the cause of justice, while reducing the use of imprisonment, which in every case should be seen as an extreme penalty. Under the rules, these measures are to take into consideration the human rights and rehabilitation of the offenders; the protection of society and the interests of victims. The rules provide guidance for the use of furlough, work release, parole remission, pardon, community service, economic sanctions, etc.[50]

Special rules in favour of women

The special status of women is acknowledged and protected by two types of provisions, "one requiring women detainees to be accommodated separately from men, and the other on the question of discrimination."

Women and discrimination

The principle of non-discrimination is fundamental to protect the rights and special status of women.

Discrimination in the enjoyment of human rights is prohibited under the principal human rights instruments. For example, Art. 2 of the Universal Declaration of Human Rights states:

> "Everyone is entitled to all the rights and freedoms set forth in the Declaration, without distinction of any kind, such as race, colour, sex, language ..... or other status."

Various human rights treaties bind parties to ensure the rights enshrined in the treaties to all without discrimination; including discrimination on grounds of sex. This type of provision is included in Art. 2 of the International Covenant on Civil and Political Rights and Art. 14 of the European Convention on Human Rights.

Art. 3 of the International Covenant on Civil and Political Rights adds an extra requirement that State parties must ensure the equal right of men and women to enjoy all civil and political rights set out in the Covenant.

There are two international instruments dealing specifically with discrimination against women: the Declaration on the Elimination of Discrimination against Women, 1967; and the Convention on the Elimination of All Forms of Discrimination against Women 1979.

Art. 1 of the Declaration states that discrimination against women "is fundamentally unjust and constitutes an offence against human dignity.[51]

Art. 2 requires all appropriate measures to be taken to abolish the laws, customs, regulations and practices which are discriminatory against women, and to establish adequate legal protection for equal rights of men and women.[52]

Art. 3 requires all appropriate measures to be taken to educate public opinion, and to direct national aspirations towards the eradication of prejudices and the abolition of practices which are based on the idea of the inferiority of women.[53]

Art. 8 of the Declaration requires all appropriate measures, including legislative measures, to be taken to combat all forms of traffic in women and exploitation of prostitution of women.[54]

A definition of "discrimination against women is set out in Art. 1 of the Convention on the Elimination of All Forms of Discrimination Against Women, which states that the term means:

> ". . . any distinction, exclusion or restriction made on the basis of sex which has the effect or purpose of impairing or nullifying the recognition, enjoyment or

exercise by women, irrespective of their marital status, on a basis of equality of men and women, of human rights and fundamental freedoms in the political, economic, social, cultural, civil or any other field."

Art. 2 of the Convention requires State parties to condemn discrimination against women in all its forms, and to agree to pursue a policy of eliminating such discrimination. The Article requires States to take a number of measures, which include embodying the principle of the equality of men and women in national constitution or legislation; adopting legislative measures prohibiting discrimination against women; establishing legal protection of the rights of women on an equal basis with men; and taking measures to eliminate discrimination against women by any person, organization or enterprise.

Art. 6 requires the States to take all appropriate measures, including legislation, to suppress all forms of traffic in women and exploitation of prostitution of women.[55]

Two aspects of non-discrimination particularly relevant to the protection of women, and of special importance to the matters considered under the next two subheadings, are the right to equality before the law and the right to equal protection of the law. These rights are enshrined in Art. 7 of the Universal Declaration of Human Rights and the same rights are repeated in Art. 26 of the International Covenant on Civil and Political Rights.

Clearly, the process of law enforcement is one of the means by which people may secure equality before the law and be given the protection of the law, and policing must be carried out in such a way that these rights are respected.[56]

Women as detainees

The rights and special status of women detainees should be recognized by all police officials.

The following requirements in relation to women detainees are emphasized:

(i) Accommodation is dealt with in rule 8 of the Standard Minimum Rules for the Treatment of Prisoners. This rule says:

(a) different categories of prisoners to be kept in separate institutions or parts of institutions, taking account of their sex, age, criminal record, etc.

(b) men and women to be kept, so far as possible, in separate institutions. In an institution which houses both men and women, the premises allocated to women are to be kept entirely separate.[57]

While, generally, the provision of separate institutions and premises for women detained in police custody is neither necessary nor feasible, the principle that they should be accommodated separately from men must strictly be complied with[58]

(ii) Women police officials to supervise women detainees.

(iii) Women detainees are to be searched by women.

Discrimination against women is dealt with in principle 5 of the Body of Principles for the Protection of All Persons under Any Form of Detention or Imprisonment. This stipulates that:

(a) the principles are to be applied without distinction of any kind, such as race, colour, sex, language, etc.

(b) measures applied under the law and designed solely to protect the rights and special status of women, especially pregnant women and nursing mothers, shall not be deemed to be discriminatory.

In order for the rights and special status of women detainees to be respected, it is necessary for:

(a) all law enforcement officials to be aware of the standards they are to comply within their treatment of detainees, and of those standards relating particularly to women;

(b) officials with command and supervisory responsibilities to ensure compliance with those standards;

(c) sufficient numbers of women police officials to be appointed, trained and appropriately deployed so that they are available to supervise and, if necessary, search women detainees;

(d) facilities for the detention of women by police to be sufficient to respect the rights and special status of women detainees - especially in respect of the requirement for women to be detained separately from men.[59]

The sensitization of police officials to the human rights of women in the process of law enforcement and the rights of women in terms of their needs and special status as people who require protection in law enforcement is also essential.

The basic message to be derived from this chapter is that human rights are not a matter under the exclusive jurisdiction of the State or its agents. Rather they are a legitimate concern of international community, which has been engaged for half a century in the setting of standards, the establishment of implementation mechanisms and the monitoring of compliance with the standards. Law enforcement officers and agencies that carry out their vital functions in a manner which respects and protects human rights bring honour not just to themselves, but to the Government which employs them and the nation which they serve. Those that violate human rights will ultimately draw the spotlight of international scrutiny and the condemnation of the international community. The challenge for the true law enforcement professionals, therefore, is at all times to enforce and uphold the law of human rights.

All these movements, studies, judicial decisions etc., have an impact on the codes of civilized countries which have started recognising the importance of reformative aspect of the punishment and treating the accused/prisoners as human beings. However, much effort is needed to incorporate the lofty international ideals, views, etc., into the statutes of various countries including India. It is also felt that the main failure is in implementing the existing provisions of the rights of the accused and of the prisoners.

(ii) Rights of Prisoners under Constitutional Law

In 1948, a movement was started in the United Nations Organisation in the form of the Universal Declaration of Human Rights to provide certain basic principles in the process of administration of justice. Some of the principles embodied in the Declaration are the equality of treatment, right to life, liberty and security of persons, freedom from torture, cruel, inhuman or degrading treatment or punishment.

The Indian Constitution which was drafted more or less at the same time has responded to the international opinion and incorporated many of the above provisions. The human rights were equally applicable not only to citizens who are free but also to those who are under legal scrutiny, namely the 'accused'. The accused is protected both constitutionally and procedurally under the Indian laws. The Common law maxim, "A man is presumed innocent until he is proved guilty" is considered as sacrosanct by the framers of the Indian Constitution. It is in this background that the constitutional provisions extended to the accused in India are examined. Part-III of the Constitution incorporates certain fundamental rights which are available to the accused.

Right to Equality

The State shall not deny to any person equality before the law or the equal protection of the laws[60] within the territory of India. The rule that like should be treated alike and the concept of reasonable classification as contained in Art.14 have been a very useful guide for the courts to determine the category of prisoners and their basis of classification into different categories.

Right to Freedom

Art.19 guarantees six freedoms to the citizens of India. Among these, certain freedoms like 'freedom of movement', 'freedom to reside and to settle anywhere in India' and 'freedom of profession, occupation, trade or business' cannot be enjoyed by the prisoners because of the very nature of these freedoms and due to the conditions of incarceration. But the other freedoms like 'freedom of speech and expression', freedom to join an association', etc., can be enjoyed by the prisoners, consistently with the limitations of the incarceration.

Doctrine of Ex-post-facto laws

Art.20, clause (1) protects the persons from ex-post-facto laws. It provides:

> No person shall be convicted by any offence except for violation of law in force at the time of the commission of the act charged as an offence, nor be subjected to a penalty greater than that which might have been inflicted under the law in force at the time of the commission of the offence.

Doctrine of Double jeopardy

The doctrine of double jeopardy means that no person can be punished more than once for the same offence. This is an important principle in the administration of criminal justice. This principle is based on the maxim "autrefois acquit and autrefois convict" which means that previous acquittal or previous conviction may be pleaded by the accused as a bar to the subsequent trial. The doctrine is founded on the English Common Law rule, "nemo debet bis vexari pro cadem causa", which means that a person may not be put twice in jeopardy for the same offence.

In Indian law, this protection is provided by Art. 20(2) of the Indian Constitution and Sec.300(1) of the Criminal Procedure Code, 1973. The Constitutional guarantee as provided by Art. 20(2) of the Indian Constitution, provides as follows:

> "No person shall be prosecuted and punished for the same offence more than once".

The protection under Art.20(2) of the Indian Constitution is narrower than the protection available in England. In India, second trial is a bar when a person has not only been prosecuted but punished also for the same offence for which he is prosecuted again. Therefore, there is no bar to a second prosecution in a case where there has been no punishment in the first trial. In *Kulwanti v. M.P. State*[61] the Supreme Court held:

> "If there is no punishment for the offence as a result of the prosecution, clause (2) of the Article 20 has no application ... and an appeal against an acquittal if provided by the procedure is in substance a continuance of the prosecution".

Sec. 300(1) Cr.P.C., 1973 provides:

> "A person who has once been tried by a court of competent jurisdiction for an offence and convicted or acquitted of such offence shall, while such

conviction or acquittal remains in force, not be liable to be tried again for the same offence, nor on the same facts for any other offence for which a different charge from the one made against him might have been made under sub-section (1) of Section 221, or for which he might have been convicted under sub-section (2) thereof".

But there are certain exceptions to this rule which are provided in sub-sections (2) to (6) of Sec. 300.

The basis of the application of Sec. 300(1) is that the first trial should have been before a court of competent jurisdiction to hear and determine the case to record a verdict of conviction or acquittal and for that purpose the Code makes a clear distinction between acquittal and discharge. It is also to be remembered that where there are two alternative charges in the same trial, the fact that the accused is acquitted in one of them will not prevent the conviction on the other.[62]

Though the same protection is also provided under Constitution,[63] there is a slight difference with Cr.P.C. The constitutional guarantee embodies only the principle *autrefois convict and not autrefois* acquit that is, previous prosecution and conviction are both necessary for claiming the plea against second trial for the same offence.

But under Sec. 300(1) Cr.P.C. it embodies both autrefois convict as well as 'autrefois acquit'. Therefore, where there has been no previous punishment or conviction, but acquittal at the end of a trial for the same offence, the person has to invoke the provisions of Sec. 300(1) of the Criminal Procedure Code.

Rule against Self-incrimination

The accused also enjoys the immunity from giving self-incriminating evidence. This guarantee contained in Art.

20(3) of the Indian Constitution provides as follows:

> "No person accused of an offence shall be compelled to be a witness against himself"

This means no one shall be compelled to give testimony which may expose him to prosecution for crime. The accused need not make any admission or statement against his own free will.

The right under Art. 20(3) of the Constitution is available only to a person accused of an offence. Formal accusation relating to the commission of an offence is sufficient to avail this right. It is not necessary that the actual trial or inquiry should have started before the court.[64]

The protection under Art. 20(3) of the Constitution is against "compulsion to be a witness". To be a witness means nothing more than "to furnish evidence" and such evidence includes oral, documentary and testimonial evidence. In other words, Art.20(3) is available only against the compulsion of accused to give evidence against himself. Compulsion means "duress" which includes threatening, beating and the like. To attract Art. 20(3) it must be shown that the accused was compelled to make the statement likely to incriminate him.

The Criminal Procedure Code 1973 also provides protection against self-incrimination of the accused. The accused is not required to make statement on oath. The accused shall not be liable to punishment for refusing to answer questions or for giving false answers to them. Sec.313 of the Criminal Procedure Code incorporates:

1) "On every inquiry or trial for the purpose of enabling the accused personally to explain any circumstances appearing in the evidence against him, the court —

(a) may at any stage, without previously warning the accused, put such questions to him as the court considers necessary;

(b) shall, after the witnesses for the prosecution have been examined and before he is called on for his defence, question him generally on the case;

provided that in summons - case where the court has dispensed with the personal attendance of the accused, it may also dispense with his examination under clause (b).

2) No oath shall be administered to the accused when he is examined under sub-sec.(1).

3) The accused shall not render himself liable to punishment by refusing to answer such questions, or by giving false answers to them.

4) The answers given by the accused may be taken into consideration in such inquiry or trial, and put in evidence for or against him in any other inquiry into, or trial for any other offence which such answers may tend to show he has committed".

Similarly, an accused person cannot be convicted on the basis of a coerced confession. Sec.164(2) of the Cr.P.C. provides as follows:

> "The Magistrate shall before recording any such confession, explain to the person making it that he is not bound to make a confession and that if he does so, it may be used as evidence against him and the Magistrate shall not record any such confession unless, upon questioning the person making it he has reason to believe that it is being made voluntarily".[65]

Thus the right of silence has been interpreted as an essential feature of fair trial.[66] In the present legal structure, the right of silence for the accused is ensured as an essential part of due process from the stage of investigation. The right of the accused not to answer and keep silent while interrogated by the police was considered by the Supreme Court of U.S.A. in *Miranda v. Arizona*.[67] The court held that if a person in custody is to be interrogated, he must first be informed in clear and unequivocal terms that he has a right to remain silent. The warning of the right to remain silent must be accompanied by the explanation that anything said can be and will be used against the individual in the court. This warning is needed in order to make the accused aware of not only of the privilege but also of the consequences of foregoing it.

In *Bijoe Emmanuel v. State of Kerala*[68], the Supreme Court read the right to remain silent as implied in the freedom of speech guaranteed under Art. 19(1)(a) of the Constitution.

Right to Fair trial

Another important principle of criminal jurisprudence is that the accused must have a fair trial. The components of the fair trial are that the trial must be held in an open court and in the presence of the accused, the accused must be made known of the charges framed against him at the earliest and that he has a right to be defended by a lawyer.

Art. 22(1) of the Indian Constitution provides that:

(a) no person who is arrested shall be detained in custody without being informed, as soon as may be, of the grounds for such arrest nor shall he be denied the right to consult and to be defended by a legal practitioner of his choice.

(b) every person who is arrested and detained in custody shall be produced before the nearest Magistrate within a period of twenty-four hours of such arrest excluding the time necessary for the journey from the place of arrest to the Court of Magistrate, and

(c) no such person shall be detained in custody beyond the said period without the authority of law.

Sec. 303 of the Code of Criminal Procedure 1973 provides:

"Any person accused of an offence before a criminal court or against whom proceedings are instituted under this Code, may of right be defended by a pleader of his choice".

Even if the accused is in police custody he is also given a reasonable opportunity of getting into communication with his counsel for the purpose of preparing his defence.

In certain cases, the accused is entitled to legal aid at the expense of the State. Sec.304(1) of Criminal Procedure Code, 1973 provides:

"Where in a trial before Court of Session, the accused is not represented by a pleader, the court shall assign a pleader for his defence at the expense of the State".

The lawyer so appointed to render service to the accused has to be reasonably remunerated for his services. Then the right to counsel is available not in the permissive sense of Art. 22(1) and its wider amplitude, but in the peremptory sense of Art. 21 confined to prison situation.[69]

Art. 21 provides:

"No person shall be deprived of his life or personal liberty except according to procedure established by law".

The Supreme Court observed[70] that the State is under a constitutional mandate to ensure speedy trial and it is the constitutional obligation of the Supreme Court to enforce the fundamental rights of the accused to speedy trial by issuing necessary direction to the State. Thus the continued detention of under-trial prisoners being totally unjustified, the court directed that these prisoners should be released forthwith as "continuance of their detention is clearly illegal and in violation of their fundamental right under Art.21 of the Constitution". It was further observed that free legal service to indigent and poor accused is implicit in the guarantee under Art. 21 because free legal service is an inalienable element of "reasonable, fair and just" procedure.

A significant question regarding legal aid is whether the accused has to ask for the lawyer where the majority of the people in a country are illiterate and backward and even literate people are not aware of their right. In *Khatri v. State of Bihar*[71], it was held that it was not necessary that the accused must ask for legal assistance. Even when there is no such demand, such aid must be made available. Further, the Supreme Court ruled that the Magistrate or the Sessions Judge before whom the accused appears, is under an obligation to inform the accused that if he is unable to engage the services of a lawyer on account of poverty or indigence, he is entitled to obtain free legal services at the cost of the State. *Suk Das v. Union Territory of Arunachal Pradesh*[72], also reiterates the same proposition. Thus the duty is cast on the Magistrate or the Sessions Judge to inform the accused concerned about his entitlement to have an engaged counsel at the cost of the State. It was further observed that this constitutional obligation to provide free legal services to the poor accused does not only arise when the trial commences but is also available when the accused is for the first time produced before a Magistrate. This right is implicit in the guarantee of the Constitution.

Another important question regarding legal aid is the qualification of a lawyer to be employed for defending the poor accused. This question was deliberated by the Supreme Court in *Kadra Pahadiya v. State of Bihar,*[73] where four undertrial prisoners were rotting in jail for more than eight years. Should it be a junior lawyer for reducing the expenditure or a "fairly competent lawyer" as demanded by the accused is the question before the Supreme Court.[74] The Supreme Court answered this question saying that the prisoners should be provided a "fairly competent lawyer". Further, the Supreme Court in *State of Maharashtra v. Manubhai Pragaji Vashi*[75] directed that the lawyer must be paid an amount fixed by the court. Finally in one sentence in Krishna Iyer J. observed[76] that to provide free legal aid is State duty and not Government charity.

Violation of free legal aid to the poor accused would render the trial bad and vitiated. The court held that a valuable right in cross-examining the prosecution witness had been lost to the accused in the absence of appointment of a counsel at the State expense.[77]

It is unfortunate that the programme of the free legal services is not successful to the extent it should have been. One of the reasons is the non-co-operative attitude of the members of the Bar. The judicial officers are also equally responsible for the non-availability of the benefits to this class of the litigants. As observed by the High Court of Gujarat,[78] where a woman or child is a party, it is equally the duty of the judicial officer concerned to let them know that they are entitled to free legal aid.

The higher judiciary in India, on the other hand, has been continuously trying its best in enforcing constitutional guarantee of free legal aid by issuing directions to the State and subordinate judiciary. Some of the Bar Associations have taken the lead in establishing legal aid cells to extend to the poor and needy accused free legal services.

In each State, Free Legal Aid Committees came into existence following the insertion of Art. 39A of the Constitution in 1976. Following this Andhra Pradesh Government had established Free Legal Aid Authority, under the chairmanship of a Senior High Court Judge. This Authority has identified the category of people who are eligible for free legal aid, economic criteria and the type of cases for which this aid can be extended. Women and children are entitled to free legal aid under this scheme.

So there is a need to review the existing provisions of the legal aid to the accused to make suitable alterations through the legislature.

Rights of 'Detenues'

International human rights standards and most national level systems make a distinction between 'detainees' and 'prisoners'. A detenue is also a detainee who is deprived of personal liberty, despite not having been convicted. A prisoner is a person deprived of liberty as a result of having been convicted.[79]

Art. 22(4) to (7) provide certain special safeguards for the 'detenues' detained under preventive detention laws. Clause (4) provides the maximum period of three months for detention without obtaining the opinion of Advisory Board. The detention beyond this period without obtaining the prior permission of the Advisory Board would render the order of detention void. Clause (5) of Art.22 guarantees two rights to a 'detenue':

(a) The authority making the order of detention must 'as soon as may be' communicate it to the person detained along with the grounds of detention and facts which led the authority to making the order.

(b) The detenue should be furnished with sufficient particulars to represent his case against the order of detention as soon as possible.

This clause imposes a duty on the detaining authority to furnish the grounds of his detention and the particulars required by the detenue to prepare his defence. Insufficient facts or particulars and the vagueness of the ground will render the detention invalid.

Clause (6) of Art. 22 provides that the authority can deny the disclosure of certain facts to the detenue in the public interest. But, on the other hand, in clause (5) the detaining authority is bound to disclose certain facts and furnish some particulars which are essential for the detenue to prepare his defence.

Under clause (7) of Art.22 there is a provision for the formation of an Advisory Board which shall be a Body free from the executive control and will be an independent and impartial body.

Position of Women under Indian Constitution – Provisions in favour of Women

Half of the Indian population consists of women. Women have always been discriminated against in silence. Self-sacrifice and self-denial are their nobility and fortitude and yet they have been subjected to all sorts of inequities, indignities and discrimination.[80]

Discrimination against women is widely prevalent all over the world. Women have been neglected in the social, economic and political development of the country in the past. Thus for ages, women have been lower in status as compared to men in the society. The post-independence era has witnessed in our country a new social awareness for the upliftment and liberation of women. With the result attempts have been made to bring about equality between men and women. Consequently, the drafting committee of the Indian Constitution incorporated certain provisions into the Constitution of India in favour of the women.

The preamble of the Indian Constitution proclaims, *inter alia*, justice, liberty and equality of opportunity and of status to all Indian citizens. A perusal of the constitutional provisions gives the impression that the makers of the Indian Constitution intended to put an end to injustice and inequality not only among different classes but also between different sexes. On the other hand, in order to promote the welfare and well-being of women and children they have enacted provisions in the body of the Constitution.

The fundamental principle relating to 'equality' is laid down in Art.14 of the Constitution. Articles 15 and 16 prohibit discrimination on certain specified grounds so as to ensure equality among all.

Art.15(1), *inter alia*, prohibits discrimination on grounds of religion, race, caste, sex, place of birth or on any one of them. Art.15(3) permits the State to make special provisions for the advancement of women and children. This provision allows special legislation for women.

For example, the mandate of Sec. 437 of the Code of Criminal Procedure, 1973 permits distinction in favour of women even if there appears to be a reasonable ground for believing that they have been guilty of an offence punishable with death or imprisonment for life.[81] In other words, this Section prohibits release of a person accused of a capital offence on bail except women and children under 16 years of age or sick or infirm persons. In *Choki v. State of Rajasthan*[82], the Rajasthan High Court has held that this provision is valid on the ground that it makes special provision for women and therefore it is protected under Art. 15(3) of the Constitution. Thus Art.15(3) reads:

> "Nothing in this Article shall prevent the State from making any special provision for women and children."

Art.16 of the Constitution of India also explicitly mentions equality of opportunities for all in public employment and prohibits the discrimination against women. It clearly states that there shall be equality of opportunity for all citizens in matters relating to employment or appointment to any office under the State and no citizen shall, on ground only of religion, race, caste, sex, descent, place of birth, residence or any of them, be ineligible for, or discriminated against in respect of, any employment or office under the State.

Art. 23 prohibits the traffic in human beings in the following terms:

(1) "Traffic in human beings and 'begar' and other similar forms of forced labour are prohibited and any contravention of this provision shall be an offence punishable in accordance with law.

(2) "Nothing in this Article shall prevent the State from imposing compulsory service for public purposes, and in imposing such service, the State shall not make any discrimination on grounds only of religion, race, caste or class or any of them."

The discrimination of women is explicitly prohibited in Art. 15 and Art. 16. In all other fundamental rights, the words 'citizen', 'person' means both male and female persons. Hence women are equally entitled to the protection of all fundamental rights along with men.

The Directive Principles of State Policy are contained in Part-IV of the Constitution of India. Though they are not enforceable by any court, still some Directives are explicitly intended to improve the status of women and for their protection.

According to Art. 39, the State shall, in particular, direct its policy towards securing—

(1) that the citizens, men and women equally, have the rights to an adequate means of livelihood, and

(2) that there is equal pay for equal work for both men and women.

(3) that the wealth and strength of workers, men and women and the tender age of children are not abused.

Art. 42 states that the State shall make provision for securing just and humane conditions of work and for maternity relief.

Art. 44 states that the State shall endeavour to secure for the citizens a uniform civil code throughout the territory of India.

As per Art. 39A, the State shall secure that the operation of legal system promotes justice, on a basis of equal opportunity and shall in particular, provide free legal aid, by suitable legislation or schemes or in any other way, to ensure that opportunities for securing justice are not denied to any citizen by reason of economic or other disabilities.

Art.51 A(e)[83] imposes a fundamental duty on every citizen, *inter alia*, to renounce practices derogatory to the dignity of women.

The Constitutional provisions detailed above contemplate equal rights between the sexes and in addition gave certain special privileges to women. However, there are no special safeguards to protect the interests of the women prisoners in the Constitution of India. The only rights available to the women accused are general in character. The interests of the women prisoners are protected only through Art. 15(3) of the Constitution. This Article permits the State to make special provisions in the existing laws or to make new laws for the benefit of women and children. Laws protecting the interests of the women in various custodies have to be made to enforce this guarantee.

Based on this background, a study is made of the existing Central and State laws regarding the rights of women in various custodies, and the findings are presented in the following chapters.

References

1. The Declaration on the Elimination of All Forms of Discrimination against Women, 1967 and the Convention on the Elimination of All Forms of Discrimination against Women, 1979.
2. Human Rights and Law Enforcement – A Manual on Human Rights Training for the Police – UN 1997 Series No.5, Paras 120 & 122, p.26.
3. Art. 1, Universal Declaration of Human Rights, 1948.
4. Art. 3, *Ibid*.
5. Art. 5, *Ibid*.
6. Art. 6, *Ibid*.
7. Art. 9, *Ibid*.
8. Art. 10, *Ibid*.
9. Art. 11, *Ibid*.
10. Art.26, ICCPR; and also the African Charter on Human and Peoples' Rights states that every individual shall be equal before the law and entitled to equal protection of the law (Art. 3); and the American Convention on Human Rights contains the same provision (Art. 24).
11. Extract from Report of National Expert Committee on Women Prisoners (1986-87) Vol. II, pp.101-102.
12. Art. 2 (1), European Convention on Human Rights, 1950.
13. Art.3, *Ibid*.
14. Art. 5(1), *Ibid*.
15. Art. 6, *Ibid*.
16. Extract from Report of National Expert Committee on Women Prisoners (1986-87), Vol. II, pp.99-101.
17. Rule 6(1) and (2), Standard Minimum Rules for the Treatment of Prisoners, 1955.
18. Rule 8, *Ibid*.
19. Rule 8(a), *Ibid*.
20. Rule 8(b), *Ibid*.
21. Rules 8(b), (c) & (d), Standard Minimum Rules for the Treatment of Prisoners, 1955.

22. Rules 30(1),(2), (3) and 31, *Ibid*.
23. Rules 8(d), 15, 16, 19 & 20(1) and 22(1), 23(1) and 37, 38, 39, *Ibid*.
24. Rules 87 & 88, Standard Minimum Rules for the Treatment of Prisoners, 1955.
25. Human Rights and Law Enforcement – A Manual on Human Rights. Training for the Police, U.N. 1997, Series no.5, Para 124, p.26.
26. Art. 9, Para 2, International Covenant on Civil and Political Rights, 1966.
27. Art. 9, Para 3, International Covenant on Civil and Political Rights, 1966.
28. Art.9, Para 4, *Ibid*.
29. Art. 9, Para 5, *Ibid*.
30. Art.10, Para 1, *Ibid*.
31. Art.14, Para 1, *Ibid*.
32. Art.14, Para 2, International Covenant on Civil and Political Rights, 1966.
33. Art.14, Para 3, *Ibid*.
34. *Ibid*., Para 7, *Ibid*.
35. Art.2, Declaration on Protection from Torture, 1975.
36. Art.3, *Ibid*.
37. Extract from Report of National Expert Committee on Women Prisoners, Vol. II, (1986-87), p.259.
38. Principle I, Declaration of Medical Ethics for Protection of Prisoners and Detainees against Torture, 1982.
39. Principle II, Declaration of Medical Ethics for Protection of Prisoners and Detainees against Torture, 1982.
40. Principle III, *Ibid*.
41. Principle IV, *Ibid*.
42. Principle V, *Ibid*.
43. Principle VI, Declaration of Medical Ethics for Protection of Prisoners and Detainees against Torture, 1982.
44. Human Rights and Law Enforcement, A Manual on Human Rights Training for the Police, UN 1997 Series No. 5, Para 130, p.28.

45. *Ibid*., Paras 392, 393, 394 & 397, p. 76.
46. *Ibid*., Para 419, p.78.
47. *Ibid*., Paras 400 & 401, p.77.
48. Ian Brownlie, Guy. S. Goodwin-Gill. "Basic documents on Human Rights", 4th Edn, 2002, Oxford University Press, p.51.
49. Human Rights and Law Enforcement – A Manual on Human Rights Training for the Police, *op. cit*,. Series No.5, Paras 141 & 142, p.29.
50. *Ibid*., Para 145, p.30.
51. *Ibid*., Para 278, p.52.
52 *Ibid*., Paras 279, 690, pp.59 and 126.
53. *Ibid*., Para 691, p.126.
54. *Ibid*., Para 692, p.126.
55. *Ibid*., Paras 693, 694, 695, p.126.
56. *Ibid*., Para 698, p.126.
57. *Ibid*., Para 412, p.78.
58. *Ibid*., Para 413, p.78.
59. *Ibid*., Para 731, p.129.
60. Art.14 of the Indian Constitution.
61. AIR 1953 SC 131.
62. *State of M.P. v. Veereshwar Rao Agnihotri*, AIR 1957 SC 592: 1957 SCJ 515.
63. Art.20(2) of the Indian Constitution.
64. *M.P. Sharma v. Satish Chandra* AIR 1954 SC 300: 1954 CriLJ 865. See also *B.R. Shah v. D.K.Guha* AIR 1973 SC 1196.
65. Further protection has been provided by the Evidence Act, 1872. Any confession made by an accused is irrelevant if it has been caused by inducement, threat or promise (Sec.24). A confession made to a police officer (Sec. 25) or a person in custody (Sec. 26) cannot be proved.
66. Art. 6 European Convention of Human Rights.
67. (1996) 384 U.S. 436. Ref. in Justice Palok Basu – "Law relating to Protection of Human Rights under the Indian Constitution and Allied Laws". First Edn., (2002) Modern Law Pub., New Delhi, p.633.
68. AIR 1987 SC 748: (1986) 3 SCC 615.

69. *M.H. Hoskot v. State of Maharashtra* 1978 CriLJ 1678 (SC): AIR 1978 SC 1548: (1978) 3 SCC 544.
70. In *Hussainera Khatoon v. State of Bihar* 1979 CriLJ 1045 (SC): AIR 1979 SC 1369: (1980) 1 SCC 98.
71. Popularly known as Bhagalpur Blinded Prisoners' case, AIR 1981 SC 928: (1981) 1 SCC 635.
72. AIR 1986 SC 991: (1986) 2 SCC 401: 1986 CriLJ 1084: referred in *Hiraman, S/o. Sakharam Borkar v. State of Maharashtra* 2000 CriLJ 4185 at p.4189 (Bom.).
73. AIR 1981 SC 939: (1981) 3 SCC 671: 1981 CriLJ 481.
74. *Ibid*.
75. AIR 1996 SC 1: (1995) 5 SCC 730.
76. AIR 2000 Journal Section 17 at pp. 19, 20 Ref. in Justice Palok Basu, *op. cit.*, p.640.
77. *State v. Ravi alias Munna* 2000 CriLJ 1125 at p.1137.
78. *Kalaben Kalbhai Desai v. Alabhai Karamshibhai Desai*, AIR 2000 Guj 232 at p.233.
79. Human Rights and Law Enforcement. A Manual on Human Rights Training for the Police, UN 1997, Series No.5, Para 381, p.75.
80. Justice K.Rama Swamy in *Madhu Kishwar v. State of Bihar* (1996) 5 SCC 125: AIR 1996 SC 1864.
81. *Suresh Kumari v. State of Haryana* 1995 (4) Crimes 643 C.P.S. 14 – Ref. Dr. S.C. Tripathi and Vibha Arora, "Law relating to women and children", 1st Edn. (2004), Central Law Publications, Allahabad, p.6.
82. AIR 1971 Raj 10.
83. Art. 51-A was added to the Constitution by the 42nd Amendment, 1976.

3

Statutory Provisions Relating to Women Prisoners in Police and Judicial Custody

This chapter deals with the existing legal provisions relating to the protection of women accused both in police and judicial custodies. For the convenience of the study, the subject is dealt under two separate sections. In the first section, the provisions under the substantive law are presented while the provisions under the procedural law are dealt with in the second section.

(i) Rights of Women Prisoners under Substantive Law (I.P.C.)

The police are the chief law enforcing authority and are duty bound to protect the life and property of the people. While performing their duties the police are expected, whenever they encounter women, to observe caution, exercise restraint and understand the constraints in their dealings. In a tradition-bound society like India, the police naturally have an added responsibility of honouring and protecting the womanhood. However, there are allegations of offences against women by the police themselves. The offences range from the lack of concern towards the complaints of females to rape of the women in police stations. In between, there are regular reports of ill-treatment of women complainants, mis-behaviour with women offenders, illegal detention, threatening, outraging the modesty, etc. Thus, of many forms of violence against women, custodial violence involving rape and molestation has clearly been on the increase. Rape in police stations or by the police is the most notorious form of violence against women. It is being reported with distressing regularity and increasing frequency over the last few years. Such reports are not confined to any particular State. There are reports from almost all corners of the country at alarming intervals. Though the exact statistics of rape in police custody are not available as most such incidents are hushed up still there are some cases brought to light by the media. A few such examples are : Rameeza Bee and Shakila cases in Andhra Pradesh, consistent police raping of Adivasi women in Madhya Pradesh, Maya Taygi case in Uttar Pradesh, Mathura case in Maharashtra, the Patiala episode in Punjab.[1]

Whenever such incidents are highlighted in the Press, the concerned State Government routinely orders either a magisterial or judicial enquiry. No one is sure of the fate of the recommendations of such enquiry committees. It is common knowledge that there are more suggestions which were not attended to than those which were implemented. So there is a need to review the custodial offences, the existing legal remedies, the suggestions already made for the prevention of such actions and make further suggestions.

The law of rape is defined in Sec. 376 of the I.P.C. The gist of the offence is that a man has a sexual intercourse with a woman against her will and without her consent. The inadequacy of the law of rape under Sec. 376 of the I.P.C. is manifested in a number of judgments.[2] One such important case is *Mathura case*.[3] The acquittal of the constables who committed rape on an innocent girl, Mathura, in the police station on the ground that there was no evidence of resistance by the victim was criticised by all sections of the society. The strong protests by women's organisations, social workers and academicians to protect the victims of rape, especially from the custodians, led to an amendment of the law of rape in 1983.[4] This Amended Act not only revised the existing Sections,[5] but also inserted new Sections[6] which provided protection for women in custody.

But custodial violence is not confined to the police alone. Similar treatment is common even in prisons and other institutional homes, shelters, centres for women under the management of State Government. There are instances of even nurses being raped or sexually abused in hospitals. Hence they are also included in the definition of 'custodial rape'.

Custodial rape

Sec. 376(2) of the I.P.C. made the following acts as custodial rape and provided severe punishment. They are–

1. A police officer committing rape in the local area to which he is appointed or in any police station whether or not situated in such local area or on a woman in his custody or in the custody of a police officer subordinate to him.[7]

2. A public servant taking advantage of his official position committing rape on a woman in his custody as such public servant or in the custody of a public servant subordinate to him.[8]

3. Any person being on the management or on the staff of a jail, remand home or other place of custody established by or under any law for the time being in force or of a women's or children's institution, taking

advantage of his official position and committing rape on any inmate of the institution.[9]

4. Any person concerned with management or being on the staff of a hospital, taking advantage of his official position and committing rape on a woman in that hospital.[10]

This Section prescribes more deterrent punishment of not less than ten years of rigorous imprisonment but which may extend to life and also fine. However, the court is empowered to reduce the minimum prescribed punishment only after recording adequate and special reasons.

Custodial sexual abuse not amounting to rape

The second important amendment made in the Penal Code in 1983 was the insertion of Sections 376B, 376C and 376D to deal with custodial sexual abuse not amounting to rape.[11] These Sections provided punishment to those persons who have taken advantage of their official position for sexual intercourse with a woman on official premises. They are -

1. Being a public servant takes advantage of his official position and induces or seduces any woman, who is in his custody or in the custody of his subordinate to have sexual intercourse with him.[12]

2. Being the Superintendent or manager of jail, remand home, or other place of custody established by or under any law for the time being in force or of a women's or children's institution, takes advantage of his official position and induces or seduces any female inmate of such jail, remand home, etc., to have sexual intercourse with him.[13]

3. Being the management or staff of the hospital takes advantage of his official position induces or seduces a

woman in the hospital to have sexual intercourse with him.[14]

Though such a sexual intercourse does not amount to rape, still the accused persons are held guilty and punishable with imprisonment extending to five years and shall also be liable to fine.

All these offences are bailable but cognizable.[15] But arrest cannot be made without warrant or without orders from the Magistrate.[16] This provision is discriminatory and advantageous to the public officials like the police, jail and hospital authorities. Taking advantage of their official position, they threaten the victim and her family, and also the witnesses. If these persons are not arrested immediately, they have ample time to destroy the evidence. An amendment in this regard is necessary so that they can be arrested without any delay. The offence should also be made a non-bailable one.

The same Amendment Act 1983, adds new Sec. 114-A to the Indian Evidence Act, 1872, which states:

> "In prosecution for rape under clause (a)(b)(c)(d) ... of sub-section (2) of Sec. 376 of the Indian Penal Code, where sexual intercourse by the accused is proved and the question is whether it was without the consent of the woman alleged to have been raped and she states in her evidence before the court that she did not consent, the court shall presume that she did not consent."

The higher judiciary has shown high concern towards women victims and this can be firmly said in as much as the testimony of a prosecutrix is considered to be the best and such victims are prime witnesses. This principle is by now well established through a plethora of judgments from the Apex Court. *The State of Maharashtra v. Chandra Prakash*

K. Jain[17] reflects the concern of the judiciary towards women who are subjected to sexual abuse. In this case, the Supreme Court, *inter alia*, denounced the society which instead of treating such victim with compassion is treating her as a 'sinner'.

In rape cases, the court must bear in mind the human psychology and behavioural probability when assessing the testimonial potency of the victims version. Krishna Iyer J. aptly observed[18]:

> "A socially sensitised judge is a better statutory armour against gender outrage such as rape than long clauses of a complex section with all the protections written into it".

A trial court will be under a legal obligation to presume that the prosecutrix did not give her consent and would be deemed to be under moral obligation to presume that no woman will come forward to make a humiliating statement against her honour of having been raped unless it was true. This view now finds favour with the Supreme Court also, as is evident from various judgments pronounced by it.[19]

New Section 53A was inserted by the Code of Criminal Procedure (Amendment) Act, 2005 to provide detailed medical examination of person accused of rape. This Section also helps the women to prove her case easily. Thus this Section says that when a person is arrested on a charge of committing an offence of rape or attempt to commit rape and there are reasonable grounds for believing that an examination of his person will afford evidence as to the commission of such offence, it shall be lawful for a registered medical practitioner employed in a hospital run by the Government or by a local authority and in the absence of such practitioner within the radius of sixty kilometer from the place where the offence has been committed, by any other registered medical practitioner, acting at the request of the police not below the rank of sub inspector, and for any person acting in good faith in his aid and under his direction, to make such force as is reasonably necessary for that purpose.[20]

The registered medical practitioner conducting such examination shall, without delay, examine such person and prepare a report of his emamination giving the following particulars.

(i) The name and address of the accused and of the person by whom he was brought.

(ii) The age of the accused.

(iii) Marks of injury, if any, on the person of the accused.

(iv) Other medical particulars in reasonable detail[21]

Further the report shall state precisely the reasons for each conclusion arrived at[22]. The registered medical practitioner shall, without delay, forward the report to the investigating officer, who shall forward it to the magistrate referred to in Section 173 as the part of the documents referred to in clause (a) of sub - section (5) of that Section[23].

Another provision[24] was introduced in Cr.P.C. by the same Amendment Act[25] to protect the victim from the blaze of media publicity. It was made mandatory for the trial of rape cases 'in-camera' except that the trial court may in its discretion permit any person to have access to the court room[26]. And further, printing or publishing of such proceedings are not lawful without previous permission of the court.[27]

Indian women are known worldwide for their decency and shy nature. In a judgment delivered the Hon'ble Supreme Court[28] while convicting three rapists of a minor girl had directed that all such trials must be held in-camera. This ruling has been widely welcomed as it will check character assassination and humiliation of the victim in public.

Another Sec. 228-A was also inserted in I.P.C. to provide that the printing or publishing of the name or any matter which may make known the identity of the victim of rape is punishable with imprisonment for a term which may extend to 2 years and with fine. But such printing or publishing is permissible only under a written order of the officer-in-charge of police station making investigation or with the authorisation in writing of the victim or if the victim is dead or a minor or of unsound mind, with the authorisation of the next kin of the victim. Further, this Section prohibits the publication of court proceedings except with the previous permission of such court and non-compliance of it is punishable with imprisonment extending upto two years and also fine.[29] But the publication of judgments of High Courts and Supreme Court does not amount to an offence.[30]

When trials are held in-camera, it would not be lawful for any person to print or publish any matter in relation to the proceedings of the case, except with the previous permission of the court as envisaged by Sec. 327(3), Cr.P.C. This would save further embarrassment being caused to the victim of sex crime. Whenever possible, it would be more desirable that the cases of sexual assaults on the females are tried by lady judges, so that the prosecutrix can make her statement with greater ease and assist the court to properly discharge its duties. The courts should, as far as possible, avoid disclosing the name of the prosecutrix in their order to save further embarrassment to the victim of sex crime.

One of the broad principles flowing from the above discussion is with respect to the right of privacy which is implicit in the right to life and personal liberty guaranteed to all persons of the country by Art.21. It is a "right to be let alone". "A person has a right to safeguard the privacy of his own, his family, marriage, procreation, motherhood, child bearing and education among other matters. None can publish anything concerning the above matters without his consent – whether truthful or otherwise and whether laudatory or critical. If he does so, he would be violating the right to privacy of the person concerned".[31]

Thus the Criminal Law (Amendment) Act, 1983 protects the privacy of the rape victim by incorporating the above provisions both in the I.P.C. and the Cr.P.C. The judiciary has also contributed in protecting the privacy of rape victim by pronouncing a landmark judgement in *State of Maharashtra v. Madhukar Narayan Mardikar*.[32] In this case, departmental proceedings were initiated against a police inspector for entering the hutment of complainant and attempting to ravish her. The police officer took the defence that the woman was of easy virtue and he had simply raided the house for illicit liquor. The Supreme Court did not hesitate to hold that "Even a woman of easy virtue is entitled to privacy and no one can invade her privacy as and when he likes. So also it is not open to any and every person to violate her person as and when he wishes. She is entitled to protect her person if there is an attempt to violate it against her wish. She is equally entitled to the protection of law". This, no doubt, is an indication of the evolution of women's rights in the criminal justice system.

From the above account, it is clear that the custodial offences, especially the incidence of rape, by the police officers are happening quite often. Despite the police being the legal custodian of the offender and therefore large responsibility is thrust on him for protecting the honour of women, the men in uniform commit the offences. Even the strict legal provisions and severe punishments imposed on the offending officers are not acting as a deterrent. It is in this context that a review of powers of police officers dealing with the women and the loopholes, if any, in the existing legal provisions under Cr.P.C. are reviewed.

(ii) Rights of Women Prisoners under Procedural Law

The Cr.P.C. is designed to create the necessary machinery for the prevention of crime, arrest of the suspected criminals, collection of evidence, determination of guilt or innocence of the suspected person in a trial and imposition of proper punishment on the guilty person. Thus, the object of Cr.P.C. is to provide a suitable mechanism and the just procedure for the enforcement of criminal law.

Though the Cr.P.C. is liberal and forward looking with the inclusion of several provisions to safeguard the interests of the accused, it has failed to distinguish between criminals in general and women as accused. The special protections given to the women accused, if any, are negligible. There is a need for special provisions for women accused at every stage as they form a different group in the Indian society in general and in the treatment from police in particular. Keeping this broad view, the provisions of Cr.P.C. are reviewed under two main headings: (i) pre-trial and (ii) during the trial.

Pre-trial procedure

The police force is an instrument for the prevention and detection of crime and is established and enrolled by every State Government under the Police Act, 1861 or under a State enactment replacing the Act of 1861.[33]

Investigation is the first stage to be conducted by the police officer or any other authorised person. It includes all the proceedings under the Code for the collection of evidence. Broadly speaking, the investigation of an offence consists of proceeding to the place of offence, ascertainment of the facts and circumstances of the case, discovery and arrest of suspected offenders, examination of various persons and the reduction of their statements into writing, search of the place and seizure of things, etc., considered necessary for the trial.

In all these stages, the Code confers wide powers on the police officers to discharge their duties subject to reasonable restrictions. Generally, the police while discharging their duties come into contact with the women in the following cases: (1) Arrest, (2) Search of place and person, (3) Detention in police lock-up, (4) Police remand, (5) Examination of women witnesses. Of these five situations mentioned above, the Cr.P.C. made special provisions with respect to search of a person and place and examination of women as witness only. Till the code was amended in 2005, there were no provisions to protect the interests of woman under arrest. Even in the case of police lock-up, where there are more chances to the police to commit offences against women, the Code is silent.

The existing provisions under Cr.P.C. in relation to women accused are as follows:

Arrest

Till 2005, no provision is provided to protect the interest of the woman accused. It was for the first time a new Sub section (4)[34] is added to Section 46 of Cr. P.C. This Sub section prohibits the arrest of a woman after sunset and before the sunrise except in unavoidable circumstances. This Sub section further says that in exceptional circumstances the woman police officer shall, by making a written report, obtain the prior permission of the judicial magistrate of the first class within whose local jurisdiction the offence is committed or the arrest is made.

In addition to this sub section (4) in Section 46 a new Section 50-A was inserted by the Amendment Act 2005. This Section imposes an obligation on a person making arrest. He has to inform about the arrest and place where the arrested person is being help to any one of his/her friends, relatives or such other persons as may be disclosed or nominated by the arrested person for the purpose of giving such information.

An another obligation imposes on the police officer is that he shall inform the arrested person his/her rights under sub-section (1) as soon as he/she is brought to the police station[35].

Further, an entry of the fact as to who has been informed of the arrest of such person shall be made in a book to be kept in the police station in such form as may be prescribed on this behalf by the State government[36].

Sub-section (4) of the same Section imposes a duty on the magistrate before whom arrested person is produced, to satisfy himself that the requirement of sub-sections (2) and (3) have been complied with respect to such arrested person.

Search of place

The police officer has the power to search a place[37] at the time of arrest. At the time of making a search of any place, an occupier of a house is under a legal duty to afford to the police and to any person acting under a warrant of arrest, all the facilities to search the house for the purpose of making arrests. If such facilities are denied or obstructions are put in the search, the police officer or any other person executing a warrant shall have power to use force for getting entry into the house for search and also for the purpose of liberating himself in case he is detained in the house.

These powers are subject to reasonable restrictions, that if any such place is an apartment in the actual occupancy of a female (not being the person to be arrested), such female being a 'purdanashin' woman - who, according to custom, does not appear in public - the police officer entering such apartment shall give notice to such female that she is at liberty to withdraw and shall afford her every reasonable facility for withdrawing, and enter it.[38]

An officer who knowingly violates the requirements of this proviso would be punishable under Sec. 166 of the I.P.C.[39]

Search of person

The police officer has the power to search an arrested person.[40] Whenever a person who is arrested cannot legally be admitted to bail or is unable to furnish a bail, the police officer making the arrest may search the person, and place in safe custody all articles, other than necessary wearing apparel found upon him. A receipt showing the articles so seized shall be given to such a person. Whenever it is necessary to cause a female to be searched, the search shall be made by another female with strict regard to decency.[41] Further, Sec. 100(3)[42] of the Cr.P.C. dealing with searches and seizures also makes it obligatory that a woman should be searched by another woman with strict regard to decency.

The words 'with strict regard to decency' in both the Sections suggest that not only should the search of a woman be made by another woman but that no male person should be present at such search.[43] But the Supreme Court has taken the view that when a male person saw from some distance something being produced from the person of a woman searched, "the search should not necessarily be illegal nor such evidence be inadmissible".[44]

Medical examination of women accused

Sections 53 and 54 of Cr.P.C. relate to the examination of the arrested person by a medical practitioner. The former relates to the examination of an accused person by a medical practitioner at the request of the police officer and the latter to the examination of an arrested person by a medical practitioner at the request of the arrested person.

Sec. 53 of the Code is intended to remove the lacuna in the old Code, by reason of which it was not possible to subject an arrested person to medical examination, without his / her consent. The Section makes this possible:

> "To facilitate effective investigation, provision has been made, authorising an examination of the arrested person by a medical practitioner, if, from the nature of the alleged offence or the circumstances under which it was alleged to have been committed, there is a reasonable ground for believing that an examination of the person will afford evidence."[45]

Sec. 54 of the Cr.P.C. on the other hand, was inserted on the recommendation of the Joint Parliamentary Committee as follows:

> "The Committee considers that a person who is arrested should be given the right to have his body examined by a medical officer when he is produced before a Magistrate or at any time when he is under custody, with a view to enabling him to establish that the offence with which he is charged was not committed by him or that he was subjected to physical injury. In view of the Committee, a person in custody is in need of this protection".

Thus Sec. 53 of the Cr.P.C. imposes an obligation upon the arrested person to subject himself/herself to a medical examination at the instance of the police to help the investigation, while Sec. 54 of the Cr.P.C. confers upon the arrested person a right to have himself / herself medically examined to establish his / her innocence, if necessary, or to show that he / she was subjected to injury while in police custody.

Where the person to be examined is a female, the examination must be made only by or under the supervision of a female registered medical officer.[46]

A new sub section (2) was inserted in Section 54 by the Amendment Act 2005. This amendment is inserted to provide a copy of the report of the medical examination of the arrested person should be furnished by the registered medical practitioner to the arrested person or the person nominated by such arrested person.

Examination of women witnesses

The Cr.P.C. has given powers to a police officer to make any person to attend before him for the purpose of investigation. According to Sec. 160(1) of the Cr.P.C. any police officer making an investigation may, by order in writing, require the attendance before himself of any person being within the limits of his own or any adjoining station who, from the information given or otherwise, appears to be acquainted with the facts and circumstances of the case, and such person shall attend as so required.

The proviso of this Section lays an obligation on the police officer with regard to the examination of women witnesses. That is to say, whenever a woman is required to be examined as a witness in connection with a case, she should not be summoned to the police station.

Prior to the Amendment Act 26 of 1955 even a child or woman, if so required by the investigating officer, was bound to attend at the place of the investigation. After the amendment, if the officer wants to examine a child below 15 years or a woman (whether Purdanashin or not), he must go to their residence. A lady even if suspected of any crime cannot be called to the police station even for the purpose of investigation and a duty is cast upon the investigating agency to examine her at the place of her residence.[47]

The Supreme Court[48] also pointed out that

> "there is a public policy, not complimentary to the police personnel, behind this legislative prescription which keeps juveniles and females from police custody except at the former's safe residence".

Apart from the above provision, the Law Commission[49] opined that when a young person below fifteen years or a woman is examined by the police during investigation, a relative or friend of such a male person or a woman or a representative of a recognised organisation interested in women and children's welfare should be allowed to be present. This point was also considered by the Law Commission in its Report on Rape and Allied Offences which favoured an amendment of Sec. 160(1) Cr.P.C. for the purpose.[50]

The court further added that if a police officer acted contrary to the proviso to Sec.160(1) of the Cr.P.C., such deviation must be visited with prompt punishment since policemen cannot be a law unto themselves while expecting others to obey the law.

If the provision is violated, and the child or woman is kept under restraint in the police station or any other place of investigation, the investigating officer may be liable to punishment under Sections 341 and 342 of the I.P.C.[51] Thus, the provision is intended to give special protection to women and children against the probable indignities and inconveniences that might be caused to them by the abuse of power by the police.

It is evident that Cr. P.C. has limited provision for protecting the accused women. The amendments made as late as 2005 gave protection to women at the time of arrest where it specifically said that women should not be arrested after the sunset and before sunrise. However the latest amendment remained silent on the mode of arrest. Sec. 46(1) specifically says that the police officer making arrest is required to actually touch or confine the body of the person. It even applies to women giving a change for male officers to misbehave with women while arresting him. Similarly there are no special provisions are provided when women are detained in police lock up, remand etc.

This lacuna in the Code has resulted in the high-handed behaviour of the police personnel. The women were routinely summoned and ill-treated by the police.

While some of the complaints against the police officials on the treatment of women remained as mere allegations, the *Mathura* and *Ramizabi* cases proved conclusively the brutality of men in uniform. The sexual assault by the custodians of law on the helpless women has touched the collective conscience of the public and the resultant condemnation has forced the Government of India to issue special instructions to the States and Union Territories through the Home Secretary, Government of India in 1980.[52]

The instructions pertain to the arrest of women, search of women suspects, women as undertrials, women in custody, etc. They are largely aimed at restraining the police force from its unlawful behaviour. They are -

(1) Arrest

Police officers are vested with wide discretionary powers of arrest. According to Sec. 46(1) of Cr.P.C., a police officer making an arrest is required to actually touch or confine the body of the person to be arrested, unless there be a submission to the custody by word or action. In case of women, their submission to the custody should be presumed unless proved otherwise and there should be no occasion for a police officer arresting a woman to touch her person. The Law Commission of India, in its one hundred thirty fifth report on 'Women in Custody' expressed the same view. The recommendation of the Commission in this regard was to add the following proviso in Sec. 46(1) of the Code:

> "Provided that where a woman is to be arrested, then, unless the circumstances indicate to the contrary, her submission to custody on an oral intimation of arrest shall be presumed, and unless the circumstances otherwise require or unless the police officer arresting is a female, the police officer shall not actually touch the person of the woman for making her arrest."[53]

It is also necessary to ensure that except in unavoidable circumstances no woman should be arrested between sunset and sunrise. If one has to be arrested during night, the police officer must obtain prior permission of his immediate superior officer and furnish written reasons thereto. If the circumstances make the arrest imminent, then the justification for making the arrest during night should be reported to the immediate superior officer without delay. In some States, only police officers of the rank of Assistant Sub-Inspector or above are empowered to effect arrest of women, and also to report all such arrestees to their Sub-Divisional Police Officers/District Superintendents of Police.

In bailable cases, bail should be granted without delay. If the offence is non-bailable the arrested woman should be remanded to judicial custody with utmost expedition. While being escorted to jail, a male relative should be permitted to accompany the escort party.

(2) Detention in police lock-up

If for good and valid reasons, an arrested woman has to be detained in police custody, it should be ensured that she is kept in a female lock-up at the police station, and where a separate lock-up is not provided for females, she should be kept in a separate room and not in the male lock-up. In addition, a male or female relative of the arrested woman should be permitted to stay on the premises of the police station and the place of custody of the arrested woman should be within his/her view. If no male or female relative is available, the services of some local female should be requisitioned and, if necessary, she should be paid for the services.

(3) Police remand

In very exceptional circumstances, the police should ask for the custody of an arrested woman on remand. Before any such request is made, a Gazetted Police Officer must satisfy himself about the grounds and arrangements made for the safety of the arrested woman.

(4) Women police

Women police, wherever available, should be utilized for dealing with women accused and, in particular, for searching their person, escorting them to jail, and keeping a watch on them while in the police lock-up.

The guidelines issued by the Union Government, it seems, were routinely passed on to the police authorities by the State Government, and men in uniform have not cared much to abide by them. The continued custodial offences against women reflect the scant regard shown to the Central Government guidelines by the police force.

The existing instructions of the Central Government are only administrative directions and they have no legal force.

If the authorities violate these instructions, the remedy is only administrative i.e., approaching the higher authorities, but there is no legal remedy. These instructions do not confer enforceable rights on women. So the Cr.P.C. should suitably be amended to incorporate these special instructions regarding arrests, detention and treatment of women in the lock-up.

The ghastly act of parading Maya Tyagi naked and the subsequent rape of her by the police has hit the headlines within three months of the issue of the guidelines. This followed the now well known petition of the reputed journalist, Ms.Sheela Barse against the custodial offences of the Bombay city police.

While disposing of the petition[54], the Supreme Court had issued certain directions to the police to follow. The directions are:

1. To keep the police lock-up in good localities where only female suspects should be kept and they should be guarded by female constables.
2. The female suspects should not be kept in a lock-up in which male suspects are detained.
3. The interrogation of female suspects should be carried out only in the presence of female police officers and female constables.
4. The Magistrate before whom the arrested person is produced should enquire from that person whether he or she was tortured or maltreated in the police lock-up. He should also inform the right to be medically examined.

In spite of the instructions of the Government of India and directions of the Supreme Court, the crimes against women in police custody are on the rise.

Recommendations of National Expert Committee

The National Expert Committee on Women Prisoners headed by Justice Krishna Iyer made the following suggestions in its report in the year 1987 under sub-heading "women and the police", with a view to protect the dignity of women under the State care and custody.[55]

1. Taking note of the special role of the women in the family, the greater probability of her being available for assisting the criminal process, the potential for abuse of her person in custody, and the lesser threat posed by her to the security of the society, it shall be the policy of the State including the police to avoid the arrest and detention of females excepting when there are special reasons recorded in writing to disregard this policy in specific situations.
2. Whenever arrest is to be made, women's submission to custody shall be presumed unless proved otherwise; there should be no occasion for a male police officer arresting a woman to touch her person.
3. Except in unavoidable circumstances, no woman needs to be arrested between sunset and sunrise.
4. Only officers of and above the rank of Assistant Sub-Inspector should effect the arrest of a woman.
5. In all cases of bailable offences, bail on her bond shall be granted forthwith by the police themselves.
6. As far as possible, in non-bailable cases also, bail should be granted unless special circumstances warrant a different course, in which case, the arrested woman shall be remanded to judicial custody with utmost expedition.
7. Such custody shall only be in a separate police lock-up for women and, where such facility is not available, in a special home or institution designated under any

law for the time being in force to receive women. At no time shall a woman arrestee be left unguarded by a woman guard or surrogate.

8. In all places of police custody, basic amenities such as living space, water, toilet, food, medical examination and care, and provisions to meet the special needs of women shall be provided.

9. The State shall, as soon as may be, draw up a charter of minimum standards of treatment, including amenities which shall obtain in police custody for custodial inmates as well as staff. The standards shall also spell out the rights and duties of inmates and staff, and shall serve as a manual of instructions and be enforceable in the manner indicated.

10. When arresting a woman, proper arrangements for the protection and care of her children shall be the responsibility of the State. Children who need to be custodialized jointly with their mothers shall enjoy rights justly needed, while in custody, in terms of food, living space, health, clothing and visitation.

11. The person of a woman shall not be searched except by a woman duly authorised by law, and in a manner strictly in accordance with the requirements of decency. Whether in custody or in transit, the arrested woman must always be guarded by a woman police or a female surrogate. While escorting, a relative may be permitted to accompany the female arrestee.

12. Whenever a woman is to be examined by the police or other investigative agency as a witness, it should be done only at her residence; nor should she be summoned to the police or investigative station unless she expresses her preference to be examined in the station.

13. Before taking a woman into custody, the police shall record the fact in relevant records and responsible officers shall ensure that 'detention' without making formal entries is strictly avoided.

14. All senior police officers visiting police stations in their official rounds must as a working rule, enquire personally into the conditions of the woman taken into custody and check the promptness with which entries are made, information forwarded, grounds of arrest furnished to the accused, etc. The result of the enquiry must be recorded by the officers.

15. Information on women in custody should be made available to recognized social organisations and individuals on request. Persons and institutions accredited as visitors should be allowed, as of right, free access to police stations and records.

16. Whenever a woman is arrested by the police without warrant, she must be immediately informed of the grounds of arrest and the right of bail.

17. In exceptional circumstances when a woman arrestee is taken to a police lock-up, the police should immediately give intimation to the nearest Legal Aid Committee or recognised legal services body which must render all necessary legal services at State expense.

18. On arrest, the police should immediately obtain from the arrestee the name of a relative or friend to whom the intimation of her arrest should be promptly given.

19. A substantial increase shall be effected in the woman component of the police force at all levels and adequate training given.

20. In endemic female crime areas, or wherever otherwise desirable, exclusive police stations, or booths and

counter within police stations, shall be set up to deal with women needing protection of, or coming in conflict with, law. Such booths and police stations shall be managed by an integrated cadre of men and women police specially trained and sensitized to deal with women.

21. Crime and arrest data gathered by the police should maintain separate streams of information on men and women. Sex-wise data should be compulsorily compiled and displayed in all police stations and reflected in all reports on crime, arrest and disposal.

22. Any violation or deviation or action on the part of any officer which defeats the policy of the above provisions shall be punished after due enquiry by a Judicial Magistrate of the first class. The nature and quantum of the punishment shall be decided by the Sessions Judge having the requisite jurisdiction. An appeal to the High Court shall be available for any aggrieved party.

23. Where the wrong is proved, the wrong-doer and, whether proved or not, the State shall make fair reparation to the victim to be determined by the sessions judge.

Recommendations of National Commission for Women

The recommendations made by the Expert Committee remained as mere recommendations since the Government failed to take any follow-up action as pointed out by Smt. Jayanti Patnaik, the then Chairperson, National Commission for Women. The National Commission for Women made the following suggestions in 1993 to the Ministry of Home Affairs after their deliberations on "Custodial Justice for Women[56]" held at New Delhi in

February 1993. The relevant suggestions include:

(1) Arrest of women, search, bail, etc.

1. Women shall not be arrested between sunset and sunrise and shall not be arrested except in the presence of women.
2. In all cases of bailable offences, bail on her bond shall be granted forthwith by the police themselves. As far as possible, in non-bailable cases also, bail should be granted unless special circumstances warrant a different course, in which case, the arrested women shall be remanded to judicial custody with utmost expedition.
3. On arrest, the police should immediately obtain from the arrestee the name of a relative or friend to whom the intimation of her arrest should be promptly given.
4. If considerations of arrestee's own safety and freedom from ensnarement by anti-social elements demand detention in public institutions, bail shall be refused to the women in her own interest, unless she specifically states her willingness to be thus released even after being alerted to the above considerations.
5. The person of women shall not be searched except by a woman duly authorised by law, and in a manner strictly in accordance with the requirements of decency. Whether in custody or in transit, the arrested woman must always be guarded by a woman police or a female surrogate. While escorting, a relative may be permitted to accompany the female arrestee.
6. Whenever a woman is to be examined by the police or other investigative agency as a witness, it should be done only at her residence. Nor should she be summoned to the police or investigative station unless she expresses her preference to be examined in the station.

(2) Exclusive custody for women

1. Police stations serving women only and exclusive lock-ups under the control of women police and like provision in women's jails should be made. This will necessitate amendment of Prisons Act and Police Act.

2. Separated space for female arrestees in every police lock-up and complete segregation of women prisoners in jail and other custody should be maintained.

3. Such custody shall only be in a separate police lock-up for women and, where such facility is not available, in a special home or institution designated under any law for the time being in force to receive women. At no time shall a woman arrestee be left unguarded by a woman guard or surrogate.

4. In all places of police custody basic amenities such as living space, water, toilet, food, medical examination and care, and provisions to meet the special needs of women shall be provided.

(3) Visitatorial provisions in custody

1. Additional provision should be made in the existing legislation conferring visitatorial rights to recognised institutions or individuals, including access to institutional and inmate records and also providing for institutional and individual accountability for lapses and excesses.

2. Information on women in custody should be made available to recognised social organisations and individuals on request. Persons and institutions accredited as visitors should be allowed, as of right, free access to police stations and records.

(4) Socio-legal counselling

In exceptional circumstances when a woman arrestee is taken to a police lock-up, the police should immediately give intimation to the nearest legal aid committee or recognised legal services body which must render all necessary legal services at State expense.

(5) Children accompanying women in police custody

When arresting a woman, proper arrangement for the protection and care of her children shall be the responsibility of the State. Children who need custodialization jointly with their mother shall enjoy the rights justly needed, while in custody, in terms of food, living space, health, clothing and visitation.

(6) Women's Assistance Police Unit

1. Women's Assistance Police Unit (WAPU) containing a cadre of men and women police with the specific task of crime prevention work and assistance to women should be set up in each district.
2. In endemic female crime areas or wherever otherwise desirable, exclusive police stations or booths and counters within the police stations, shall be set up to deal with women needing protection of, or coming in conflict with law. Such booths and police stations shall be managed by an integrated cadre of men and women police specially trained and sensitized to deal with women.

For further strengthening the existing legal provisions and safeguards, the Criminal Procedure Code (Amendment) Bill, 1994, containing the following important amendments, having a direct bearing on human rights, namely,

1. Prohibition of arrest of women before sunrise and after sunset.

2. Mandatory provision for conveying information about detainees to their friends/relatives nominated by them.
3. Furnishing a copy of the medical report to the detainee when requested.
4. Mandatory judicial inquiry in case of alleged death, disappearance and rape in custody, should be expeditiously passed by the Parliament.

At the time of trial procedure

Criminal cases have to make a long journey of investigation, enquiry, trial, etc. Thus the procedural law consists of hundreds of provisions relating to enquiry, trial etc., to determine the guilt or innocence of the undertrial prisoner. Unfortunately, the Cr.P.C. is silent in providing protection to women prisoners in judicial custody except in certain conditions.

Bail

In case of bailable offences the accused is entitled to bail as a matter of right if he/she is prepared to give bail. If the police officer and the court thinks that the arrested person is indigent and is unable to furnish surety, instead of taking bail from such person, discharge him/her on executing a bond without sureties for his/her appearance[58].

Further explanation says that when a person is unable to give bail within a week of the date of his arrest, it shall be sufficient ground for the officer or the court to presume that he/she is an indigent person[59].

A person who is accused of bailable offence has to remain in jail for his/her inability to furnish bail. Therefore Section 436 (1) is amended[60] to make a mandatory provision that if the arrested person is accused of bailable offence and is indigent and cannot furnish surety, the court shall release him/her on his/her execution of a bond without sureties.

There had been instances where undertrial prisoners were detained in jail for periods beyond the maximum period of imprisonment provided for the alleged offence. Therefore a new Section 436-A is being inserted in the code to provide that where an undertrial prisoner other than the one accused of an offence for which death has been prescribed as one of the punishment, has been under detention for a period extending to one-half of the maximum period of imprisonment provided for the alleged offence, he/she should be released on his/her personal bond, with or without sureties. It is also proposed to provide that in no case will an undertrial prisoner be detained beyond the maximum period of imprisonment for which he/she can be convicted for the alleged offence.

But in case of non-bailable offences, it is a discretionary power vested on the officer-in-charge of police station and on court. In non-bailable offences, a distinction is made between offences punishable with death or imprisonment for life and other offences.

Sec. 437(1) of the Cr.P.C., 1973 says that the accused shall not be released on bail, if there appears reasonable ground for believing that he has been guilty of an offence punishable with death or imprisonment for life. However, the court may direct that any person under the age of sixteen years or any woman or any sick or infirm person accused of such an offence be released on bail,[61] after recording its reasons in writing for doing so.

There is no direct authority of the Supreme Court on this issue, whether the word 'may' has to be read as "shall". But the Supreme Court has made some observations in *Gurucharan Singh v. Delhi Administration*.[62]

> "In other non-bailable cases, the court will exercise its judicial discretion in favour of granting bail subject to sub-sec.(3) of Sec.437, Cr.P.C., if it deems necessary

to act upon it, unless exceptional circumstances are brought to the notice of the court which may defeat proper investigation and a fair trial, the court will not decline to grant bail to person who is not accused of an offence punishable with death or imprisonment for life. It is also clear that when an accused is brought before the Court of Magistrate with the allegation against him of an offence punishable with death or imprisonment for life, he has ordinarily no option in the matter but to refuse bail subject, however to the first proviso to Sec.437(1), Cr.P.C. and in case where the Magistrate entertains a reasonable belief on the materials that the accused has not been guilty of such an offence. This will, however be an extraordinary occasion since there will be some material at the stage of initial arrest, for the accusation or for strong suspicion of commission by the person of such an offence".

So far as the High Courts are concerned there is controversy regarding the interpretation of the word 'may' in the first proviso to Sec.437 of the Cr.P.C. 1973.

Some of the High Courts expressed the word 'may' is only directory and not mandatory and held that bail cannot be granted only on the ground that accused is a woman.[63] Some other High Courts took the contrary view that the word 'may' used in the proviso means "shall" and hence it is mandatory and held that a woman is entitled to release on bail.[64]

The word "may" has been interpreted by the Hon'ble Supreme Court[65] as follows:

"There is no doubt that the word "may" generally does not mean "must" or "shall" but it is well settled that word "may" is capable of meaning of "must" or "shall" in the light of the context. It is also clear that

> where discretion is conferred upon a public authority coupled with an obligation the word "may" which denotes direction should be construed to mean a command. Sometimes a legislature uses that word "may" out of deference to the high status of authority on whom power and obligation are intended to be conferred".

For instance, the words 'may take cognizance' under Sec. 190(1)(b) of the Cr.P.C. are to be read as "must take cognizance" i.e., the magistrate is bound to take cognizance of any cognizable offence brought to his notice. Thus he has no discretion in this case because it is violative of Art.14 of the Indian Constitution.[66]

According to the interpretations of the Supreme Court[67] and some of the High Courts, especially Rajasthan High Court,[68] the word "may" in proviso first of Sec.437 Cr.P.C. has to be read as "must" or "shall". Thus this proviso being mandatory, the court is under obligation to release the accused persons including women on bail.

Keeping in view, the status of women in India, this proviso was inserted under Sec. 437 Cr.P.C. to avoid women being kept in custody as far as possible.

It is an obligation on the part of the court to interpret the law as it is and release the women accused on bail liberally even if there are reasonable grounds to believe that she has been guilty of an offence punishable with death or imprisonment for life.

Dispensing with personal appearance of women accused before court

It is an established and cardinal principle of criminal jurisprudence that in all criminal proceedings, the evidence against the accused should be recorded in his/her presence and in an open court so that the accused will have an opportunity to challenge the evidence and can defend his/her case. But in certain cases, the court may dispense with the personal attendance of the accused and permit him/her to appear through a pleader.

The following are the relevant provisions under Cr.P.C.

Secs. 205 and 273 of the Cr.P.C. provide for exemption of an accused from personal attendance before the court.

Sec.205(1) of the Code reads thus:

> Whenever a Magistrate issues a summons he may, if he sees reason so to do, dispense with the personal attendance of the accused and permit him to appear by his pleader.

Sec.273 reads thus:

> Except as otherwise expressly provided, all evidence taken in the course of the trial or other proceedings shall be taken in the presence of the accused, or when his personal attendance is dispensed with, in the presence of his pleader.

Both Sections provide for the exemption of the accused from personal attendance, but they refer to different stages of the proceedings. Thus Sec. 205(1) deals with the initial appearance of the accused person before the Magistrate who issues summons, while Sec.273 deals with the presence of the accused person at the trial and empowers the presiding officer, whether he is a Magistrate, Sessions Judge or Judge of the High Court to dispense with the personal attendance of the accused at the trial.[69]

In 1951, the Calcutta High Court expressed its view that a purdanashin woman[70] has to be exempted from personal attendance, in cases involving no moral turpitude.

Other High Courts have also taken similar views[71] in dispensing with the personal appearance of purdanashin women. They further exempted those accused who are highly placed public functionaries and persons rendering public service.

The High Court of Gauhati in *M.J. Marjina Begum and Others v. Matakhal Ali,*[72] while dealing with the necessity of seeking attendance of the women accused in a criminal trial by the learned Magistrate, held that:

> "Women should not be asked to appear in person in court unless there are some strong reasons for insisting upon their personal presence in court. Discretion in their favour ought to be liberally exercised in view of the social conditions that exist today".

The use of the expression "if he sees reason so to do" clearly indicates that the power conferred by Sec. 205(1) is discretionary and no hard and fast rule can be laid down, as to the manner in which it is to be exercised. It has to be considered after giving due consideration to the attendant circumstances. No sweeping generalizations can be made. The court should be generous in exempting accused persons from personal appearance. Such appearance is the rule in criminal cases of a serious nature, involving moral turpitude and punishable with imprisonment for some length of time. The courts should consider the nature of the aberration alleged, prima facie material for acceptance of such allegation, the possibility of malafide allegation and prejudice if any likely to be caused if personal attendance is not made. The courts have to weigh the inconvenience likely to be caused to an accused if he is required to be absent from his vocation, profession, trade, occupation and calling for attendance in court, against the prejudice likely to be caused if he does not appear in court. Whenever personal attendance is insisted upon, there is indubitably some harassment to the accused and the courts have to see that this harassment is not out of proportion to the seriousness of the allegation, the severity of possible punishment on conviction and the nature of allegations as they stand out prima facie. Court is expected to exercise its discretion after considering comprehensively all the details. Courts should normally dispense with the personal appearance when it concerns a purdanashin woman, highly placed public functionary . . . . . and the like.[73]

In *Tilotama Kar v. Ranjitarani Satpathy* case,[74] the Orissa High Court held that "although there is no exception in law that merely because an accused is a purdanashin woman, discretion must be exercised in her favour, yet it should be reasonably exercised in consideration of habits and customs of the country and the prejudice caused to a woman when she is required to attend any court regularly. In a conservative society normally such appearances are looked down. Public appearance of women still continue to be a taboo in a conservative society. The mere fact that an accused is a purdanashin lady does not entitle her to remain exempted all the time even if her presence is required for proper conduct of the case. As a matter of right, exemption from personal appearance cannot be claimed.

While dealing with an application for dispensing with the personal attendance the court should not take too technical or stringent a view. The approach should be to see whether personal appearance is absolutely necessary for the purpose of the case.

In *Kaveri v. State*,[75] the facts of the case were that two ladies were shown as absconders in the charge sheet and it was pleaded that as they were purdanashin ladies, they should be exempted from personal attendance and the fact that the accused were married women and residing with their respective-in-laws, there was no scope of their absconding or fleeing from justice. Taking these factors into consideration, the Orissa High Court dispensed with the personal appearance of the accused petitioners.

The Karnataka High Court in *Shakuntala v. Virupanna S*,[76] after referring to the relevant provisions of law and of the High Court of Guwahati[77] made it abundantly clear that the criminal courts should not be unduly strict and harsh in the matter of securing personal attendance of the women accused in a criminal proceeding against them and that they should normally adopt a liberal and humane approach in the matter of granting them exemption from personal attendance when so requested by an advocate. This duty on the part of the learned trial judges gains all the more importance considering the social milieu and ethos peculiar to the Indian society. While dealing with an application of any woman accused for her exemption from personal attendance in a criminal trial against her, the criminal courts must keep themselves informed of the religious and cultural susceptibilities, gender susceptibilities such as the sense of shame, modesty and stigma with which a woman accused of a crime would usually be overtaken during her trial in a criminal court; and the social and religious customs and practices of the particular community to which a woman accused belongs, placing constraints on her public appearance viz., a purdananshin lady.

In this case, the petitioner was a widow who was a permanent resident of Bangalore city and the court where she was being tried is at a distance of about 200 km from Bangalore. So an application under Sec. 205 Cr.P.C. was filed on her behalf to exempt her from personal attendance at the trial in the case. The Karnataka High Court granted exemption from personal appearance during her trial unless her presence is essential at any particular stage of the trial proceeding to avoid failure of justice.

From the above account, it is clear that women need to be treated differently though there is no such distinction in the term 'accused'. The personal appearance of the women accused, involved in non-serious cases, may be done away with. The very atmosphere of the court itself, where a large number of undertrials and other accused are gathered, is a punishment for the women accused to become a part of that group. Waiting for her turn from morning to evening keeps her away from house and children. The social stigma attached to the accused is also unbearable. The insistence to appear before court in all hearings and at every stage of the trial is an avoidable harassment to the women.

Therefore, it is suggested that a new provision may be inserted in Sec.205 and also in other parts of Cr.P.C. so that the presence of the women accused whether pardanashin or not, may be dispensed with at the trial. Depending on the severity of the offence and the need for her presence the women accused may still be summoned.

Release on probation

Sec. 360(1) of the Cr.P.C. comprises two classes of cases –

(1) Sub-section (1) relates to release on probation of good conduct on bond, and

(2) Sub-section (3) relates to release on or after admonition.

The conditions laid down in sub-sec.(1) for release on probation are:

(a) That the accused is either -

   (i) a person of 21 years or above, convicted of an offence punishable with fine only or imprisonment for 7 years or less; or

   (ii) a person under 21 years or a woman, convicted of an offence which is not punishable with death or imprisonment for life;

(b) that no previous conviction has been proved against the accused;

(c) the court convicting him or her considers that having regard to the age, character or antecedents of the offender and the circumstances in which the offence was committed, it is expedient that the offender should be released on probation of good conduct, instead of sentencing him at once to any punishment.

Then the court, whether trial court, appellate court or the High Court or Court of Session when exercising its powers of revision, may deal leniently with a person who has committed an offence for the first time by releasing him on probation of good conduct instead of awarding him punishment so as to give a chance to the offender to reform himself and to protect him from becoming a regular criminal by association with hardened criminals in jails.

In *State of H.P. v. Sheelan Devi*[78] the learned Sessions Judge convicted the accused respondent Sheelan Devi under Sec. 436[79] IPC and instead of sentencing her he extended the benefit of the provision of Sec. 360 read with Sec. 361[80] of the Cr.P.C. and ordered her release after executing a personal bond for a period of 3 years.

Himachal Pradesh High Court held that sub-section (1) of Sec. 360 of the Cr.P.C., in terms, *inter alia*, lays down that even in the case of any person under 21 years of age or any woman, as in the instant case, the conviction should be of an offence not punishable with death, or imprisonment for life, meaning thereby, that in case they are convicted of the offences which are punishable with death or imprisonment for life the provisions of Sec. 360 of the Cr.P.C. would not come into operation and as such the court has no power whatsoever to release such a person on probation.

Women who commit offences which are not punishable with death or life imprisonment and first offenders must be released on probation instead of putting them behind bars.

Death sentence on pregnant woman

When any person is sentenced to death by a Court of Session, the sentence shall not be executed unless it is confirmed by the High Court.[81] When the sentence is confirmed by the High Court, the Court of Session shall issue a warrant to the Superintendent of the prison in which the prisoner is confined to cause the sentence to be carried into effect.[82] If a woman sentenced to death is found to be pregnant, the High Court shall order the execution of the sentence to be postponed and may, if it thinks fit, commute the sentence to imprisonment for life.[83]

In *State of Tamil Nadu v. Nalini,*[84] in respect of the assassination of Rajiv Gandhi, the former Prime Minister of India, all the 26 accused had been sentenced to death by the trial judge. The Supreme Court finally confirmed the conviction only on six accused. Of the six persons convicted of the murder, the death sentence was imposed only on four accused and one of them is Nalini.

Because Nalini is a woman and a mother of the child who was born while she was in custody, K.T. Thomas J. felt that the death penalty should be converted to life sentence.

According to him, the following were the relevant considerations in the case of Nalini:-

> "Another consideration which we find difficult to overlook is – she is the mother of a little female child who would not have even experienced maternal huddling as that little one was born in captivity. Of course, the maxim 'justicia non novit patrem nec matrem' (justice knows no father nor mother) is a

> pristine doctrine. But it cannot be allowed to reign with its rigour in the sphere of sentence determination. As we have confirmed the death sentence passed on father of that small child, an effort to save its mother from gallows may not militate against 'jus gladii' so that an innocent child can be saved from orphanhood."

But Wadhwa and Quadri JJ who confirmed the death sentence felt from the facts that "the participation of Nalini was not the result of helplessness but a well-designed action with her free will to make her part of the contribution to the unholy plan and wicked conspiracy."

However, the Governor of Tamil Nadu State commuted the death penalty against Nalini to life sentence for reasons similar to those given by Thomas J.

Thus one question that arises often in relation to pregnant women and mother-and-baby units is whether this class of women should ever be given custodial sentences. One supporter of this point of view is James Anderson, Governor of a British Prison. In a memorandum to the Prison Department he argued:

> "It seems to me that a mother giving birth to a baby should always be given an opportunity to make a fresh start and that a caring and compassionate society should, if anything, err on the side of leniency. I doubt very much whether the community would be exposed to any undue risk and if we are serious about reducing sentence length I suggest a humane start could be made in this direction."[85]

The Chairman of the National Expert Committee also agreed with this view and expressed his opinion that the option must be given to the woman to go into or out of prison after explaining to her the advantages and disadvantages. Further, he opined that once the nutrition and medical attention is strengthened for expectant mothers and mothers and babies inside prison, they have a better chance in a well-run jail than if they are back home where medical neglect, inaccessibility to hospitals, nutritional illiteracy and general poverty imperil both mother and baby.

It is submitted that instead of giving an option to women to go into or out of prison, it is better to provide necessary medical assistance and nutritious food for both mother and baby.

Other critics have frowned upon remanding in custody pregnant women and mothers of young babies. Some of them give birth while in custody and may eventually be released as innocent. A Report from the Howard League for Penal Reform states:

> "The Chairman of the Parliamentary All Party Penal Affairs Committee, Robert Kilroy Silk, M.P., has commented. It is particularly important that women should not be imprisoned at the sensitive time of childbirth unless there are reasons of the most powerful kind for doing so. It is clear from these very disturbing figures that this is far from being the case at present. Before imprisoning a pregnant woman or mother with young children, a court should have to show that there is no alternative to doing so because the woman's imprisonment is essential to protect the public."[86]

Judges and Magistrates require a thorough sensitization and orientation for handling judicial proceedings relating to women. The judiciary while passing a sentence should understand the responsibility of a woman towards her children. Hence, a lenient view has to be taken in case of women offenders who are mothers or pregnant women. A statutory amendment is to be made keeping in view the welfare of the newly born baby or infant child. Whenever a woman sentenced to death is found to be pregnant instead of postponing the death sentence on her, it should be commuted to life imprisonment. An amendment in Cr.P.C. is needed for this purpose, keeping in view the welfare of the child.

Recommendations of National Expert Committee

The Expert Committee on women prisoners has taken into consideration all the observations made by the judiciary in various cases involving women and finally came out with the following recommendations under the sub-heading women and judiciary.[87]

1. In protecting the rights of the women in the criminal justice process from arrest through release, the judiciary has special responsibility to ensure that the principles and purposes of this Code are implemented. Judicial officers shall always respond to the distressed call of women in custody irrespective of their jurisdiction or status in the judicial hierarchy.
2. When produced before the Magistrate, he or she shall invariably ask the woman of the treatment given to her by the police and of any other special problems she encounters in her situation. Every effort shall be made to resolve those special difficulties and in cases where an immediate solution is not possible within the law, the Magistrate may explain the position to her and initiate appropriate action for redress.
3. Except in extreme situations when detention is desired, the Magistrate shall release the woman on her own bond, the conditions of which shall be explained to her by the Magistrate.
4. No judicial remand of women will be allowed except in those institutions which are completely under the control of women officials.

5. If considerations of arrestee's own safety and freedom from ensnarement by anti-social elements demand detention in public institutions, bail shall be refused to the woman in her own interest, unless she specifically states her willingness to be thus released even after being alerted to the above considerations.

6. In the disposition of women to custody or otherwise the Magistrate must enquire and direct that suitable arrangements for the welfare of her children be made in a manner that protects the rights of children.

7. Speedy trial of all cases involving women is a legal and moral requirement. All magistrates shall proceed with such trials with utmost expedition, with due regard to the principle of limitation where applicable. Special tribunals and procedures to carry out this directive shall be organized by Government in consultation with the High Court.

8. To the extent possible, the State shall set up Women's Courts to try women offenders. Where joint trial with man is involved, the courts may use their discretionary power whether to hold joint or separate hearings.

9. Right to legal aid in criminal proceedings is a fundamental right. In the case of women, free legal aid shall be given from the time of arrest and the Magistrate shall ensure that adequate legal services are provided.

10. Magistrate shall inform women, when first produced, of their right to legal aid at State expense and direct the provision of necessary services. They shall also explain the nature and scope of the proceedings against her and her rights in it.

11. When women are examined in court as accused or as witnesses, due courtesy and decency shall be shown. If circumstances so demand in the interest of modesty

and privacy of women, the trial may be held *in camera* or the woman may be examined on commission through women advocates.

12. Long cross-examinations and repeated examinations may be avoided in the case of women and, if necessary, information may be sought by affidavit and/or interrogatories.

13. Representation of women at all levels in the judiciary is essential to promote gender justice and women may be appointed in adequate numbers, among others, for processing cases involving women.

14. In courts processing cases involving women, the court staff should consist of sufficient number of women employees in order to avoid personal difficulties which women accused or women witnesses may face with the male dominated institutions and cadres.

15. Sentences and sentencing in respect of women offenders may have to take note of the solidarity of the family and the woman's unique role and needs. Except when unavoidable, custodialization shall not be resorted to. Community based treatment of women being ideal for them, their children and society, it is desirable to prefer such disposition.

16. While sentencing women to imprisonment or any form of custodialization, suitable arrangements should be made for the custody and welfare of their children.

17. Courts will take continuing interest in the welfare of women in custody and ensure that they receive proper treatment, including psychiatric and habilitative services.

18. Magistrates shall make frequent visits to jails and custodial institutions within their jurisdiction and shall file periodic reports to the superior judicial officers on the status and condition of women in such institutions.

19. In case of women in custody for long periods, premature release by reducing the sentence by courts may be considered. Parole, furlough and other forms of supervised release may be widely resorted to.

20. Short term sentences of less than six months may be totally avoided in case of women. Similarly simple imprisonment which is demoralizing and wasteful shall be avoided.

21. Where, owing to small numbers, the woman's custodialization amounts to solitary confinement, the court shall move for her immediate release unconditionally, or on probation or parole as may be deemed fit.

22. In the disposition of women offenders, courts should mandatorily call for and give due regard to the probation officer's report and to the report of medical/ psychiatric examination. Where probation officers are not available, probation investigation should be entrusted to recognized and accredited institutions and individuals.

23. Women, unless economically independent, shall not be sentenced to fine and alternatives such as admonition, conditional discharge, probation under supervision, etc., should be resorted to.

24. The courts shall not sentence any mentally sick woman or retardates to prison and shall ensure the immediate transfer of any existing cases of non-criminal and criminal lunatics to mental homes for therapeutic and habilitative care.

25. Insufficient escorting staff or facilities shall not be used as grounds for postponing the hearing or disposition of women. Whenever necessary, surrogate escorts should be used. In addition, the State Government through the Social Welfare Department should

develop an escort corps to serve the escorting requirements of female inmates in various custodial situations.

Recommendations of National Commission for Women

Further, the National Commission for Women also contributed their bit for custodial justice of women by making the following recommendations to be implemented by the Ministry of Home, Government of India.[88]

1. When women are examined in court as accused or as witnesses, due courtesy and decency shall be shown as the circumstances so demand; and in the interest of modesty and privacy of women, the trial may be held in camera or the women may be examined on commission through women advocates.
2. In the disposition of women offenders, courts should mandatorily call for and give due regard to the probation officer's report and to the report of medical/psychiatric examination. Where probation officers are not available, probation investigation should be entrusted to recognized and accredited institutions and individuals.
3. Right to legal aid in criminal proceedings is a fundamental right. In the case of women, free legal aid shall be given from the time of arrest and Magistrate shall ensure that adequate legal services are provided.
4. Magistrate shall inform women, when first produced, of their right to legal aid at State expense and direct the provision of necessary services. They shall also explain the nature and scope of the proceedings against her and her rights in it.
5. In the disposition of women to custody or otherwise the Magistrate must enquire and direct that suitable

arrangements for the welfare of her children be made in a manner that protects the rights of children.

The National Expert Committee for Women Prisoners, 1987 made elaborate recommendations regarding the protection of women in police and judicial custody. The National Commission for Women has also made its own recommendations in 1993 on the same subject. These recommendations made by those bodies are more or less the same and repetitive in their content. Despite all these well meaning recommendations whose implementation may not cause any extra expenditure, the executive sadly remained silent. This shows the lack of concern on the part of the executive towards the helpless women in custody.

The I.P.C. and Cr.P.C. contain several hundreds of provisions dealing with several aspects of the crime and administration of justice. However the provisions which are exclusively made for women are so negligible that they can be counted on one's fingers. As such, the custodial justice for women is a far cry, resulting in crime against women in the custody. Lack of protective provisions for the women in custody, in particular police custody, has started drawing the attention of the public in the early eighties.

The concerted efforts of the academicians, public-spirited activists and the judiciary resulted only in the amendment of rape laws in I.P.C. and inclusion of relevant provisions in Cr.P.C. and Evidence Act. The Government and the Supreme Court have also independently issued separate instructions and directions respectively to curb the menace of custodial offences in police stations.

References

1. Extracts from the Memorandum prepared on 1 May, 1980 by Dr. Upendra Baxi, Dr. Raghunath Kelkar and Dr. Lothika

Sarkar. Professors of Law, Delhi University submitted to the Home Minister, Law Minister and Members of Parliament. Ref in Anwarul Yaqin and Badar Anwar. "Protection of Women under the Law. An Annotated Bibliography" (1982); Deep and Deep Publications, New Delhi (p. 177) and also in Vimal Balasubrahmanyan, "Rape-Mortality Norms Remain" in "In Search of Justice". First Edn. (1990), Shubhada Saraswat Prakashan, Pune, pp.108, 112, 114.

2. *Sidheswar Ganguly v. State of West Bengal*, AIR 1958 SC 143: 1958 CriLJ 273: *Tukaram & another v. State of Maharashtra*, AIR 1979 SC 185: *Bharawada Bhoginbhai Hirjibhai v. State of Gujarat*, AIR 1983 SC 753: (1983) 3 SCC 217: 1983 CriLJ 1096.
3. *Tukaram & another v. State of Maharashtra*, AIR 1979 SC 185: 1978 CriLJ 1864: (1979) 2 SCC 143.
4. Indian Penal Code (Amendment) Act 43, 1983.
5. Secs. 375 & 376, Indian Penal Code, 1860.
6. Secs. 376A to 376D, *Ibid*., Ref in R.P. Kathuria, "Law of Crimes and Criminology", Vol. 3 (2001) Vinod Publications (P) Ltd., Delhi, pp. 2894, 2895, 2913, 2915.
7. Sec. 376(2)(a), Indian Penal Code, 1860.
8. Sec. 376(2)(b), *Ibid*.
9. Sec. 376(2)(c), *Ibid*.
10. Sec. 376(2)(d), *Ibid*.
11. Law Commission of India, 135th report on 'Women in Custody' (1989), Para 3.3, page 15.
12. Sec. 376B, Indian Penal Code, 1860.
13. Sec. 376C, *Ibid*.
14. Sec. 376D, *Ibid*.
15. Criminal Law (Amendment) Act, 43 of 1983.
16. Column 4 of First Schedule of Criminal Procedure Code, 1973 – Ref. in Dr. Awasthi, "Law of Bails and Remand", 2nd Edn. (2002), Ashoka Law House, New Delhi, p.150.
17. AIR 1990 SC 658: 1990 Cri LJ 889, (1990) 1 SCC 550.
18. *Krishan Lal v. State of Haryana* (1980) 3 SCC 150: AIR 1980 SC 1252.
19. *Bharawada Bhoginbhai Hirjibhai v. State of Gujarat*, AIR 1983 SC 753: 1983 CriLJ 1096: (1983) 3 SCC 217.

20. Sub-sec (1) of Sec 53 A of Cr PC 1973.
21. Sub-sec (2), *Ibid*.
22. Sub-sec (3), *Ibid*.
23. Sub-sec (5), *Ibid*.
24. Sec. 327(2) and (3), Criminal Procedure Code, 1973.
25. Criminal Law (Amendment) Act, 43 of 1983.
26. Sec 327(2), Criminal Procedure Code, 1973.
27. Sec. 327(3), *Ibid*.
28. *State of Punjab v. Gurmit Singh*, AIR 1996 SC 1393, 1996 CriLJ 1728: (1996) 1 SCJ 566.
29. Sec.228-A(3), IPC 1860 is inserted by the Criminal Law Amendment Act, 1983 (43 of 1983). Ref in P.S.A. Pillai. "Criminal Law", 9th Edn., (2000) Butterworths, New Delhi, pp.732-733.
30. Expl. to Sec.228-A(3), *Ibid*.
31. *R. Raja Gopal v. State of Tamil Nadu*, AIR 1995 SC 264: (1995) 2 SCJ 86: (1994) 6 SCC 632.
32. 1991 CrLJ 187: AIR 1991 SC 207.
33. Examples: Delhi Police Act, 1978, Bombay Police Act, 1951, West Bengal Police Act, 1952.
34. Inserted by the Code of Criminal Procedure (Amendment) Act, 2005 (25 of 2005), S.6 (w.e.f. 23-6-2006).
35. Sub-section (2) of Section 50-A., *Ibid*.
36. Sub-sec (3)., *Ibid*.
37. Sec. 47, Criminal Procedure Code, 1973.
38. Proviso of sub-sec.(2) of Sec.47, Criminal Procedure Code, 1973.
39. Sec.166 IPC provides; "whoever, being a public servant, knowingly disobeys any direction of the law as to the way which he is to conduct himself on such public servant intending to cause, or knowing it to be likely that he will, by such disobedience cause injury to any person shall be punished with simple imprisonment for a term which may extend to one year, or with fine, or with both".
40. Sec. 51, Criminal Procedure Code, 1973.
41. Sub-Sec.(2) of Sec.51, Criminal Procedure Code, 1973.
42. S.100(3) Cr.P.C. reads: "Where any person in or about such place is reasonably suspected of concealing about his person

any article for which search should be made. Such person may be searched and if such person is a woman, the search shall be made by another woman with strict regard to decency".

43. *Motilal v. State* (1958) 24 Cut.L.J. 445 (447) Ref. in D.D. Basu, "Criminal Procedure Code, 1973" (1979), Dum Dum Park, Calcutta, p.118.

44. *Kamalabai v. State of Maharashtra* AIR 1962 SC 1189 Para 3. Ref in S.C. Sarkar – "Sarkar on Criminal Procedure, 8th Edn. (2004) Indian Law House, Delhi, p.110.

45. Notes on clauses on the Bill of 1970, Ref. in D.D. Basu. "Criminal Procedure Code, 1973" (1979), Dum Dum Park, Calcutta, p.238.

46. Sec. 53(2), Criminal Procedure Code, 1973.

47. (1989) 1. Sim LC 288 at 298 Ref in N.D. Basu. "Basu's Code of Criminal Procedure", Vol. I, 9th Edn., (2002) Ashok Law House, New Delhi, p.795.

48. *Nandhini Satpathy v. P.L.Dani*, AIR 1978 SC 1025: 1978 CriLJ 968.

49. Law Commission of India, One Hundred thirty-fifth report on 'Women in Custody', (1989), Para 2.11, p. 5.

50. Law Commission of India, 84th Report (Rape and allied offences : Some questions of Substantive Law, Procedure and Evidence (1980) Para 3.24 to 3.25, p.18.

51. Cf. *Raja v. State of Haryana* (1971) 3 SCC 945 (Para 13).

52. Ministry of Home Affairs through its letter No. 9/18/79 to the Judicial Cell dated 10th and 14th March, 1980.

53. Law Commission of India, One hundred and thirty fifth report on 'Women in Custody' (1989), Para 2.2, p.3.

54. *Sheela Barse v. State of Maharashtra*, 1983 CriLJ. 642: AIR 1983 SC 378: (1983) 2 SCC 96.

55. Report of National Expert Committee on Women Prisoners (1986-87), Vol. I, pp.316-319.

56. "Custodial Justice for Women": National Commission for Women, (1993), p.3.

57. Sita Ram Singh. "Human Rights and Policing in India" (1997) CriLJ 125-128.

58. See Sec. 436 Cr.P.C. 1973.

59. Inserted by the Code of Criminal Procedure (Amendment) Act, 2005 (25 of 2005), S.35 (w.e.f. 23-6-2006).
60. Amendment Act, 2005.
61. First proviso to Sec. 437(1), Criminal Procedure Code, 1973.
62. AIR 1978 SC 179: 1978 CriLJ 129.
63. *Pramod Kumar v. Smt. Sadhana Rani*, 1989 CriLJ. 1772. *Smt. Chandra Kala v. State of Rajasthan* 1991 Raj Cric 426 (Raj): *Chandrawati v. State of U.P.* 1992 CriLJ. 3634: *Lahari Bai v. State of Rajasthan* 1996 CriLJ 682 (Raj).
64. *Smt. Choki v. State of Rajasthan*, AIR 1957 Raj 10: *Collector of Monghyr v. Keshav Prasad Goenka*, AIR 1962 SC 1614. *Shakuntala Devi v. State of U.P.*, 1986 CriLJ. 365. *Kane, W/o. Manguram v. State* 1987 CriLR. (Raj) 312: *Smt. Rameshwari Devi v. State* 1979 CriLR (Raj) 601. *Smt. Durga v. State of Rajasthan*, 1981 Raj. Cri.C 100 (Raj). *Smt. Madani v. State of Rajasthan* 1980 CriLR (Raj.) 499. *Smt. Uchhab Kanwar v. L.R. of Ram Swaroop*, AIR 1995 Raj 209.
65. In *State of U.P. v. Joginder Singh*, AIR 1963 SC 1618: 1963 (2) CriLJ. 529, Para No.8, also refer to *Wasim Beg v. State of U.P.*, AIR 1998 SC 1291.
66. *Agarwal v. Smt. Ram Kali* (Constitution Bench) AIR 1968 SC 1: 1968 CriLJ 82 A.C.
67. *State of U.P. v. Joginder Singh*, AIR 1963 SC 1618: 1963, CriLJ 529. *Wasim Beg v. State of U.P.* AIR 1998 SC 1291.
68. *Smt. Choki v. State of Rajasthan*, AIR 1957 Raj 10: *Collector of Monghyr v. Keshav Prasad Goenka*, AIR 1962 SC 1614. *Shakuntala Devi v. State of U.P.*, 1986 CriLJ. 365. *Kane, W/o. Manguram v. State* 1987 CriLR. (Raj) 312: *Smt. Rameshwari Devi v. State* 1979 CriLR. (Raj) 601. *Smt. Durga v. State of Rajasthan*, 1981 Raj. Cri.C 100 (Raj). *Smt. Madani v. State of Rajasthan* 1980 CriLR (Raj.) 499. *Smt. Uchhab Kanwar v. L.R. of Ram Swaroop*, AIR 1995 Raj 209.
69. *Zain Yar Jung v. Raghotam* AIR 1957 Andhra 468.
70. *Rajyalakshmi v. State* (1951) 46 C.W.N. 221. Ref. in S.C. Sarkar, "Sarkar on Criminal Procedure", 8th Ed. 2004, Indian Law House, Delhi, p.735.
71. *Sushila Devi v. Sharada Devi* 1961, CriLJ 819. *Jagadguru Sachidananda Shankara Bharati Swami of Sri Kudli Sringeri Mutt*

v. State of Mysore, AIR 1969 Mys. 96: 1969 CriLJ 423. *Raghunath Das v. Hari Mohan Pani* 1988 CriLJ 1573.

72. 1978 CriLJ NOC 292 (Gau).
73. These aspects were highlighted in *K.Narayana Patra v. Gopinath Sahu* (1991) 2 Orissa LR 401: 1991 CriLJ 3219.
74. (1992) 1 Orissa LR 437. Ref. in *Kaveri v. State* 1995 CriLJ 224 in Para 3.
75. 1995 CriLJ 224.
76. 2001 CriLJ1129.
77. 1978 CriLJ NOC 292 (Gau).
78. 1986 CriLJ 245.
79. Sec.436 IPC: Mischief by fire or explosive substance with intent to destroy house, etc.
80. Under section 361, the court is required to record special reasons in its judgement as to why in any case where the court could not have dealt with an accused person under section 360 of the Code or under the provisions of the Probation of Offenders Act, 1958.
81. Sec. 366, Criminal Procedure Code, 1973.
82. Sec. 413, *Ibid*.
83. Sec. 416, *Ibid*.
84. AIR 1999 SC 2640.
85. Women in Penal System – page 9. Ref to Report of National Expert Committee on Women Prisoners (1986-87), Vol. I, p.84.
86. Women in Penal System – page 9. Ref to Report of National Expert Committee on Women Prisoners (1986-87), Vol. I, p.84.
87. Report of National Expert Committee on Women Prisoners (1986-87) Vol. I, p.319.
88. Custodial Justice for Women – National Commission for Women, (1993), p.3.

4

Statutory Provisions Relating to Women Prisoners in Prison Custody

In this chapter, an attempt is made to review the status of women in prison custody. The statutes and rules made to protect the interest of women held in prison are presented. Protective provisions under Prisons Act, 1894 and Andhra Pradesh Prisons Rules (A.P. Jail Manual), 1979 are listed. The recommendations of National Expert Committee on Women Prisoners, 1987 and National Commission for Women, 1993 are presented and discussed. An attempt is made to compare the provisions in existing Prisons Rules in Andhra Pradesh and the recommendations made by Committee, Commissions etc. Some of the draft Prison Reform Bills were obtained and the important reformatory provisions in those bills are presented.

(i) Rights of Women Prisoners under Prisons Act of 1894

A prison, in all ages, was the place meant for law-breakers among others. In medieval times where the word of the King was final, the punishment was severe and jail was treated as a place for ill-treatment of sentenced persons. However, with the advent of democratic concept, there have been reforms on all issues in the society. Jails turned out to be not only a place where the law-breakers serve their sentences but also a place meant for reformation.

The principle that despite the detention, the human dignity should be respected was accepted. Accordingly a number of laws were enacted around the world. Though India was under colonial rule, it made several Acts for criminal justice.

All these laws gave the appropriate government powers to exercise control on the jail administration and proper treatment of prisoners. All these laws contain some provisions for the reformation of the prisoners, which is a pre-requisite for a healthy society. Borstal School Act, Habitual Offenders Act, Civil Jails Act, 1874, the Prisons Act, 1894, the Prisoners Act, 1900, the Identification of Prisoners Act, 1920, Exchange of prisoners Act, 1948, Transfer of Prisoners Act, 1950, the Prisoners (Attendance in Courts) Act, 1955, etc., contain provisions for the administration of prisons as well as treatment of prisoners. Besides these laws which extend to the whole country, there are several laws enacted by different State Governments to suit the local needs and to meet the internal conditions. From these Acts, it is evident that the executive had ample powers in the administration of prisons. Even the judiciary was silent and accepted this position till the eighties.

However, overcrowding in prisons, prolonged detention of under-trial prisoners, unsatisfactory living conditions, lack of fair treatment programmes and allegations of indifferent and even inhuman approach of prison staff have repeatedly attracted the attention of the critics over the years.

The existing laws have miserably failed not only in solving these problems in prisons, but also in caring to protect the dignity of the women prisoners. The women prisoners require a different kind of treatment at different stages of their life based on the social conditions. This fact has been ignored by the law makers. The women were never considered as a separate entity and were treated under the common term 'Prisoners'. May be at that time, the rate of criminality among women was low or the number of female convicts was negligible. Whatever might be the reasons, the women prisoners were not treated on a separate footing. So very few provisions were incorporated into the statutes which deal exclusively on the rights and issues concerned with women prisoners.

Though several studies were made on the general conditions of prisoners and their treatment in jails vis-à-vis the laws, and the rules governing the prison administration, very few attempts were made to study the issues from the female prisoner's perspective.[1]

The Prisoners Act, 1900 consolidated the law relating to prisoners confined by the order of the court. The Prisoners (Attendance in Courts) Act, 1955 provides rules and procedure for the attendance of prisoners in courts in person for obtaining their evidence or for answering criminal charges. The Transfer of Prisoners Act, 1950 provides a mechanism for the inter-State transfer of prisoners. These enactments do not contain any special provisions to protect the interests of women prisoners.

It is only the Prisons Act, 1894 that contains merely two provisions for the protection of women prisoners. This Act also had not provided for the needs of the contemporary correctional thinking.

The following are the special provisions contained in the Prisons Act, 1894 which are meant to protect the women prisoners.

Separation of prisoners

There is a provision regarding the separation of prisoners. It provides:

"In a prison containing female as well as male prisoners, the females shall be imprisoned in separate buildings, or separate parts of the same buildings in such a manner as to prevent their seeing or conversing or holding any intercourse with the male prisoners.[2] Unconvicted criminal prisoners shall be kept separate from convicted criminal prisoners".[3]

Safety from fellow prisoners

In order to ensure the physical safety of the inmates from other fellow prisoners, it is provided that before admission of a prisoner into the jail, he shall be searched and any article which is found during search shall be handed over to the Jailor. In case of women prisoners the search shall be carried out by a Matron under the general or special orders of the Medical Officer.[4]

(ii) Rights of Women Prisoners under Andhra Pradesh Prisons Rules, 1979

(A.P. Jail Manual)

The Prisons Act, 1894 insisted that the women prisoners should be placed in separate building or separate parts of the building so as to separate them from male prisoners. In 1986-87, the National Expert Committee on women prisoners recommended separate institutions/annexures for female prisoners.

Following these recommendations, the prison department of the Government of Andhra Pradesh (A.P.) has established two women prisons exclusively managed by women officers and staff. The State Jail for Women, Hyderabad, has an authorised capacity of 120 while the State Jail for Women, Rajahmundry, can accommodate 200 women prisoners. Apart from these, the female prisoners in Andhra Pradesh convicted for less than one month are confined to separate barracks/cells in the other central prisons located at Warangal, Visakhapatnam and Cuddapah. Even the 9 district jails and other 147 sub-jails in the State are provided with separate barracks and cells for lodging the women undertrials. Women prisoners sentenced to imprisonment exceeding one month by courts in the Telangana region are committed to the State Jail for Women, Chanchalguda, Hyderabad. While all women who are convicted for a jail term exceeding one month by the courts in the entire Coastal and Rayalaseema region of the State are committed to the State Jail for Women, Rajahmundry.

Separation of female prisoners

Under Sec. 27 of the Prisons Act, 1894 in case of a prison having both male and female prisoners, female prisoners shall be so separated from the male prisoners so as to prevent their seeing, conversing or holding any intercourse with the male prisoners. Under the same Section unconvicted female prisoners shall have to be kept apart from convicted female prisoners.

Female prisoners shall, as far as possible, be classified and separated, not only the unconvicted from the convicted but also adolescents from older prisoners, habituals from non-habituals and prostitutes and procuresses from respectable women.[5]

The undertrials and convicts are treated differently to a large extent except that a few provisions are common to both the categories of prisoners. At the time of admission into the prison both the undertrials and convicts are searched and medically examined without any distinction. Restrictions on the movements of the female prisoners are also common. Except for attending to the court, the prisoners of both types are not allowed to move out of their enclosures. Similarly, the restrictions on the entry of outsiders into an enclosure is also common. Both the undertrials and convicts are permitted to correspond and also have interviews with their advocates, relatives and other visitors. There are no separate provisions as such for such activities of undertrials and convicts.

Undertrial prisoners

According to Sec. 27 of the Prisons Act, 1894, unconvicted criminal prisoners (undertrial prisoners) shall be kept apart from convicted criminal prisoners. These prisoners are of two classes, i.e., special and ordinary.[6] The courts shall make the initial recommendation based on their social status, education and habit of life.[7] As far as possible, undertrial prisoners shall be confined each in a cell. The undertrial ward shall also be divided, if possible, into separate divisions, so that prisoners who have been in prison before shall be separated from those committed for the first time, adolescents from adult offenders and special class from the ordinary class.[8] They are allowed to receive or purchase uncooked packed food, clothing, bedding and other necessaries like soap, oil and tooth powder with their money. They are also allowed to receive these articles from their friends and relatives. A written undertaking shall be given by the undertrial prisoners and the supplier of food that they are responsible for any mishap that may happen. The Superintendent of the Jail has the authority to disallow or discontinue this concession at any time.[9] An undertrial prisoner who has no sufficient clothing of his own may be provided with the same at Government cost. Similarly soapnut and washing soda may be given to those who are unable to get the same at their own cost.[10] They are permitted to wear shoes or chappals, if provided by relatives or friends or at their own cost.[11]

Undertrials are allowed to read books in the prison library and they shall be allowed to purchase any daily newspaper.[12] They shall not be subjected to more restraint than necessary for their safe custody.[13] No undertrial prisoner shall be required to labour[14] but they shall be required to keep their yards, wards, cells and bedding clean, and also they shall not be compelled to perform duties of a degrading nature.[15]

The Superintendent is responsible for the production of the undertrial prisoners before the court, at the appointed time and shall make suitable arrangements with the police for necessary escort. The responsibility of providing escort and producing them before the court rests entirely with the police.[16] When women undertrial prisoners are taken from courts to prison or vice-versa, they shall be provided with conveyances where the distance to be traversed by them exceeds 1.60 kms. Conveyance may also be provided for shorter distances in cases in which, for reasons of health or custom or other valid reasons, failure to make such provision would cause undue hardship to them.[17] Undertrial prisoners shall be brought before the Magistrate at least once in 15 days for the purpose of remand.[18]

Admission of female prisoners

Under Sections 24 and 25 of the Prisons Act, 1894, prisoners shall be searched on admission and all weapons and prohibited articles shall be taken from them. In the case of female prisoners, the search and examination shall be carried out by the Matron under the general or special orders of the Medical Officer.

As per Rule 242 of the A.P. Prisons rules, on admission to jail all female prisoners shall be required to wash themselves and their clothing thoroughly. As per Rule 243, after washing, they shall be searched by a female Warder. Search and washing of female prisoners are to be conducted in a female yard or respective cells and not in the presence of other prisoners. Search is to be conducted with due regard to decency and with reasonable privacy.

At this search, every article whether clothing, bedding, jewellery, money or otherwise, shall be taken away from female prisoner on her admission to the jail.[19] All articles removed from a prisoner shall be dealt as prisoner's property.[20] But female prisoners shall be allowed to retain in moderation certain ornaments such as '*tali*', wedding ring, bangles etc. The articles will in no case be supplied at the expense of the Government. But the Superintendent may deprive these articles to any of the female prisoners for such a period as he thinks fit for disciplinary reasons.[21]

Every newly admitted prisoner shall be medically examined and all entries such as of age, height, weight, health and class of labour shall be made promptly in the Medical Sheet.[22]

Though the prison rules make it mandatory that upon admission of a person into prison a medical examination shall be conducted, the National Human Rights Commission (NHRC) "noted with dismay that, in many prisons, this has remained a mere procedural formality, presumably because of a lack of adequate medical staff, on the one hand, and an equal lack of concern on the part of the prison administration to follow the required procedure, on the other".[23]

The NHRC, therefore, felt it necessary to develop a format in respect of the medical examinations that should be conducted. The format was so devised as to benefit from modern techniques that are used in the preparation and maintenance of medical data and dossiers. It would place particular emphasis on the metabolic, nutritional and general medical status of the prisoner, particularly in relation to communicable diseases. The format included an indication by the examining Medical Officers as to the nature of the medical and diet regimen that should receive particular attention. Such a format of the initial medical examination results should be accurate and comprehensive so that whenever serious ailments are discovered or suspected, the format would, indeed, become the starting point for an effective and humane management of the health condition of the prisoners. The format also would indicate, wherever necessary, the need for confirmatory tests. In its efforts to devise the most appropriate format, the NHRC has been assisted by a committee of seven experts, who have since submitted their draft for the approval of the NHRC. In the interim, the NHRC recommended to all State Governments that all those who are in jail custody should be tested for tuberculosis, with their informed consent, and that, on the basis of such tests, appropriate remedial steps be initiated promptly.[24]

The NHRC in its Annual Report for the year 1998-99 felt that many lives could have been saved if proper medical examinations had been carried out at the time of the admission of a prisoner and if this had been followed up with periodical medical checks. Acting with the help of an expert group, it devised a proforma for the health screening of prisoners and directed Chief Secretaries of all States to ensure that medical examinations of all prisoners were conducted in accordance with that proforma. It also directed that monthly progress reports should also be communicated.[25]

Lack of medical facilities and negligence and carelessness on the part of jail authorities often result in the death of some prisoners. For example, one Mr. Bhagwan Ishwara Patil in Kolhapur Central Jail, Kalamba died due to a heart-attack and he was not given prompt medical attention despite his request. His plea for removal to a hospital for urgent treatment fell on the deaf ears of the Superintendent, Senior Jailor, and the Jailor. The jail authorities instead of sending Mr. Patil to the hospital for medical treatment, threatened him against making false pleas. The Bombay High Court directed the State Government to establish and continue to maintain a prison hospital as required under the Maharashtra Prison (Prison Hospital) Rules 1970, which shall be manned by a Medical Officer, Class I.[26]

Restrictions on female prisoners

No female prisoner shall, on any pretext, leave or be permitted to leave or be removed from the enclosures set apart for females, except for release, transfer or attendance at court, or under the order of the Superintendent for any other legitimate purpose.[27]

Every female prisoner authorised to leave the female enclosure shall ordinarily be accompanied by the Assistant Matron or a female Warden from the time she leaves the enclosure till she returns to it or quits the prison premises.[28]

Restriction on female enclosure

No adult male shall enter or be permitted to enter the female ward of any prison by day unless he has a legitimate duty to attend to there and is accompanied by the Assistant Matron or a female Warden while he remains therein. No adult male shall enter it at all by night except in an emergency. He shall then enter a distinct report of his visit with the reason and hour thereof in his report book.[29] Male Wardens acting as escorts to visitors and officials shall remain outside the enclosure.[30]

The locks of the enclosure and compartments where females are confined shall be different from those in use in other parts of the prison, so that the keys of the latter may not open the former. The keys of the female enclosure shall be kept in a separate glass fronted box next to the general key box. The key of this box shall be kept either by the Jailor or Assistant Matron according to local circumstances. In case of serious emergency such as fire or attempted suicide in the female enclosure, the Senior Warden on duty in the prison at the time shall break the glass, take out the keys and hand them over to the female section after having sent messages summoning the Jailor, Assistant Matron and Medical Officer.[31]

Diet

The State Government shall lay down a dietary scale for female prisoners keeping in view their calorification requirements as per medical norms. Every female prisoner shall be entitled to receive food daily at the prescribed time according to the prescribed scale. The diet of the individual prisoner may be modified on the recommendation of the Medical Officer.[32] Special diet to all classes of prisoners are provided on festival days.[33] If any complaint is made by a prisoner regarding the quantity, quality or cooking of the food, it shall be inquired into by the Jailor.[34]

Nursing mothers may be allowed, in excess of the ordinary labour rations, such articles of the diet as the Medical Officer may direct; the cost of the same shall be debited to extra provision.[35] Thus special consideration was provided to nursing female prisoners. It is submitted that such special consideration may be extended even to pregnant prisoners.

Clothing and bedding

State Government shall lay down suitable scales for the clothing and bedding of the female prisoners in accordance with the local climate requirements.[36] Extra clothing and bedding shall be issued to the sick, aged and infirm on the recommendation of the Medical Officer.[37]

Hospital clothing & bedding

Every female prisoner shall, on admission to hospital, be supplied with hospital clothing and bedding. In infective cases clothing and bedding are to be thoroughly disinfected.[38]

Personal hygiene - health, cleanliness

The hair of a female prisoner shall not be cut without her consent, except on account of vermin or dirt or when the Medical Officer deems it requisite on the ground of health and cleanliness and then the hair of such prisoner shall not be cut closer than necessary for the purpose of health and cleanliness. They shall each be provided with 8 gms of coconut oil daily for dressing the hair and 15 gms of soapnut powder twice a week for bathing. Female prisoners shall be supplied with a comb each and be allowed the use of a looking glass, one in each cell and one or two in each ward being provided.[39] Irrespective of her classification, each female prisoner shall be supplied with eight sanitary towels per mensem to maintain cleanliness during her menstrual period.[40]

Amenities

Married Hindu female prisoners may be permitted to wear bangles and they will be provided at the prisoner's expenses. If a female prisoner has no bangles or if the bangles break, she should be supplied with four plastic bangles at Government cost, where religion or custom makes the wearing of bangles obligatory.[41]

All married Hindu female prisoners whose husbands are alive should, on religious ground, be allowed to wear a small red mark (*kumkum*) on their foreheads. The female prisoners should be supplied with *kumkum* worth 25 paise per month in accordance with local customs at Government cost. These married Hindu female prisoners may also be allowed to wear *'mangala sutras'* and nose-rings according to their customs.[42]

A register should be maintained in every female prison by the Assistant Matron, for recording the regularity of the menses of female prisoners and the treatment given to them by the Medical Officer, if necessary, for any irregularity.[43] In all registers and returns the numbers and names of female prisoners shall be written in red ink.[44]

Sanitation

Women prisoners should be employed for conservancy work in women's institutions / annexures provided they volunteer for such work. If women prisoners are not available for this work, part time paid female scavengers should be appointed. Under no circumstances should male scavengers be allowed to enter the areas where women offenders are kept.[45]

Commenting on manual scavenging, the NHRC in its annual report 1997-98 observed as follows:

> "It is a matter of grave and unacceptable social injustice that even after 50 years of independence, the country permits the construction of dry latrines and the practice of manual scavenging. Realising how demeaning the practice of manual scavenging is, the Government of India has legislated twice in regard to this matter; to prohibit the construction of dry latrines and the employment of manual scavengers and announced a package of measures for the rehabilitation of the affected families who have given up their earlier work."

Noting, however, that very little had been done by the Central as well as the State Governments to enforce the legislation banning construction of dry latrines and to provide meaningful rehabilitation and dismayed by the continuance of the inhuman and degrading practice of manual handling of night soil, the Chairperson of the NHRC addressed a letter to the concerned Central Ministers and urged them to take positive steps to achieve this very important social goal.[46]

Education

Educational facilities should be provided in jails[47] during prescribed hours. Every prison shall be provided with a library of approved books, periodicals, newspapers, etc.[48] An elementary school with a qualified teacher should be established in each central prison and district jail. Prisoners may be supplied with a slate, pencil and other writing materials at the Superintendent's discretion,[49] either at the Government's or prisoner's cost.

Recreation

Female prisoners are entitled to recreation. The recreational activities inside the jail for women include indoor games like draughts and carrom and outdoor games like ring-tennis to be played regularly by the prisoners.[50] In addition to it group music, community and folk dances, educational films, arts and crafts[51] are to be provided as a recreation.

Vocational training and labour

All prison labour shall be divided into three main classes - hard, medium and light[52], basing upon the severity of punishment imposed on prisoners. No female convict shall, under any pretext, be employed outside the female enclosure of any prison.[53] They shall ordinarily be employed in cooking, or in the preparation of articles of food, such as pounding, husking or sifting grain and the like, but shall not be employed in grinding grain except as a punishment. Whenever possible they shall be given instruction in needle-work such as knitting, etc., and such other domestic industries as will be useful to them after release.[54] The tasks allotted to female convicts shall be from one half or two-thirds of those prescribed for male convicts.[55] The task to be imposed on any female convicts shall not exceed three-fourths of the task for hard labour prescribed in respect of adult male convicts.[56]

Female prisoners and their children

Female prisoners shall be allowed to keep their children up to five years of age in prison if the child cannot be placed with relatives or otherwise properly provided for. The children born in prison may remain with their mothers up to five years of age if they cannot be otherwise suitably disposed of. The Medical Officer shall determine the age of children not born in prison.[57]

No child shall be admitted into or retained in prison if it has attained the age of five years. Upon reaching the age of five years, the child may be handed over to a relative or guardian as per the wishes of the female prisoner provided such relative or guardian is willing to take care of the child. In case no relative or guardian is forth-coming, the case of the child may be reported to the nearest Magistrate of the First Class to be dealt with under the provisions of the Children Act.[58]

Children in prison shall be allowed such diet and clothing as the Medical Officer may order for them.[59]

When a female prisoner dies in prison leaving a child, the Superintendent shall inform the District Magistrate concerned who shall make necessary arrangements for the care of such a child. Should no friend or relation be found willing to take care of the child, the District Magistrate shall either place it in an approved institution or entrust it to some respectable person.[60]

Release and transfer of female prisoners

Release: Before a female prisoner is released, timely notice shall be sent to her relations or friends to enable them to attend at the prison and receive her. If no relative or friend appears on the day of the release, she may be sent to her home with the incharge of the female Warden should the Superintendent consider this course desirable.[61]

Female prisoners who are released from prisons shall be provided with conveyances where the distance to be traversed by them exceeds 1.6 km. Conveyances may also be provided for shorter distances in cases in which, for reasons of health, or customs, or other valid reasons, failure to make such provision would cause undue hardship to them. If necessary, the children of the female prisoners shall also be provided with batta and railway ticket.[62]

Transfer: Sec. 26 of the Prisons Act, 1894, requires that all prisoners, previous to transfer, shall be examined by the Medical Officer, who shall certify that they are free from any illness rendering them unfit for removal.

Whenever a female convict is transferred to a Home under orders of Government to pass the unexpired portion of her sentence there, the final date of her release including the remission earned in prison should be communicated to the officer-in-charge of the Home and the Inspector General.[63]

When women prisoners are taken from one prison to another on transfer, they shall be provided with conveyance where the distance to be traversed by them exceeds 1.6 km. Conveyances may also be provided for shorter distances in cases in which, for reasons of health, or custom, or other valid reason, failure to make such provision would cause undue hardship to them.[64]

When a female prisoner is transferred, a female Warden shall accompany her. The presence of a female Warden does not affect the responsibility of the police for the safe custody of female prisoners in transit.[65] During the transit, female and juvenile prisoners shall be separated from adult prisoners.[66]

Safety measures

A bell or gong must be provided in the female section so that attention may be attracted in case of emergency.[67] Some means of rapid communication must be provided between the main gate and the Assistant Matron's or Jailor's Quarters, either by a messenger or by an electric bell or similar contrivance. In some cases, it might also be desirable to have electric bell communication between the female enclosure and the main gate.[68] If the alarm from female section should merely be a complaint of illness or similar occurrence where a short delay would not matter, the Senior Warden, shall send for the Assistant Matron or Jailor.[69]

Interviews and communications with person

Every newly convicted prisoner including a female prisoner shall be allowed reasonable facilities for seeing or communicating with his/her friends, relatives or legal advisers with a view to the preparation of an appeal or to the procuring of bail and shall also be allowed to have interviews or to write letters to his/her relatives, friends or legal advisers, once or twice or often if the Superintendent considers if necessary, to enable her to arrange for the management of his/her property or other family affairs.[70] Suitable arrangements for writing letters and petitions for female convicts shall be made according to local circumstances.[71]

The Superintendent of Central Prisons, Rajahmundry and Hyderabad respectively may permit the prisoners to have interviews with their relatives who are inmates of State Jail for Women, Rajahmundry and local jails of Hyderabad respectively, when both parties are willing to have interviews with one another. In such cases, the prisoners of Central Prison, Rajahmundry are to be taken to the State Jail for Women, Rajahmundry and those of Central Prison, Hyderabad to local jails of Hyderabad and vice versa under the police or Warden escort.[72]

The Superintendent shall fix the day and hours at which all interviews shall be allowed and no interview shall be allowed at any other time except with the special permission of the Superintendent. A notice of the interview hours shall be posted outside the prison.[73]

Every interview shall take place in a special part of the prison appointed for the purpose, if possible at or near the main gate provided that interviews with female prisoners shall, if practicable, take place in the female enclosure, provided also that if a prisoner is seriously ill, the Superintendent shall permit the interview to take place in the hospital and a condemned prisoner shall ordinarily be interviewed in the cell. However, the Superintendent may for special reasons to be recorded in writing, permit an interview to take place in any part of the prison.[74]

Every interview with a convicted prisoner shall take place in the presence of a prison officer who shall be responsible that no irregularity occurs and who shall be so placed as to be able to see and hear what passes and to prevent any article being passed between the parties. The Assistant Matron or a female Warden shall be present at the interviews of female prisoners. Conversation at the interview shall not be permitted in any language not readily understood by the prison officer present.[75] Any interview may be terminated at any moment, if the officer present considers that sufficient cause exists.[76] The time allowed for an interview shall not ordinarily exceed half an hour, but may be extended by the Superintendent at his discretion.[77]

The right of the Press to interview a prisoner in jail and the power of jail authorities to prohibit such interview came up for consideration before the Supreme Court in *State v. Charulata Joshi*.[78] The Apex Court referred to the law laid down by itself in *Smt. Prabha Dutt*[79] and *Sheela Barse*[80] cases.

In *Prabha Dutt* case, the Supreme Court observed that the Constitutional Right to Freedom of speech and expression conferred by Act. 19(1)(a) of the Constitution which includes the freedom of the Press is not an absolute right and does not confer any right on the Press to have an unrestricted access to the means of information.

In *Sheela Barse* case also the court took a similar view that the access of the Press has to be controlled and regulated. The pressmen are not entitled to uncontrolled interviews and that those who receive permission to have interviews will have to agree to abide by reasonable restrictions as contained in the Jail Manual. Therefore, any permission granted by the court would be subject to the provisions contained in the Jail Manual itself.

Bearing in mind the ratio in the aforesaid two judgments the Supreme Court in *Charulatha* case held that no court would pass a blanket order mechanically without applying its mind and also without knowing the mind of the authorities. The court reiterated that the Press does not have an unfettered right to interview prisoners in jail.

Handcuffs

Under Sec.58 of the Prisons Act, 1894 no prisoner shall be put in irons or under mechanical restraint by the Jailor of his own authority, except in case of urgent necessity. No female prisoner shall, under any circumstances, be fettered.[81] No fetters shall be imposed for the purpose of security on any female prisoner who, by reason of age, physical infirmity or serious illness in the opinion of the Medical Officer, is unfit to be placed in fetters.[82] Handcuffs may be imposed upon any female prisoner who is violent, or dangerous, but in no case, except where the prisoner is likely to injure herself, should they be kept longer than twenty-four hours at a time and even then they should occasionally be removed to give the arms relief.[83] Apart from that a female prisoner shall be liable to be handcuffed as a means of restraint under the same conditions as a male prisoner.[84]

Under Sec. 56 of the Prisons Act, 1894, the Superintendent of a Prison, subject to such rules as may be laid down by the Inspector General with the sanction of the State Government, and if he considers it necessary (with reference to either the state of a prison or the character of a prisoner) for the safe custody of any prisoners that they should be confined in irons, may so confine them.

Death sentence on pregnant women

When any person is sentenced to death by a Court of Sessions, the sentence shall not be executed unless it is confirmed by the High Court.[85] When the sentence is confirmed by the High Court, the Court of Sessions shall issue a warrant to the Superintendent of the prison in which the prisoner is confined to cause the sentence to be carried into effect.[86]

If a woman sentenced to death is found to be pregnant, the High Court shall order the execution of the sentence to be postponed and may, if it thinks fit, commute the sentence to imprisonment for life.[87]

The preceding rules[88] are applicable to female prisoners under sentence of death except that –

(a) no female shall be fettered, and hand-cuffs shall not be used unless the Superintendent is of the opinion that the women might seriously injure herself if not restrained by these means; and

(b) the duty of searching shall be performed by the Assistant Matron and in her absence by a female Warden and that of guarding by female Wardens.

If a female prisoner sentenced to death be found to be pregnant, the fact shall be certified by the Medical Officer and shall be noted by the Superintendent on the warrant, which shall be returned to the Sessions Judge for the orders of the High Court under Sec. 416 of the Code of Criminal Procedure, 1973.[89] If a female prisoner sentenced to death declares herself to be pregnant and the Medical Officer is unable to certify to the truth or otherwise of the statement, he shall record the fact in writing, and the interval of time necessary, to enable him to satisfy himself on the point. The statement shall be attached to the warrant and forwarded to the Sessions Judge, a copy being kept for record.[90] When the execution of a female has been suspended under either of the two last preceding rules, it shall not afterwards be carried out without the orders of Government, for which the Superintendent shall apply through the Inspector General.[91]

Visitors of jail

The visitors of jail shall include ex-officio, ex-officio non-official and non-official visitors. The official, non-official and ex-officio non-official visitors of each jail shall constitute a Board.

The following are the ex-officio visitors of the jail in their respective jurisdictions:

(a) Sessions Judges and Additional Session Judges, Chief Metropolitan Magistrate, Hyderabad, District Collector shall inspect all matters relating to general administration and management of jails.

(b) Director of Medical and Health Services shall inspect all matters relating to Medical Administration, Health, Sanitation, Water supply and dietary.

(c) District Educational Officers shall inspect convict schools in jails and religious and moral education of prisoners.

(d) Director of Industries may inspect all matters relating to industries.

(e) Chief Inspector of Factories may inspect factories in jails.

Provided that in the case of the State Jail for Women, Rajahmundry and Hyderabad, the Inspectresses of Girls Schools, Rajahmundry and Hyderabad and not the District Educational Officer, shall be the ex-officio visitor.[92]

The Senior Fire Officer of the town where a Fire Station is functioning or any other fire officer of higher rank having jurisdiction over the fire station in that town shall be an ex-officio visitor to the jail in the town. He will confine his inspection to those branches of the work and administration which come within the purview of his ordinary official duties.[93]

Ex-officio non-official visitors include members of the Andhra Pradesh Legislative Assembly and members of the Andhra Pradesh Legislative Council. They visit the jails in their respective constituencies provided that the members of the Legislative Council elected by the members of the

Legislative Assembly under Art. 171(3)(d) and those nominated by the Governor under Art. 171(3)(e) of the Constitution of India shall be ex-officio non-official visitors to all jails in the whole of the State.[94] However, it should be noted, that A.P. Legislative Council was abolished in 1980's and the State presently has the unicameral system.

The Government may, in consultation with the Inspector General, nominate any officer in the service to be a visitor of all or any of the jails in the State.[95]

The Government may fix at such figure as they may think fit the number of persons to be non-official visitors in respect of any jail.[96] There shall generally be six non-official visitors for each central prison and special jail. For each District Jail, there shall be three non-official visitors.

There shall also be two lady non-official visitors for each central prison and one for each district jail in which female prisoners are confined and five lady non-official visitors for the State Jail for Women, Rajahmundry and Hyderabad.[97]

These non-official visitors shall be appointed by Government on the recommendation of the Inspector General who will propose the names in consultation with the concerned District Collectors. The term of these visitors shall be two years and they shall also be eligible for reappointment on the expiry of the term.[98]

The official, non-official and ex-officio non-official visitors of each jail constitute a Board of which the District Collector shall be the ex-officio chairman. It shall be the duty of the Chairman to arrange rosters for weekly visits[99] to the jail so as to give each visitor his due turn and to send out a notice intimating whose turn it is to visit the jail in the coming week. There is no fixed day of visiting jail and the visitors are left free to visit jail on any working day that suits them. There shall also be a quarterly meeting of the Board of Visitors on such a day as the Chairman may determine, which shall be attended by the official and non-official visitors. The visit should be between 8 A.M. and 5 P.M. only.[100] Any non-official visitor who fails to visit for a period of two months shall be liable to be removed from the list of visitors.[101]

A visitor may verify about the living conditions of the prisoners. He/She may verify that the food and clothing supplied to the prisoners is in accordance with the scales laid down.[102] The Board shall hear any complaints from the prisoners and satisfy themselves about the quality of food.[103]

Special rules with respect to female prisoners

The Board of visitors to a jail may visit the female yard of the jail collectively. Individual male visitors shall not be permitted to enter the female yard of the jail, unless it is necessary to pass through it in order to reach the male yard.[104]

Lady visitors shall have the same powers and duties as the male visitors except that their functions shall extend only to the female prisoners and the female yard. They shall not enter the male yard of the prison, unless it is necessary to pass through it in order to reach the female yard.[105] An escort is to be provided to each visitor throughout their inspection.[106] The visitor after completion of the visit to the jail will record the date and hour of his visit along with any remarks or suggestions, if any, in the visitors book prescribed by Sec.12 of the Prisons Act, 1894.[107]

Any police officer not lower in rank than an Inspector shall for the purpose of discharging his duties be permitted to enter the jail. He shall interrogate or interview the prisoners with the permission of the Superintendent of

Police or District Collector or Commissioner of Police in writing and in the presence of a superior police officer permitted to interview the prisoners.[108]

A list of visitors shall be posted in a conspicuous place near the main gate of the prison.[109]

In dealing with writ petition number 3899/96,[110] the Bombay High Court passed an order on 24th November 1996 directing that the State shall appoint a nominee of the NHRC as an ex-officio or non-official visitor to each of the 33 prisons in the State. In this connection, it needs to be recalled that under the Maharashtra Visitors of Prisons Rules, 1962, there is a need for a Board of visitors consisting of ex-officio and non-official visitors in respect of each of the prisons in the State. The court requested the Commission to nominate eminent persons from the fields of correctional administration, juvenile welfare, etc., for undertaking regular visits to jails as envisaged under the rules. Responding to the orders of the court, the Commission nominated persons for each of the 33 prisons in Maharashtra and the State Government, subsequently notified them as visitors. Guidelines to enable the visitors to focus on the key aspects of the administration of jails are being prepared to assist them in their responsibilities.

The National Human Rights Commission hoped that these non-official visitors, acting on behalf of the NHRC, will play a significant role in watching over prison conditions in the State.[111]

All India Committee on Jail Reforms (1980-83) (Mulla Committee)

Till the appointment of the Mulla Committee in the year 1980, the State Governments have followed the guidelines framed by the conference of State Chief Secretaries in 1979 for the administration of prisons. The Mulla Committee was appointed to make a comprehensive review of the prison administration in the country. This Committee had submitted its report on jail reforms to the Home Ministry on 31st March, 1983. It had suggested many measures for effecting reforms in the criminal justice system. The Committee felt that the lack of national commitment on the goals and objectives of prison administration was the cause for not framing the modalities for achieving them. Having said so, the Mulla Committee formulated a draft on the National Policy on Prisons and recommended for its adoption by the Government of India. It also recommended the creation of a permanent National Commission of Prisons, a body under the Ministry of Home Affairs. The objective was to bring about uniformity in various States and Union Territories regarding the prison management, treatment of prisoners, etc. As a whole, the Committee tried to evolve a National Policy on Prisons and Prisoners.

The goals and objectives in the proposed National policy on Prisons and Prisoners need to be examined. The creation of a Department of Prisons and Correctional Services dealing with adult and young offenders is one of the suggestions made. The institutional care, treatment, after care, etc., of the prisoners will be the responsibility of that department. That department will also deal with the probation and other non-institutional services. The State should evolve a proper mechanism to avoid unnecessary detention of undertrials. This can be achieved, as per the recommendations, by speeding up trials, simplification of bail procedures, and periodic review of cases of undertrial prisoners. It was also sugggested that undertrial prisoners shall, as far as possible, be confined in separate institutions. Government should make legal provisions for alternatives to imprisonment, such as community service, forfeiture of property, payment of compensation to victims, public censure, etc. Similarly, the Probation of Offenders Act, 1958 should be implemented effectively and widely.

The Mulla Committee was highly critical of the living conditions in prisons. The Committee observed that the living conditions in jails are far below the normal human dignity and felt that better conditions of accommodation, hygiene, sanitation, food, clothing, medical facilities, etc., are needed. The one novel idea it put forward was the visits of jails by selected eminent public men, under official authority, and to submit an independent report to the appropriate authorities about their impression of jails.

The Committee suggested that probation, after-care, rehabilitation and follow-up of offenders be made to form an integral part of the function of the department of prisons and correctional services. It advocated a permanent monitoring system to continuously monitor and periodically evaluate the implementation of the proposed plans. The Committee suggested liberal state funding for all such rehabilitation activities and functioning of the monitoring committees.

The Mulla Committee felt that the problems of women prisoners are different and the Jail Superintendents must deal with them differently. The needs of women are different and their sociological backgrounds also differ. In the absence of proper orientation for the jail staff, the Committee commented, the custodial justice to women prisoners have become a problem.

In view of this comment, the Jail Reform Committee (1980-83) headed by Justice Mulla has made some recommendations.[112] The following are the relevant extracts from the report of the All-India Committee on Jail Reforms (1980-83):

All police investigations involving women must, as far as possible, be carried out in the presence of a relative of the accused or her lawyer and of a lady staff member. Women should not be called to the police station for investigation.

Police personnel should treat women with due courtesy and dignity during investigation and while they are in police custody.

Women kept in police lock-up should invariably be under the charge of a woman police official and while in transit they should always be accompanied by women escorts.

A separate place with proper toilet facilities should be provided on court premises for women prisoners awaiting production before presiding magistrates.

Bail should be liberally granted to women undertrial prisoners, and those not able to furnish surety may be released on personal re-cognizance.

The Probation of Offenders Act, 1958 should be extensively used for the benefit of women offenders in order to keep them away from prisons as far as possible.

Women prisoners should be lodged in separate institutions/annexes meant exclusively for them. Till arrangements as recommended above are made, enclosures for women in common prisons should be so renovated as to ensure that women prisoners do not come in view of male prisoners during their passage to and fro from these enclosures. The enclosures should have a 'double lock system' - one lock outside and the other inside; the keys of the latter remaining always with a woman guard inside. This would prevent entry of male staff into these enclosures without proper authority.

All prisons/annexes for women must be staffed by women personnel only. No male staff should enter the women's jail, unless accompanied by a female staff member.

Where there are sufficiently large numbers of women prisoners, a whole time lady Medical Officer should be deputed. This lady Medical Officer should attend to the medical needs of women prisoners and also to those of family members of the staff. At other prisons, arrangements should be made for part time lady Medical Officers. If the number of women prisoners is too small to justify the appointment of a lady Medical Officer, the woman Medical Officer from the nearest hospital may be deputed to visit the jail once a week and as often as necessary where there are seriously ill-patients.

In view of the status of the women in the family and the society, their special needs and problems in the society and their vulnerability while in prisons, special consideration has to be given to segregation, protection, care, treatment, training and rehabilitation of women offenders.

Three years have elapsed since the Mulla Committee submitted its report when the Government of India has once again decided to appoint a National Expert Committee on Women Prisoners in 1986. This committee was headed by Justice V.R. Krishna Iyer.

Recommendations of National Expert Committee (NECWP)

The National Expert Committee toured the different states and made a detailed study of the problems faced by the female prisoners in the country. The Committee observed that the smaller number of women prisoners can't be considered as a valid ground for non-formulation of a national policy on custodial justice for women and made the following recommendations[113] for securing the gender justice for women at various stages of the criminal justice system.

1. All custodial premises for women prisoners should have a private, secured and therapeutic environment.
2. As far as possible, each State should have at least one or more separate jails for women.

3. There should be separate custodial facilities for convict and undertrial women. Separate institutions or reception centres, where undertrial and remanded women when necessary may be kept, should be set up in larger cities, district headquarters, and in female crime endemic areas. Where convicts and undertrials are currently housed in one institution, they must be kept apart in separate wings until independent facilities are set up.

4. Proper medical facilities and medical examination of women inmates on admission and periodically thereafter are to be ensured in all custodial centres including prisons, jails, sub-jails, etc.

5. Qualified lady doctors and nurses should be attached on a visiting basis to every female prison and custodial centre with women inmates.

6. Expectant mothers in custody shall be shown special consideration by way of medical and nutritional care, education in child rearing and mother craft and assigned work in accordance with their expectant status.

7. Women suffering from contagious diseases shall be placed in isolated care or at a health facility, if necessary, until they recover.

8. Scale of diet for women prisoners shall be strictly according to medical norms and special extra diet shall be given if medically prescribed.

9. Standard clothing should be allowed to every female prisoner and extra clothing to sick and old may be granted as medically advised.

10. For personal hygiene, female prisoners may be provided with comb, mirror, washing soap, bath soap, oil, sanitary napkins, etc.

11. The accommodation, cleanliness and sanitation provided to female prisoners shall conform to the prescribed standard and norms.

12. Work in prison shall not be treated as punishment but as habilitative therapy.

13. Female prisoners shall be paid equitable remuneration for their work in prison. Wages paid shall be of a habilitative value. Out of their earnings, they will be allowed to purchase essential articles for their use while in custody, and to save and/or remit to their families.

14. The menial duties in the female prisons or ward shall not be assigned to inmates and no monetary or non-monetary incentive should be applied to such work. The prison budget should provide for this function as a routine staff expense.

15. As far as practicable, women prisoners shall be imparted training which will make them economically self-sufficient and capable of functioning independently in society. Choice of skill taught will be related to marketability and independent earning potential. Some representative trades are: home science, mother craft, nursing, handloom weaving, hosiery, toy-making, ceramics, stationery articles, gardening, fruit preservation, electronics, etc. In addition, socially useful knowledge such as use of bank, post office, health centre, employment exchange, saving schemes, etc., will be imparted to the prisoners. Educating women in their rights, status, role and capabilities will be mandatory.

16. A reasonable number of interviews with the relatives and unlimited opportunities to write letters to them and receive letters from them should be allowed to the female prisoners.

17. Compulsory education for illiterate prisoners shall be provided. Literate prisoners will be motivated to pursue further learning.

18. Recreational facilities, books and reading materials, etc., should be provided to female prisoners and they should be encouraged to use them. This should include the use of religious books of the prisoner's choice. Pursuit of painting, music, theatre, etc., shall be encouraged as part of correctional therapy.

19. Female prisoners shall be classified on the basis of the age groups, nature of crime, type and length of sentence, etc., and correctional treatment of a prisoner shall be related to her specific problem and situation. For this purpose, treatment personnel trained in correctional approaches shall be appointed.

20. In no circumstances should girls be imprisoned or kept in mixed custody with adult women.

21. Habitual offenders, prostitutes and brothel keepers must be kept separate from other inmates in prisons.

22. No mentally afflicted women should be placed in prison and steps for their immediate transfer to mental homes must be effected.

23. Women and children held as victims or in protective custody or required for the purpose of giving evidence must not be kept in jails and should be transferred to designated welfare and protective homes.

24. Inmates with children require the special attention of prison authorities and suitable orders may be taken from court to ensure the interests of both mother and child.

25. As far as possible, children of inmates may not be kept within adult jails and visits by children to the inmates may be liberally allowed. In cases where imprisonment

is unavoidable, children of prisoners must have rights per se in terms of food, spare clothing, education, recreation, visitations, etc.

26. At the time of release of the child, on account of reaching maximum permissible age, the court and the prison/custodial management shall ensure that the mother-child link is not severed.

27. Probation, parole and other non-institutional modalities of corrective treatment shall be widely used in case of women offenders, save in exceptional cases where specified considerations of prisoner's or state security limit such options.

28. Women who pose no security risk and meet other suitability criteria may be housed in open jails where work facilities related to their agricultural or other occupational background should be available.

29. Women illegally detained in jails on ground of destitution, begging or vagrancy may be rehabilitated in appropriate institutional and community-based services and modalities.

30. No female prisoner shall be liable to any form of corporal punishment or use of handcuffs, fetters or isolation as a form of disciplining.

31. No female prisoner shall be punished without being informed of her offence and allowed an opportunity to explain her conduct. Exceeding the sentence is illegal. For any custodial excess or neglect, the responsible staff shall be dealt with severely and promptly.

32. Female prisoners shall be searched by female wardens in the presence of other senior women personnel with strict compliance to privacy and decency.

33. Complaints from female prisoners shall be registered, investigated and promptly remedied. A grievance box may be provided for this purpose. No harm should come to any complainant as a result of articulating her grievance or for deposing against custodial staff.

34. The prison manual must be physically available in every jail for easy reference by inmates and staff or accredited visitors.

35. A separate volume of the prison manual should deal with the custody and treatment of female and should be circulated amongst staff and inmates or for reference by accredited visitors.

36. Rights, special privileges and duties of women prisoners, should be widely publicised within the prison and each inmate should have full right of access to information in this regard.

37. Before a female prisoner is released, her relatives shall be informed and where no relative exists or shows up, the released prisoner shall be sent with a female escort.

38. Appropriate assistance shall be rendered to every female prisoner on release whether during or after completion of sentence. For this purpose, a centre for assisting released prisoner shall be set up to service a cluster of prisons and custodial institutions on an area-wise basis. Even without the centre, the prison authorities shall take necessary steps to arrange the rehabilitation of the released prisoner either through the family, the relief centre or a voluntary organisation.

39. After care and short-stay homes for women prisoners may be established in every state to serve those prisoners who are homeless or rejected by their families.

40. Women's representation in prison services must be enhanced and adequate compensation given to them

in lieu of lack of promotion opportunities on account of fewer job openings and in recognition of the demanding and stressful nature of their work. Adequate training and retraining should be provided for female custodial and prison staff to enable them to update their skills.

41. Apart from female staff in women's jail, there shall be a women D.I.G. in the State-Headquarters, preferably from the prison service, to specially look after the work relating to women prisoners.

42. Democratization of prison administration must be systematically engendered and a new prison culture based on humane and constitutional values developed. For this purpose, both pre-service training and sensitisation are necessary for male and female cadres associated with the administration of prisons.

43. Legal aid and counselling through professional bodies assisted by para-legal and social workers should be institutionalized in every prison and custodial institutions. Law schools and schools of social work should be encouraged and permitted to render socio-legal counselling service to the inmates.

44. Visiting Committees to Jails should be constituted in consultation with professional bodies and University departments of law, criminology, social work and social sciences from the neighbouring area. Visitors should be nominated on the basis of merit, public spiritedness, activist record and actual time likely to be made available to the visitorial function.

Rules for Superintendence and Management of Female Prisoners

For realising these principles, the National Expert Committee on Women Prisoners has suggested a set of Rules for the Superintendence and Management of Female Prisoners and Children with them in jails.[114] These rules cover various aspects of segregation and classification; admission, property; dependent children; general treatment and daily routine; clothing and equipment; accommodation, cleanliness and sanitation; amenities, letters and interviews; vocational training and labour; medical facilities; legal aid; counselling and restorative measures; facilities for foreign nationals; education; premature release and transfer; social relations and aftercare; insane and mentally ill female prisoners; discipline, punishment, requests and complaints; and female personnel.

Subsequently, the Supreme Court[115] also directed that steps should be taken to shift the wardens at the end of every three years. [This principle had been adopted by the State of Punjab for its Jail Manual (Chapter VI, Rule 273)]. The Administration should change the rules regarding the transfer of Wardens. Such transfers will indeed be helpful in restoring discipline in the jail and to emphasise that those who are incharge of the jail administration from bottom to top must develop the proper approach to deal with the prisoners and undertrials.

The prison conditions have to provide the proper atmosphere, leadership, environment, situations and circumstances for the desired regeneration to achieve true purpose of rehabilitation to the prisoner. Members of the staff of jail must be made cognizant of this responsibility and that awareness must be reflected in their conduct.

Recommendations of National Commission for Women

The National Commission for Women (NCW) has, after due consideration culled out some of the recommendations which were made earlier by the National Expert Committee which were not implemented by the Government, though the implementation of those would not mean any significant strain on the public exchequer. So the NCW in its report on custodial justice for women has made separate recommendations in the year 1993 to the Ministry of Home affairs for speedy consideration and implementation by the executive for the women in custody.[116]

In addition to most of the recommendations of the NECWP, the NCW recommended the following for immediate implementation.

1. No female prisoner shall be liable to any form of corporal punishment or use of handcuffs, fetters or isolation as a form of disciplining.

2. As far as possible, each State should have at least one or more separate jails for women.

3. There should be separate custodial facilities for convicts and undertrial women. Separate institutions or reception centres, where undertrial and remanded women, when necessary, be kept, should be set up in larger cities, district headquarters, and in female crime endemic areas. Where convicts and undertrials are currently housed in one institution, they must be kept apart in separate wings until independent facilities are set up.

4. Visitor's committees for jails should be constituted in consultation with professional bodies and University Departments of Law, Criminology, Social Work and Social Sciences from the neighbouring area. Visitors should be nominated on the basis of merit, public spiritedness, activist record and actual time likely to be made available to the visitorial function.

5. A women DIG should be appointed in State Head Quarters, preferably from the prison service, particularly to look after the work relating to women prisons, women prison staff and women prisoners.

6. Women Superintendents of separate prisons for women should be made functionally autonomous.

7. Prisoners' Council or Bandi Sabhas should be set up for every prison to help airing prisoners' grievances and difficulties.

8. Socio-Legal Counselling Cells should be set up in every prison for women inmates.

9. Legal aid and counselling through professional bodies, assisted by para-legal and social workers, should be institutionalized for all prisons and custodial institutions. Law Schools and Schools of Social Work should be encouraged and permitted to render socio-legal counselling service to the inmates.

10. Released Prisoners' Aid Societies should operate in every district to provide a single-window assistance towards habilitation and mainstreaming of the released women prisoners.

11. Before a female prisoner is released, her relatives shall be informed, and when no relative exists or shows up, the released prisoner shall be sent with a female escort to her destination.

12. Appropriate assistance shall be rendered to every female prisoner on release whether during or after completion of sentence. For this purpose, a centre for assisting released prisoners shall be set up to service a cluster of prisons and custodial institutions on an area-wise basis. Even without the centre, the prison authorities shall take necessary steps to arrange the rehabilitation of the released prisoner either through the family, the relief centre or a voluntary organization.

13. After-care and short-stay homes for women prisoners may be established in every state to serve those prisoners who are homeless or rejected by their families.

14. Expectant mothers in custody shall be shown special consideration by way of medical and nutritional care, education in child rearing and mother craft.

It is necessary that a large dose of good living conditions should be introduced into the jail life. The Administrators of jail have to take into consideration this aspect and try to generate a sense of humanism in officers and those in the ranks below them so that the prisoners should have direct contact with them and benefit by every contact with those officers in getting round to the right approach in life.

The prison reforms became a prime agenda for both Central and State Governments during the last decade of 20th Century. This resulted in the drafting of several new laws relating to prison administration and prisoner reformation at the central level.

The Indian Prisons Bill, 1996: It is based on the draft prepared by the National Human Rights Commission and circulated among States and Union Territory Governments. The comments and suggestions made by different Governments were taken into consideration and finally emphasised the need to bring the existing Indian prison system in tune with the changing pattern of the society and modern criminology and penological thinking.

The Bill clearly specified that the administration should deal with the prisoner in conditions compatible with human dignity. It has suggested a comprehensive plan regarding sanitation, health care and food of prisoners.[117] It also emphasised the need for an effective and adequate strategy for prison management. It further suggested the establishment of advisory boards for the development of prisons and correctional services under the Chief Secretary of the concerned State.[118]

The Prison Administration and Treatment of Prisoners Bill 1998: The National Human Rights Commission has formulated a draft of the Prisons (Administration & Treatment of Prisoners) Bill, 1998 based on an outline of the Indian Prisons Bill, 1996 which is referred to earlier. The basic objective of the Bill is to introduce a progressive legislation on prisons. The Bill has incorporated all basic and relevant points of the earlier legislations and Manuals on the Indian Prison administration. The Bill has given larger emphasis on the development of prison infrastructure with necessary amenities.[119] The Bill recognised some new categories of prisoners such as security risk prisoners, persons suffering from infectious diseases, mentally ill persons, drug addicts, people involved in socio-political agitations, political or otherwise preventive detenues.[120] The Bill also gave due attention to issues like after-care, rehabilitation of prisoners, open institutions, prison facilities, etc. It also suggested some amendments to I.P.C. and Cr.P.C. in relation to punishment and imprisonment under various Sections.[121]

The Prison Management Bill, 1998: This draft Bill was prepared by the Government of India on the basis of the above two Bills prepared by National Human Rights Commission (NHRC). This Bill aims at consolidating and amending the Indian laws in relation to prisons. This Bill recognises the rights and duties of the prisoners and also enumerated the duties of the prison staff. According to this Bill, every prison officer shall at all times avoid all contacts calculated to unduly irritate any prisoner, treat every prisoner with tact, humanity and impartiality. They shall maintain strict discipline and enforce all laws and rules and regulations in order to discharge all of the duties assigned to him/her.[122] The Bill has given special attention to the protection of undertrial prisoners. The State Governments shall provide to every unconvicted prisoner transport facility to carry them to the Court of Law and also provide adequate strength for the police force for the protection of the remand prisoners during the period when they are taken out of the prison.[123]

Unfortunately, the three aforesaid Bills on the prison reforms drafted in tune with the International Human Rights standards could not be placed before the Parliament so far. This reflects on the lack of sincerity of the Government of India in implementing prison reforms.

The Prisons Act, 1894 was mainly intended for punishing the culprit. It suffers from not having reformative and rehabilitative aspects. Moreover, there are hardly any provisions in this Act for safeguarding the interests of the women prisoners. So the Act should be suitably amended for protecting the interests of the female prisoners in order to attain custodial justice particularly in terms of reformative and rehabilitative provisions. Compared with this, The A.P. Prisons Rules, 1979 (A.P. Jail Manual) are highly progressive having incorporated the modern aspects of jail administration.

The medical facilities for the convicts through a qualified lady doctor and nurses, special consideration for expectant mothers and nursing mothers were also taken care of in the A.P. Prisons Rules of 1979. The other aspects like diet, clothing, cleanliness, accommodation, remuneration to prisoners, interviews with friends, relatives, etc., are also incorporated into prison rules. The rules on handcuffing, or fetters are also liberalised even before the Krishna Iyer Committee recommended them. A perusal of the A.P. Prisons Rules, 1979 revealed that almost half of the National Expert Committee recommendations are already there and are followed by the jail administration in the State. It may be concluded that Andhra Pradesh is far ahead of other States in jail administration. But still some of the National Expert Committee recommendations are not incorporated in the jail manual even though they were made a decade and half ago.

There is an urgent need for adopting a National Prison Rules with suitable, exclusive provisions for safeguarding the interests of the women prisoners, keeping in view the peculiar status in which women are placed in India.

References

1. One such study was by the National Expert Committee on Women Prisoners (1986-87).
2. Sec. 27(1), The Prisons Act, 1894.
3. Sec. 27(3), The Prisons Act, 1894.
4. Scc. 24(3), *Ibid*.
5. R. 817, The A.P. Prisons Rules, 1979.
6. R. 730, A.P. Prisons Rules, 1979.
7. *Ibid*.
8. R. 739, *Ibid*.
9. R. 733, *Ibid*.
10. *Ibid*.
11. R 735, A.P. Prisons Rules, 1979.
12. R 736, *Ibid*.
13. R 738, *Ibid*.
14. R 732, *Ibid*.
15. R 740, *Ibid*.
16. R 741(2), *Ibid*.
17. R.741(6), *Ibid*.
18. R 749, *Ibid*.
19. R 244, A.P. Prisons Rules, 1979.
20. R 244(1), *Ibid*.
21. R 244(2), *Ibid*.
22. R 246, A.P. Prisons Rules, 1979.
23. N.H.R.C. Annual Report, (1997-98), Para 3.30, p.17.

24. National Human Rights Commission – Annual Report (1997-98), Para 3.31, p.17.
25. *Ibid*. (1998-99), Para 3.43.
26. *Muktaram Sitaram Shinde v. State of Maharashtra*, 1997 Cri LJ 3458 (Bom.).
27. R 818(1), A.P. Prisons Rules, 1979.
28. R 818(2), *Ibid*.
29. R 819(1), *Ibid*.
30. R 819(2), *Ibid*.
31. R 820, A.P. Prisons Rules, 1979.
32. R 394(2), *Ibid*.
33. R 397, *Ibid*.
34. R 407, *Ibid*.
35. R 410(2), *Ibid*.
36. R 428, A.P. Prisons Rules, 1979.
37. R 429, *Ibid*.
38. R 597, *Ibid*.
39. R 821, A.P. Prisons Rules, 1979.
40. R.415, *Ibid*.
41. R 831, *Ibid*.
42. *Ibid*.
43. R 825, *Ibid*.
44. R 829, *Ibid*.
45. R 824, A.P. Prisons Rules, 1979.
46. NHRC Annual Report (1997-98), Para 9.1, p.32.
47. R 294, A.P. Prisons Rules, 1979.
48. R 290 and R 291 and Note under R 291, *Ibid*.
49. R 295, *Ibid*.
50. R 831(5)(c), *Ibid*.
51. *Ibid*.
52. R 437, *Ibid*.
53. R 449, *Ibid*.
54. R 450, A.P. Prisons Rules, 1979.

55. R. 831(b), *Ibid*.
56. R 450, *Ibid*.
57. R 828(1), *Ibid*.
58. R 828(2), A.P. Prisons Rules, 1979.
59. R 828(3) and R410(1), *Ibid*.
60. R 578(6), *Ibid*.
61. R 826, *Ibid*.
62. R 827, A.P. Prisons Rules, 1979.
63. R 830, *Ibid*.
64. R 1062(3), *Ibid*.
65. R 1051, *Ibid*.
66. R 1059, *Ibid*.
67. R 820(V), A.P. Prisons Rules, 1979.
68. R 820(vi), *Ibid*.
69. R 820(iv), *Ibid*.
70. R 489(1), *Ibid*.
71. R 818(1), *Ibid*.
72. R 494(3), A.P. Prisons Rules, 1979.
73. R 495, *Ibid*.
74. R 496. *Ibid*.
75. R.497, A.P. Prisons Rules, 1979.
76. R 498. *Ibid*.
77. R 499. *Ibid*.
78. 1999 Cri.L.J. 2273.
79. *Prabha Dutt v. Union of India*, AIR 1982 SC 6; 1982 CriLJ 148.
80. *Sheela Barse v. State of Maharashtra* (1988) (1) Bom CR 58 at p.64 Ref in Justice Palok Basu, "Law relating to Protection of Human Rights under the Indian Constitution and Allied Laws", 2002 First Edn., Modern Law Publications, New Delhi at p.869.
81 R 822, A.P. Prisons Rules, 1979.
82. R 549, *Ibid*.
83. R 548(2), *Ibid*.
84. R 822. *Ibid*.

85. Sec.366, Criminal Procedure Code, 1973.
86. Sec. 413, *Ibid*.
87. Sec. 416, *Ibid*.
88. R 783, A.P. Prisons Rules, 1979.
89. R 797, A.P. Prisons Rules, 1979.
90. R 798, *Ibid*.
91. R 799. *Ibid*.
92. R 26(1). A.P. Prisons Rules, 1979.
93. R 26(2). *Ibid*.
94. R 26(3), *Ibid*.
95. R 26(4), A.P. Prisons Rules, 1979.
96. R 27(1), *Ibid*.
97. R 27(2), *Ibid*.
98. R 27(3) and (4), *Ibid*.
99. **Note** to the R.28(1), *Ibid*.: The roster for weekly visits and attendance at the meetings of Board shall not apply in the case of Director of Medical and Health service and to the officers of the Departments of Industries and Factories who have jurisdiction all over the State.
100. R 28(1), A.P. Prisons Rules, 1979.
101. R 28(2), *Ibid*.
102. R 29(1), *Ibid*.
103. R 29(2), *Ibid*.
104. R 29(3), *Ibid*.
105. R 30(1), *Ibid*.
106. R 30(2), A.P. Prisons Rules, 1979.
107. R 31(1), *Ibid*.
108. R 35(1) and (2), *Ibid*.
109. R 38, *Ibid*.
110. *Muktaram Sitaram Shinde v. The State of Maharashtra*, (1997) CriLJ 3458.
111. N.H.R.C., Annual Report (1997-98), Para 3.36, p.18.

112. 'Custodial Justice for Women and Children' – National Commission for Women (1994), p.37.
113. Report of National Expert Committee on Women Prisoners (1986-87), Vol. I, pp.322-327.
114. *Ibid.*, pp.332-350.
115. *Sanjay Suri v. Delhi Administration*, Delhi, AIR 1988 SC 414: 1988 CriLJ 705 at 709.
116. 'Custodial Justice for Women' – National Commission for Women (1993), p.3.
117. The Indian Prisons Bill, 1996, Ch. V, pp.5 to 7.
118. *Ibid.*, Ch. XVI, p.25.
119. The Prison Administration and treatment of Prisoners Bill, 1998, Chapter II, pp.7-9.
120. *Ibid.*, Ch. II, pp.9-10.
121. *Ibid.*, Schedule 3, pp.69, 71.
122. The Prison Management Bill, 1998, Ch. IV, p.4.
123. *Ibid.*, Ch. VI, pp.8-9.

5

Statutory Provisions Relating to Women Prisoners in Non-penal Custody

Besides police custody, judicial custody and prison custody which were discussed in the earlier chapters there are two other types of custody, namely, social welfare and mental health custodies. These two are collectively referred to as non-penal custodies.

The Constitutional spring board for social welfare custody lies in Art. 41 of the Indian Constitution. The Article provides that "State shall, within the limits of its economic capacity and development, make effective provisions for securing the right, among others, to public assistance in cases of unemployment, old-age, sickness and disablement and in other cases of underserved want". When read with Art. 23, which deals with "prohibiting traffic in human beings", the direction of Art. 41 constitutes the animating principle behind the social welfare and mental health custodial institutions.

The social welfare custodial institutions, operationally, come under the jurisdiction of Social Welfare Departments of respective State Governments. There is a variety of nomenclature and designations in each State under which the social welfare custodial institutions are operating. The National Expert Committee on Women Prisoners has listed some of the names in use, namely, District Shelters,

Reception Centres, Protective Homes, After-Care Service Homes, State Homes for women, Destitute Homes, Shelter Homes, Vigilance Homes, Short-stay Homes, Beggar Homes, etc. Since the names of the Homes is not exactly suggestive of the functioning, the Committee suggested the streamlining of these hybrid names into more acceptable nomenclatures and fewer substantive categories.[1] The Committee further suggested that in order to achieve the objective of the institutes the name should be crystal clear.

The report categorised the existing social welfare custodial institutions into:

(a) *Ashram* – like residential 'homes' or 'shelters' and short-stay homes for poor, destitute and widowed women or girls or those with a variety of family problems such as desertion, etc., but with no background of offence or socially deviant behaviour.

(b) Institutions for the reception and detention of prostitutes or women and girls rescued from brothels by voluntary or police action, under the erstwhile Suppression of Immoral Traffic Act (now Immoral Traffic [Prevention] Act).

(c) Institutions for the reception and detention of women arrested for public begging, under Beggars Act or similar social welfare enactments.

(d) Institutions for the reception and custody of children with problems and young offenders under the erstwhile Children's Act (now Juvenile Justice Act).[2]

(e) Institutions for the reception and detention of mentally disturbed and retarded women or girls in need of protection, custody and treatment.

(f) Short-term aftercare homes and hostels, aiming at preparation for economic self-reliance and social rehabilitation.

Of the above listed institutions, the present study is restricted to the institutions holding prostitutes, women or girls rescued from brothels under relevant Acts and the provisions therein.

(i) Immoral Traffic (Prevention) Act, 1956

Prostitution is the oldest profession in every civilization and is carried on even now in almost all countries. It is regarded as a social evil which has to be curbed and if possible eradicated from the civil society. In this direction, Government has promulgated various laws to check the spread of prostitutions, but the profession continues to grow. Traffic in women for the purpose of prostitution which is popularly called as 'flesh trade' has now crossed the national boundaries. Young women are lured into prostitution under some pretext or the other. Since this profession involves not only the health of individuals but also the health of the society, it has drawn the attention of law makers.

In the pre-independent India, there was no separate law to curb prostitution except that there were two sections dealing with the subject in the Indian Penal Code.[3] The post Independence period witnessed the enactment of a number of legislations to protect and confirm the rights on Indian women to enable them to lead a dignified life. One of the important legislations enacted on the subject of prostitution was the Suppression of Immoral Traffic in Women and Girls Act, 1956, popularly known as SITA. This Act was later amended and renamed as Immoral Traffic (Prevention) Act, 1956[4] for punishing those who are engaged in human traffic.

The Act has identified nine conducts of prostitutes or others associated with them as criminal actions.[5] This act deals substantially with women and provides specific guidelines for their arrest, sentencing, corrective detention, safe custody and protective care, apart from delineating sentences applicable to those (men and women) caught dealing with and profiting from immoral traffic in women.

This Act also gave power to the State Governments to make Rules for carrying out the purposes of the Act effectively.

The Act has contemplated a specific machinery for the enforcement of the prevention of human traffic.

(a) A Special Police Officer not below the rank of Inspector of Police is to be appointed by the State Government for a specified area in the State.[6]

(b) The District Magistrate may, if he considers it necessary, confer upon any retired police or military officer as a Special Police Officer with respect to cases or class of cases.[7]

(c) The Special Police Officer of an area shall be assisted by such number of subordinate police officers, including women police officers wherever practicable.[8]

(d) Non-official advisory body consisting of not more than five leading social workers of that area (including social workers, wherever practicable) may associate with the Special Police Officer to advise him on questions of general importance regarding the working of the Act.[9]

(e) The Central Government may appoint a number of police officers as trafficking police officers to investigate an offence under this Act where sexual exploitation of persons is committed in more than one State and such officer will discharge all functions as are exercisable by Special Police Officer under this Act.[10]

(f) If necessary the State Government in consultation with the High Court may establish one or more Courts of Judicial Magistrates of First Class or Metropolitan

Magistrates in any area for the purpose of speedy trial of offences under this Act[11]

(g) If necessary the Central Government in consultation with the High Court may establish one or more Courts of Judicial Magistrates of First class or Metropolitan Magistrates for the speedy trial of offences committed in more than one State.[12]

Special procedures regarding arrest

Arrest without warrant can be made only by the Special Police Officer (S.P.O.) or under his direction or guidance or subject to his prior approval.[13] The Special Police Officer or trafficking police officer is vested with wide powers, subject to reasonable restrictions. Sec. 15 of the Act confers powers on the S.P.O. to enter and search premises without warrant whenever he reasonably believes that an offence punishable under the Act has been or is being committed in respect of a woman or girl living in any premises and that the search of the premises with warrant cannot be made without undue delay. However, the recording of the reasons is a condition precedent to effect a search warrant.[14] Ignoring it would amount to ignoring the material part of the provision on a search.[15]

Before making a search, the officer issues an order in writing to two or more respectable inhabitants and one of whom shall be a woman to attend and witness.[16]

The officer is entitled to remove all persons found in the premises.[17] He must produce such persons before the appropriate Magistrate.[18] It is mandatory under the new Act that she shall be examined by a registered medical practitioner for the purpose of determination of her age, injuries, sexual disease, etc.[19]

Not satisfied with the existing provisions for protecting the women under this Act, the Government has added, in course of time, some additional provisions to further protect the safety of the women and girls held under this Act.

A proviso to sub-sec.(2) of Sec.15 was inserted[20] because of the difficulty faced by the S.P.O. in getting respectable women inhabitants of the locality to attend and witness the search. After the amendment,[21] it is not necessary that the respectable woman inhabitant should be from the locality in which the place is to be searched. A new sub-sec.6A of Sec.15 was added[22] to further safeguard the interests of persons likely to be affected by a search without warrant by a special police officer. This Section lays down that an S.P.O. making a search under Sec. 15(1) shall be accompanied by at least two women police officers and where any woman removed is to be interrogated it shall be done by a woman police officer and if no woman police officer is available, the interrogation shall be done only in the presence of a lady member of a recognised welfare institution or organisation. Thus an officer is now required to be accompanied by at least two women police officers during a search made under Sec. 15 as and when available.

Trial procedure

Where a Magistrate has a reason to believe from the information received from the police or from any other authorised person or otherwise that any person is living, or is carrying on, or is being made to carry on prostitution in a brothel, he may direct a police officer not below the rank of sub-inspector to remove such a person found, if any, in such premises and produce her before him.[23]

This Act also speaks about intermediate custody of women and girls removed under Sec.15(4) or rescued under Sec.16(1). When a Special Police Officer after removing a person, is for any reason unable to produce her before the appropriate Magistrate, he shall forthwith produce her before the nearest Magistrate who shall pass such orders as he deems proper for her safe custody until she is produced before the appropriate Magistrate, provided that no person shall be

(i) detained in custody for a period exceeding 10 days from the date of the order, or

(ii) restored to or placed in the custody of a person who may exercise a harmful influence over him/her.[24]

When the person is produced before the appropriate Magistrate, after giving her a reasonable opportunity of being heard, cause an inquiry regarding the age, character and antecedents of the person and the suitability of her parents, guardians or husband for taking charge of her and the nature of influence which the conditions in her home are likely to have on her if she is sent home. For this purpose, the Magistrate may direct the Probationary Officer to inquire into the above circumstances and the prospects of her rehabilitation.[25]

While an inquiry is made, the Magistrate may pass such orders as he deems proper for the safe custody of the person not exceeding three weeks from the date of the order and shall not be kept in the custody having harmful influence over her.[26]

Where the Magistrate is satisfied, after making an inquiry as required under sub-sec.(2)

(a) that the information received is correct; and

(b) that she is in need of care and protection;

he may, subject to the provisions of sub-sec.(5), make an order that such person be detained for such period, being not less than one year and not more than three years, as may be specified in the order, in a protective home, or in such other custody as he shall, for reasons to be recorded in writing, consider suitable.

The Magistrate while discharging his functions under sub-sec.(2), may summon a panel of five respectable persons, three of whom shall, wherever practicable, be women to assist him and may, for this purpose, keep a list of experienced social welfare workers, particularly women social welfare workers, in the field of suppression of immoral traffic in persons.[27]

The word 'may' occurring in Sec.17(5) has been interpreted by the Supreme Court as "shall" and therefore it is incumbent on Magistrate to summon a panel of five respectable persons as envisaged by Sec.17(5).[28]

A person who is carrying on prostitution may make an application to the Magistrate within the local limits of whose jurisdiction she is carrying on prostitution for an order that she may be kept in a protective home or provided care and protection by the court.[29] The Magistrate may, pending enquiry, direct that the person be kept in such a custody as he may consider proper.[30] After conducting enquiry, including an inquiry by a Probation Officer into the personality, conditions of home and prospects of rehabilitation of the applicant, the Magistrate may pass an order, after recording reasons, that the applicant be kept in a

(i) protective home, or

(ii) corrective institution, or

(iii) under the supervision of a person appointed by the Magistrate, for such period as may be specified in the order.[31]

No court inferior to that of a Metropolitan Magistrate or a Judicial Magistrate of first class, shall try any offence under Sections.3, 4, 5, 6, 7 or 8 of this Act.[32]

Sec. 10-A deals with detention in a corrective institution. It provides, "where (a) a female offender is found guilty of an offence under Sec. 7 or Sec. 8, and (b) the character, state of health and mental condition of the offender and the other circumstances of the case are such that it is expedient that she should be subject to detention for such term and such instruction and discipline as are conducive to her correction, it shall be lawful for the court to pass, in lieu of a sentence of imprisonment, an order of detention in a corrective institution for such term, not being less than two years and not being more than five years, as the court thinks fit. Provided that before passing such an order (i) the court shall give an opportunity to the offender to be heard and shall also consider any representation which the offender may make to the court as to the suitability of the case for treatment in such an institution, as also the report of the Probation Officer appointed under the Probation of Offenders Act, 1958, and (ii) the court shall record that it is satisfied that the character, state of health and mental condition of the offender and the other circumstances of the case are such that the offender is likely to benefit by such instruction and discipline as aforesaid."

If the State Government is satisfied that it is necessary for the purpose of providing speedy trial, it may establish one or more Courts of Judicial Magistrate of the 1st class to try cases only under this Act.[33]

The Central Government also has the power to establish Special Courts for the purpose of providing speedy trial of offences under this Act.[34]

Provisions under IPC, 1860

Besides the above Act, there are various provisions in the Indian Penal Code for protecting the women from becoming the victims of flesh trade. Sec. 366 of IPC deals with the offence of inducing a woman to compel, in order that she may be forced or seduced, to illicit intercourse. Sec. 366A deals with the offence of inducing a minor girl to go from any place or to do any act with the intention or knowledge that she will be forced or seduced to illicit intercourse. Sec. 366B deals with offence of importation of girl from foreign country and Sec. 372 deals with selling of minor girls for purposes of prostitution, etc., and Sec. 373 deals with the offence of buying a minor for the purpose of prostitution, etc.

Provisions under CrPC, 1973

Criminal Procedure Code, 1973, contains very few provisions for the protection of women. If a woman is wrongfully confined either in general or for an unlawful purpose, the court has power to pass an order for restoration of such females.[35]

Protective home

Rescued women and girls must not be handed over to the police custody but to custodial institutes. The women and girls found in the flesh trade are to be sent to protective homes, where in addition to informal education, they receive some form of vocational training. The expression "protective home"[36] means an institution, by whatever name called (being an institution established or licensed as such under Section 21) in which persons, who are in need of care and protection may be kept under this Act and where appropriate technically qualified persons, equipment and other facilities have been provided, but does not include-

(i) a shelter where undertrials may be kept in pursuance of this Act, or

(ii) a corrective institution.

The expression 'protective home' comprehends a shelter where female undertrials are kept. But Sec. 2(g) of the Act has not used the term 'undertrials' in the restrictive sense of including only those in respect of whom an inquiry is being made under the provisions of Sec. 17 of the Act.[37]

Thus the protective homes under the amended Act[38] refer only to institutions where women and girls rescued from prostitution may be kept. But the Act is silent with respect to the quality of rehabilitative care and training.

By incorporation of a new clause in Sec. 2(g) stating that the protective homes should have appropriate technically qualified persons, equipment and other facilities, it mandates that in protective homes women should not only live in dignity but also find means of gainful employment.

Sec. 21 of the Act provides procedure regarding the establishment of protective home or corrective institution.

Under the amended Act the protective homes can be started by the State Governments or some private persons, preferably women, after obtaining necessary licence from the Government. The licence shall be for a specified period, renewable after the inspection by the authority and depending upon satisfactory running of home. The licence is not transferable. The Government has the right to amend the rules aimed at improving the living standard of the inmates of the home. The inmates can be transferred from one home to another for the reasons recorded and for the good of the inmates. All the existing homes prior to the amended Act have to obtain licence within a period of six months after fulfilling all the conditions. A licence is subject to cancellation or suspension, if the home is found to be not running satisfactorily.

Recommendations of National Expert Committee

The National Expert Committee made a thorough study of not only the penal custodies but also of the non-penal custodies and came out with the following recommendations for the running of the non-penal custodial institutions and also the treatment to be given for the women placed in such institutions.

1. The custodial conditions in non-penal institutions shall be superior to those in penal institutions and in no event shall be below the standard prescribed for female prisons.

2. A manual for non-penal custodial institutions shall be developed and all institutions and their inmates, as well as accredited visitors shall have access to copies of it.

3. Institutions shall be set up to service specified client groups in a specialized manner. No indiscriminate mixing of various categories of clients shall be allowed. Undertrial or convicted women shall not be placed in such institutions under any circumstances.

4. Model rescue homes and the beggar homes shall be set up for women in every metropolitan area and in such urban or district centres where the need to service these categories of women is greater.

5. Beggar homes for women and like institutions shall be centres of corrective treatment and rehabilitation and not for mere detention.

6. All existing programmes of socio-economic assistance to women shall also encompass women in non-penal custodial institutions both while in custody and on release.

7. Inmate's Councils or *Sanstha Sabhas* should be set up in every custodial institution to enable inmates to interface meaningfully with each other and with the custodial staff.

8. Socio-legal counselling cells should be set up in every non-penal custodial facility for women to assist in their socio-economic and emotional rehabilitation.

9. Legal aid camps and wherever possible *Lok Adalats* should be organised periodically in custodial centres. Voluntary agencies may be encouraged to give legal literacy and to assist in securing redress for inmates both in civil and legal matters.
10. Accredited voluntary organizations should be allowed to visit and invigilate the wholesome enforcement of the Code and the manual in the institutions.
11. Visitors appointed should be eminent people and should be selected in consultation with professional bodies and university departments of law and social work, and with due regard to active, activist record and actual availability of time.
12. Women students of law and social work, and women's groups should be encouraged and permitted to render services to inmates of non-penal custodial institutions.
13. Special steps should be taken by custodial authorities at the time of release of inmates to assist in their rehabilitation through close liaison with their families and/or recognized voluntary organizations.
14. A very strict accreditation process and machinery should be operative in order to discourage delinquent institutions and honour competence.
15. Children of women inmates require considerable handling and all endeavours in custody shall be toward reinforcing the inmate's links with the child.
16. Wherever children need to be custodialized with the inmate mother, the institution shall make adequate provisions either in the institution or elsewhere. In all such cases, the custodialized child shall enjoy rights per se to food, space, clothing, care, education, etc.
17. Literacy and skills training shall be mandatory for all inmates irrespective of their grounds or nature of custody.

18. Custodial staff shall be sensitized toward a humanist approach to management of the inmates and to pay due regard to their innocence in law.

19. Custodial neglect, abuse or excess shall be dealt with due severity and the management or the State shall be liable for compensation to the victim.

20. The State social welfare departments should develop and escort corps of specially trained persons who can service the escorting needs of various institutions.[39]

Women are exploited in the society in many ways - the worst form of exploitation being the exploitation of her body for commercial purposes. This exploitation under the profession of prostitution has been existent for several centuries. During certain period this profession was stratified while at certain places that profession was sanctified. As such the problem of prostitution remained as a social problem. Any social problem, as was proved, cannot be tackled by the criminal justice system. Still, the successive governments made legislations to curb the immoral traffic.

The Immoral Traffic (Prevention) Act, 1956 has some provisions to protect the women and girls, like the involvement of women police or women social worker at the time of search of the place and during interrogation. The Act has contemplated the protection of women and girls from the harassment of male police officers for money or sexual favours by the involvement of women police or women social workers at the time of search of the place and during interrogation. On the face of it, Sec. 13(3a) of the Act[40] appears to be adequate enough to protect the dignity of women though they are in prostitution. However, the fact remains that the said Section has given a convenient leverage to circumvent the very purpose of involving women in search and interrogation. The involvement of women in assisting the special police officer, as per the Act, is only 'whenever practicable'. Thus, it is left to the discretion of the special police officer who leads the raiding party to include the women police. The special police officers can avoid the women police by simply making the situation 'impracticable'.

So, it is needed that the term 'whenever practicable' in Sec. 13(3a) be deleted and the inclusion of women police be made mandatory.

A chance was given, through the Act, for prostitutes to reform themselves. States were asked to open protective homes to accommodate prostitutes if they wish so through the intervention of a Judicial Magistrate.

Such protective homes, as per Sec.21 of Act, can also be established and maintained by a private person after obtaining necessary licence from the designated government authority. Though such private homes are not opened in the State of Andhra Pradesh till date, the possibility of those running brothel houses, pimps, other anti-social elements obtaining the licence for running protective homes and continuing prostitution in such homes can't be ruled out. In a market driven society, which is unfolding in India, governed by the law of supply and demand, the prostitution could become a profitable business. So the minimum that should be done is to plug the loopholes and make the enforcing authorities more responsive and the State more considerate in providing infrastructure for the establishment of more protective homes.

The rehabilitation of prostitutes is an urgent necessity, but the Act is silent on that aspect. So it is important that certain changes are made in the Act to regulate this social evil called prostitution. It is essential to prevent the women caught under this Act from returning to the profession. This could be possible only through adequate and suitable rehabilitation mechanisms.

The prostitutes are routinely released on bail and the persons who pay for their bail are invariably the brothel house keepers, pimps or those associated with their flesh trade. In case of their failure to furnish the bail bond the prostitutes are in practice remanded to jail.

Those who are detained under this Act require a long term treatment for rehabilitation. There is no use in sending them to jail, instead they should be sent to protective homes. The drafting of special counsellors who are in the know of the problems of prostitutes is required. The children of prostitutes are the immediate sufferers and are also likely successors into the profession. Such children must be separated and their emotional and psychological problems tackled with understanding. Bringing them up in an atmosphere devoid of any social stigma will not only boost their confidence but also influence their mother to come out of the profession.

The prostitutes who are willing to give up prostitution may be engaged in remunerative work or imparted certain amount of training in skilled jobs basing on their ability, aptitude and qualification.

(ii) Mental Health Act, 1987

Another major area where the rights are yet to be articulated and processes streamlined was the case of people suffering from mental diseases. Women in mental distress if caught in the criminal justice system suffer greater deprivation and humiliation than men, for which the system has no effective remedy. It is here criminals and non-criminals are treated alike by the system. The laws in this regard are designed to protect the society and not so much the mentally retarded.[41]

The right to habilitation and to reasonably competent medical attention are implicit in the fundamental rights under Articles 14 and 21 of the Indian Constitution.[42] A scientific classification of mental patients for accommodation and treatment is also a reasonable imperative. Every mentally ill person has the right to competent treatment when he is confined in a psychiatric institution. The Right to competent treatment as a human right of a disabled person may be read into Art. 21 of the Constitution.[43]

The law relating to lunatics is contained in the Indian Lunacy Act, 1912. In 1987, the Lunacy Act was repealed and replaced by the Mental Health Act.[44] This Act is a beneficial legislation intended solely for the benefit of the mentally ill persons. It also provides facilities and protection to the mentally ill persons and safety of their properties.

The Mental Health Act, 1987 contemplated the establishment of psychiatric hospitals and psychiatric nursing homes for the admission, treatment and care of the mentally ill.[45] These hospitals or nursing homes can be established in four groups, namely:

(1) for the persons below the age of sixteen,

(2) for the persons who are addicted to alcohol or any other drugs,

(3) for the persons who have been convicted,

(4) for other cases

The Central or State Government has to establish four such hospitals[46] and separate arrangement for each group has to be provided.

Under this Act, Sec. 2(l) defines a mentally ill person as

> "A person who is in need of treatment by reason of any mental disorder other than mental retardation"

A person who is merely mentally retarded does not, in general, come within the ambit of the Mental Health Act, 1987. The expression 'mental disorder' itself is not defined in the Act but if the mental disorder is of such a nature or magnitude that treatment is needed, then the person suffering from it would become a mentally ill person.

Sec. 2(m) defines 'mentally ill prisoner' means a mentally ill person for whose detention in, or removal to, a psychiatric hospital, psychiatric nursing home, jail or other place of the safe custody, an order referred to in Sec. 27 has been made;

In this chapter, the various provisions under Mental Health Act, 1987 relating to two categories of women in the mental health custody are studied. a) Those who are wanderers, considered dangerous and arrested by the police for public safety and then referred to mental health custody by the court. b) Prisoners who are mentally disturbed and referred to mental health custody by prison authorities.

Thus, the criteria for admission of mentally ill persons is to prevent them from committing any crime which incidentally is also the object of criminal law.

The following are some of the relevant provisions relating to admission, detention, treatment, etc., of mentally ill women admitted through the order of court or a convicted or remand prisoner through jail.

Admission of mentally ill person as a preventive means

The police officer within the local limits of his jurisdiction can take into protection the wandering mentally ill person for the safety of others.[47] Such a person shall be produced before the nearest Magistrate by the police officer within 24 hours of taking him into protection. In computing the period of 24 hours, the time taken in journey from the place where he was taken for protection to the court room is to be excluded.[48] The police will not detain any person without informing him of the grounds for the taking into protection of such person. If the person is not capable of understanding the grounds it will be stated to his friend or relative.[49] This is in consonance with the principle of detention and arrest under the Criminal Procedure Code and also in conformity with the principle of natural justice. This Section is meant not only for the benefit of such a mentally ill person but also as a preventive measure to protect others, where he has a reason to believe to be dangerous by reason of mental illness.

Sec. 24 prescribes the procedure in respect of mentally ill persons taken under protection and produced before the Magistrate under Sec. 23(3). The Magistrate will make an inquiry which will satisfy him that there are grounds to proceed further and after examining him/her by a medical officer and assessing his/her capacity to understand, pass a reception order authorising detention in a mental institution. The Magistrate will not send the mentally ill person to any psychiatric hospital, if the friend or relative of the mentally ill person offers an undertaking that he will take proper care of the said person and he/she will not be dangerous to his/her life or the life of others. The Magistrate if so satisfied with the undertaking under a bond with or without sureties for the amount to be fixed by the Magistrate will hand him/her over to his friend or relative. The provision for release on bond is discretionary and is to be exercised judicially. The procedure is very elaborate and is in the welfare and interest of the mentally ill.

Admission of mentally ill prisoner

An order under Sec.30 of the Prisoners Act, 1900, or under Sec. 144 of the Air Force Act, 1950, or under Sec.

145 of the Army Act, 1950, or, under Sec. 143 or Sec. 144 of the Navy Act, 1957, or under Sec. 330 or Sec.335 of the Code of Criminal Procedure, 1973, directing the reception of a mentally ill prisoner into any psychiatric hospital or psychiatric nursing home, shall be sufficient authority for the admission of such a person to such a hospital where he is lawfully transferred for detention.[50]

The Andhra Pradesh Prisons Rules, 1979, under Rule 844, it is laid down that "no lunatic shall be transferred to the mental hospital at Visakhapatnam or Hyderabad until the Medical Officer of the prison has examined and has certified that he/she is in a fit state to travel".[51] The lunatic is to be provided with sufficient clothing[52] and food[53] during the journey.

Every female lunatic, when sent to the mental hospital at Visakhapatnam or Hyderabad, shall be accompanied by a female warden or attendant or relative, in addition to the usual escort.[54]

Provisions under Cr.P.C. 1973

Sec. 328 of the Code provides that, when during the course of an enquiry a Magistrate has reason to believe that a person is incapable of defending himself due to unsoundness of mind, a medical assessment of the accused is to be ordered. If the medical examination confirms the incapacity of the accused the Magistrate is required to postpone the enquiry. A similar procedure has to be followed by the court when unsoundness of mind rendering the accused incapable is discovered or pleaded during the course of the trial.[55]

The trial is postponed because an accused who is of unsound mind at the time of enquiry or trial would not be able to exercise his right of selecting a counsel and imparting necessary instructions for conducting his defence to his best advantage. If the enquiry or trial is proceeded with in his absence the accused cannot impart instructions for cross-examination and cannot render any explanation with regard to the circumstances appearing against him in the course of his examination under Sec. 342 Cr.P.C. The rationale for postponement emanates from the norm of fair trial – one of the basic premises of fair procedure.[56]

On postponement, the accused can either be discharged on a bond of safe custody to his relatives or detained in safe custody in jail or a mental hospital till he recovers sufficiently to stand trial.[57] There is no limitation in law on the period of such postponement.

Protective measures for mentally ill persons

Sec.81 of the Mental Health Act, 1987 contains a comprehensive provision for punishing indignity or cruelty to mentally ill persons. The provision reads as under:

(1) No mentally ill person shall be subjected during treatment to any indignity (whether physical or mental) or cruelty.

(2) No mentally ill person under treatment shall be used for purposes of research, unless-

 (i) Such research is of direct benefit to him for purposes of diagnosis or treatment;

 or

 (ii) Such person, being a voluntary patient, has given his consent in writing or where such person (whether or not a voluntary patient) is incompetent by reason of minority or otherwise to give valid consent, the guardian or other person competent to give consent on his behalf, has given his consent in writing, for such research.

(3) Subject to any rules made in this behalf under Sec. 94 for the purpose of preventing vexations or defamatory communications or communications prejudicial to the treatment of mentally ill persons, no letters or other communication sent by or to a mentally ill person under treatment shall be intercepted, detained or destroyed.

This Section is applicable to persons of both sexes and the prohibition of indignity or cruelty should, of course, take care of harassment of women or torture also. No doubt, serious harassment of a sexual nature is not specifically focused. But the Indian Penal Code took sufficient care of serious sexual offences, including seduction committed by the Superintendents or other officers in charge of custodial institutions.[58]

However, the penalty provided for the infringement of Sec. 81 is rather mild and it is provided in Sec. 85 which reads:

> "Any person who contravenes any of the provisions of this Act or of any rule or regulation made thereunder, for the contravention of which no penalty is expressly provided, shall, on conviction, be punishable with imprisonment for a term which may extend to six months, or with fine, which may extend to five hundred rupees, or both".

The punishment of imprisonment up to six months, provided by Sec. 85 may not be adequate, particularly where the victim of the malpractice is a woman. There is a need for higher punishment, to deal adequately with subtle forms of sexual and other harassment in respect of mentally ill patients.[59]

Appointment of visitors

Psychiatric hospitals and psychiatric nursing homes must have at least five visitors in the scheme of the Mental Health Act, 1987. Sec. 37 provides as under:

(1) The State Government or the Central Government, as the case may be, shall appoint for every psychiatric hospital and psychiatric nursing home, not less than five visitors, of whom at least one shall be a medical officer, preferably a psychiatrist, and two social workers.[60]

(2) The head of the Medical Services of the State or his nominee preferably a psychiatrist shall be an ex officio visitor of all psychiatric hospitals and psychiatric nursing homes in the State.[61]

(3) The qualifications of persons to be appointed as visitors under sub-section (1) and the terms and conditions of their appointment shall be such as may be prescribed".[62]

Sec.37 of the Act which envisages the formation of a five member visiting team to each hospital has not made any mention about the gender composition of team. It is necessary that a separate team is constituted for female enclosure and all those visitors be females. If it is not immediately feasible it should be made mandatory for the inclusion of at least one woman in the present team.[63] The inclusion of women in the team will give necessary confidence for the mentally ill to interact and also prevent the sexual abuse of women patients. The woman member in the team can better understand the problems of women inmates and make suitable suggestions.

Visitors for mentally ill prisoners

Where any person is detained as per Sec. 27 of the Act, the Inspector General of Prisons, where such a person is detained in jail and all or any three of the visitors including at least one social worker appointed under sub-section (1) of Sec. 37, where such person is detained in a psychiatric hospital or psychiatric nursing home, shall, once in every three months, visit such person at the place where he is detained, in order to assess his state of mind and make a report to the authority under whose order such person is so detained.[64]

The medical officer in charge of a psychiatric hospital or psychiatric nursing home, shall once in every six months, make a special report regarding the mental and physical condition of the person so detained under sub-sec.(1), to the concerned authority.[65]

Sub-section 4 says that every person who is detained in a jail under the provisions of various Acts referred to in sub-sec.(1) shall be visited at least once in every three months by a psychiatrist, or, where a psychiatrist is not available, by a medical officer empowered by the State Government in this behalf. Such psychiatrist or medical officer, as the case may be, shall make a special report regarding the mental and physical condition of such person to the concerned authority.[66]

Removal: Any mentally ill person[67] may, in accordance with any general or special order of the State Government, be removed from any psychiatric hospital or psychiatric nursing home to another hospital or nursing home within the State.[68]

Similarly, the State Government may make such general or special order as it thinks fit directing the removal of any mentally ill prisoner from the place where he is for the time being detained to any psychiatric hospital, psychiatric nursing home, jail or other place of safe custody in the State or in any other State with the consent of the Government of that other State.

Legal aid to mentally ill persons

Sec.91 of Mental Health Act, 1987 provides for legal aid to the mentally ill-person in any proceeding where he is not represented by any legal practitioner at State expense. The law on the subject is based on the principle that nobody is to be considered as accused unless so decided by a competent court. So every person has the right to defend himself, but owing to poverty if a person is unable to engage a lawyer, the legislature has considered the desirability of providing legal aid.

Recommendations of National Expert Committee

The National Expert Committee is unanimous in its belief that the prison cannot be an ideal place for the treatment of criminal or non-criminal lunacy. They further expressed that those designated as lunatics must not be sent to prison for placement and opined that jail is no place for the mentally distressed individuals. The Committee urged the elimination of the reference to 'jail' in the definition of 'mentally ill prisoner'[69] and if the word 'jail' is deleted from the above definition, the visits of IG prisons to visit prisons to assess the state of mind of the person and related provisions should also be deleted.[70] The Committee noticed that mental health infrastructure is under-equipped and under-staffed, and also observed that though most of the patients are fit for their discharge, the procedure for their release is either cumbersome or ineffective. After observing the miserable conditions and maintenance of mental hospitals and the pathetic situation of women in mental custody, they recommended the following measures to improve the custody of the women in mental asylum.[71]

1. Mentally disturbed women are entitled to proper medical care and to education, training and rehabilitation. A companion-right of the female retardate is freedom from sexual or other exploitation.

2. Mentally disturbed women shall not be detained in prison and they shall be given proper treatment in mental hospitals. Those that are currently in prison shall be immediately transferred to a mental health facility.

3. At no time shall mentally ill women be left unguarded by women escort or guards.

4. Juvenile girls who are mentally sick must receive special therapeutic attention and protection from physical or other exploitation, and must be custodialized separately from adult female retardates.

5. Institutional facilities in accordance with the Mental Health Act should be established in every State for rendering psychiatric justice to patients.

6. Conditions in mental hospitals should strictly conform to the medical standards, and supervisory staff should be personally responsible for ensuring them.

7. Watchdog committees of social activists should be constituted for each mental home or hospital and they should file reports after periodic inspection. Such reports should be a basis for continued recognition and accreditation of the concerned institutions.

8. Medical and custodial staff in mental homes and hospitals found negligent must be severely dealt with.

9. Legal aid camps must be organised in mental homes and all reprocessual and legal help rendered to inmates to overcome any difficulties arising from their custodialization.

10. The present distinction between criminal and non-criminal lunatics is unsatisfactory and ought to be substantiated or disproved through appropriate mental health research. The State should encourage research in that direction.

11. The State may utilize the services of a nationally reputed mental health institution (NIMHANS) to streamline and upgrade mental health facilities and approaches.

12. Custodialization and treatment of the mentally distressed should appropriately reflect modern care and therapeutic approaches. Greater use of community based and supervised options, including day care centres for the mentally ill, and open, non-cellular custodial residences, etc., should be promoted.

13. In the thereapy and habilitation of the mentally ill women, their families shall be consulted and closely associated wherever possible.

14. Training should be given to custodial as well as medical staff in mental homes and hospitals to understand and deal sensitively with the mentally ill. Similar sensitization will be necessary in case of staff of all penal and non-penal custodial centres (viz., police, prisons, welfare homes, etc.).

The Mental Health Act, 1987 intended to help the mentally ill patients and those who became mentally ill during custody or while serving the sentence. However, the Act has not distinguished between the male and female patients and their separate needs.

The Act is also silent on the training or rehabilitation of the mentally ill patients. Such programmes are not suggested for the sick or patients recovering from mental illness.

As per the Act, the mentally ill prisoner can be held in a separate enclosure within the jail, and such a prisoner should be visited by the I.G. of Prisons once in 3 months to assess the state of mind of such a detainee. The I.G. of prisons is a qualified police officer and is not trained in psychiatry, and as such he may not be in a position to make a proper assessment of the mental health of a person. So a competent trained psychiatrist may be entrusted with the job of visiting the mentally ill prisoner to make proper assessment. It is better if the mentally ill prisoner is immediately shifted to the care of a psychiatrist.

References

1. Report of National Expert Committee on Women Prisoners (1986-87), Vol. I, p.189.
2. The Juvenile Justice Act, 1986 was repealed by the Juvenile Justice (Care and Protection of Children) Act, 2000.
3. Secs. 372 & 373 IPC – Prohibit the buying and selling of a person under the age of 18 years for the purpose of prostitution, sexual intercourse or immoral purpose.
4. Act No.44 of 1986 w.e.f. 26-1-1987.
5. (i) Brothel keeping, Sec.3(1).
   (ii) Abetment of Brothel keeping - Sec.3(2).
   (iii) Living on the earnings of prostitution – Sec.4.
   (iv) Procuring, inducing or taking a person for purpose of prostitution – Sec.5.
   (v) Detaining a person in premises where prostitution is carried on – Sec.6.
   (vi) Prostitution in or in the vicinity of public places – Sec.7(1).
   (vii) Abetment of prostitution in public place – Sec.7(2).
   (viii) Seducing or soliciting for purpose of prostitution – Sec.8.
   (ix) Seducing of persons by those having custody over them – Sec.9.
6. Sec.13(1)&(2), Immoral Traffic (Prevention) Act, 1956.
7. Sec.13(2A), *Ibid*.
8. Sec.13(3)(a), *Ibid*.
9. Sec.13(3)(b), *Ibid*.
10. Sec.13(4), *Ibid*. (inserted by Act 44 of 1986).
11. Sec.22A, *Ibid*.
12. Sec.22AA, Immoral Traffic (Prevention) Act, 1956.

13. Sec.14, *Ibid*.
14. Sec.15(1), *Ibid*.
15. AIR 1970 SC 1396; 1970 CriLJ 1279 (SC). Ref in Bhatnagar's "Law relating to Women and their Rights" Second Edn., (1998) Ashoka Law House, New Delhi, p. 547.
16. Sec.15(2), Immoral Traffic (Prevention) Act,1956.
17. Sec.15(4), *Ibid*.
18. Sec.15(5), *Ibid*.
19. Sec.15(5A), *Ibid*.
20. Inserted by Act No.46 of 1978, w.e.f. 2-10-1979.
21. Sec.15(2), Immoral Traffic (Prevention) Act, 1956.
22. Inserted by Act 44 of 1986 w.e.f. 26-1-1987.
23. Sec.16(1), Immoral Traffic (Prevention) Act, 1956.
24. Sec.17(1), *Ibid*.
25. Sec.17(2), *Ibid*.
26. Sec.17(3), Immoral Traffic (Prevention) Act, 1956.
27. Sec.17(5), *Ibid*.
28. *Sangeeta v. State* 1995 CriLJ 3923.
29. Sec.19(1) Immoral Traffic (Prevention) Act, 1956.
30. Sec.19(2), *Ibid*.
31. Sec.19(3), *Ibid*.
32. Sec.22, *Ibid*; For details of these sections, please refer to Foot Note No.5.
33. Sec.22A(1), Immoral Traffic (Prevention) Act, 1956.
34. Sec.22AA, *Ibid*.
35. Sections 97 and 98, Criminal Procedure Code, 1973.
36. Sec.2(g), Immoral Traffic (Prevention) Act, 1956.
37. 1963 All.L.J. 434. Ref in Bhatnagar's "Law relating to Women and Their Rights", Second Edn. (1998), Ashoka Law House, New Delhi, p.511.
38. Act No. 44 of 1986.
39. Report of National Expert Committee on Women Prisoners, (1986-87), Vol. I, p.327.
40. For details of the Section refer to p. 4.

41. Report of National Expert Committee on Women Prisoners (1986-87), Vol. II, p.258.
42. *Ibid*., Vol. I, p.23.
43. *Ibid*., p.25.
44. Received the assent of the President on May22, 1987 and published in the official Gazette of India (Extra) Part-II, Section I, dated 22nd May, 1987, pp.1-36. Ref in Bholeshwarnath, "Mental Health Act, 1987"; First Edn. (1990), Eastern Book Company, Lucknow, p.1.
45. Sec.5, Mental Health Act, 1987.
46. Sec.6 prohibits any private psychiatric hospital or nursing home without licence. Secs.7 to 12 deal with licence.
47. Sec. 23(1), Mental Health Act, 1987.
48. Sec.23(3), *Ibid*.
49. Sec.23(2), Mental Health Act, 1987.
50. Sec.27, Mental Health Act, 1987.
51. R. 844, The A.P. Prisons Rules, 1979.
52. R 845, *Ibid*.
53. R.846, *Ibid*.
54. R.848, *Ibid*.
55. Sec.329, Criminal Procedure Code, 1973.
56. Kelkar, R.V. "Outlines of Criminal Procedure", (1984), Eastern Book Company, Lucknow, p. 239.
57. Sec.330, Criminal Procedure Code, 1973.
58. Secs..376(2)(d) & 376D, Indian Penal Code, 1860.
59. Law Commission of India in its 135th Report on 'Women in Custody', recommended a new Section, 84A in the Mental Health Act, 1987, in the following terms – 84A. Penalty for contravention of Sec.81 – "Any person who controvenes the provisions of Sec.81 shall, on conviction, be punishable with imprisonment for a term which may extend to two years or with fine which may extend to five thousand rupees or with both".
60. Sec.37(1), Mental Health Act, 1987.
61. Sec.37(2), *Ibid*.

62. Sec.37(3), *Ibid*.
63. Law Commission of India in its 135th Report on 'Women in Custody' recommended that Sec. 37(1) should be amended by adding after the words "two social workers" the words "of whom at least one shall be a woman, wherever practicable".
64. Sec.39(1), Mental Health Act, 1987.
65. Sec.39(3), *Ibid*.
66. Sec.39(4), *Ibid*.
67. Other than a voluntary patient referred to under Sections 15 & 16.
68. Sec.47(1), Mental Health Act, 1987.
69. Sec.2(m), Mental Health Act, 1987.
70. Report of National Expert Committee on Women Prisoners (1986-87), Vol. I, p.200.
71. *Ibid*., pp.329-330.

6

Judicial Contribution to Custodial Justice

Justice is administered as per the law enacted by the legislature. All such legislative provisions meant for the protection of women in various custodies – police, judicial, prison, social welfare and mental health-are discussed in previous chapters. Some of these legislative provisions have evolved over a period of time through the efforts of the judiciary. The Supreme Court with an extraordinary vision and innovative approach has tried to bridge the gap between law and justice by giving a new interpretation of the law to meet the existing standards of human rights as enunciated in various fora. The attempt of the higher judiciary in protecting the interests and dignity of the prisoners in general and of women prisoners in particular is presented in this chapter through a discussion of the judgments delivered on various issues concerning the prisoners. However, it should be noted that only important land-mark cases are discussed to make it a focussed presentation. Issues relating largely to women prisoners are given prominence in this chapter.

It is generally agreed that custodial justice has invoked in recent times a fair amount of scrutiny by the judiciary. While the earlier judicial directives were focused on the conditions of prisons and prisoners, more recently, social welfare and mental health institutions as well as police custodial institutions have attracted judicial intervention.

The provocation for the judiciary to address itself to such matters, the Expert Committee felt, has come from "executive inaction and disproportionate response of the legislature". The court's constitutional power of intervention has been invoked to prevent and eradicate custodial abuses and malpractices and to safeguard the rights and status of convicted and undertrial prisoners - especially women in police or protective custody and juveniles in welfare custody.[1] The main thrust of the judgments delivered on custodial situations and rights of women prisoners in cases like *Upendra Baxi v. State of U.P.*,[2] *Sheela Barse v. State of Maharashtra*[3], *Rakeshchandra Narain v. State of Bihar*[4] has been the identification of the modalities and actual arrangements to protect the dignity of women in custody and to render custodial justice to them.

(i) Judicial Contribution to Police Custody

Arrest: The police are the law enforcing agency. But if it becomes a law-violating wing, no doubt, it is for the judiciary to protect the rights of the victims from the hands of the police. In India, the Supreme Court has played a vital role in combating custodial violence in police stations.

The Supreme Court expressed its worries and serious concerns towards torture and deaths in police custody in several cases.[5] Similarly, the Supreme Court's concern on police atrocities and handcuffing has also been expressed in various cases.[6] The Supreme Court issued directions from time to time to protect the rights of arrested women. The first in the series are the directions given in *Sheela Barse v. State of Maharashtra*.[7]

Mrs. Sheela Barse, a journalist of repute, complained of custodial violence on women prisoners who are confined in police lock-up in the city of Bombay. The petitioner interviewed 15 women prisoners in Bombay Central Jail with the permission of the Inspector General of Prisons and five of them told to have been assaulted in police lock-up. While disposing the petition filed by Sheela Barse, the Supreme Court gave the following directions.

(i) Police lock-ups should be selected in reasonably good localities where only female suspects should be kept and they should be guarded by female constables. Female suspects should not be kept in a police lock-up in which male suspects are detained.

(ii) Interrogation of females should be carried out only in the presence of female police officers/constables.

(iii) Whenever a person is arrested by the police without warrant, he/she must be immediately informed of the ground of arrest, and in the case of every arrest it must immediately be made known to the arrested person that he/she is entitled to apply for bail.

(iv) Whenever a person is arrested by the police and taken to the police lock-up, the police shall immediately give intimation of the fact of such arrest to the nearest Legal Aid Committee and such Legal Aid Committee will take immediate steps for the purpose of providing legal assistance to the arrested person at State cost provided he/she is willing to accept such legal assistance. The State Government shall provide necessary funds to the concerned Legal Aid Committee for carrying out this direction.

(v) A City Sessions Judge, to be nominated by the Principal Judge of the City Civil Court, preferably a lady judge, if there is one, shall make surprise visits to police lock-ups in the city periodically with a view to providing the arrested persons an opportunity to air their grievances and ascertaining the conditions in the police lock-ups and to find out whether the requisite facilities are being observed and the directions given by the Court are being carried out. If it is found as a result of inspection that there are any lapses on the part of the police authorities, the City Sessions Judge shall bring them to the notice of the Commissioner of Police and if necessary to the notice of the Home Department and if even this approach fails, the City Sessions Judge may draw the attention of the Chief Justice of the High Court to such lapses. This direction in regard to police lock-ups at the district headquarters shall be carried out by the Sessions Judge of the District concerned.

(vi) As soon as a person is arrested, the police must immediately obtain from him/her the name of any relative or friend whom he/she would like to be informed about his/her arrest and the police should get in touch with such relative or friend and inform him/her about the arrest.

(vii) The Magistrate before whom an arrested person is produced shall enquire from the arrested person whether he/she has any complaint of torture or maltreatment in police custody and inform him that he/she has the right under Section 54 of the Cr.P.C., 1973 to be medically examined. Undoubtedly, Section 54 of the Cr.P.C. provides for the examination of an arrested person by a medical practitioner at the request of the arrested person, and it is a right conferred on the arrested person. But, very often, the arrested person is not aware of this right and on account of his/her ignorance, he/she is unable to exercise this right even though he/she may have been tortured or maltreated by the police in the police lock-up. It is for this reason that the Court gave a specific direction requiring the Magistrate to inform the arrested person about this right of medical examination in case, he/she has any complaint of torture or maltreatment in police custody.

In *Joginder Kumar v. State of U.P.*[8], the Supreme Court issued the following directions for effective enforcement of the fundamental rights guaranteed under Art.21 & 22(1) of the Constitution.

(i) An arrested person being held in custody is entitled if he desires to have one friend, relative, or other person, who is known to him or likely to take an interest in his welfare, told as far as practicable that he has been arrested and where he is being detained.

(ii) The police officer shall inform the arrested person when he is brought to the police station of this right.

(iii) An entry shall be required to be made in the diary as to who was informed of the arrest.

It is the direction of the Supreme Court that the above requirements shall be followed in all cases of arrest till legal provisions are made in this behalf.

In a matter relating to custodial violence and arrest of female persons, the Bombay High Court in C.C. *Welfare Council of India v. Government of Maharashtra*[9] issued the following directions to the State Government.

(i) The State of Maharashtra is directed to constitute a committee consisting of its Home Secretary, Law Secretary and Director General of Police within 15 days from today for going into all the aspects of custodial violence by the police in the State and suggest comprehensive measures and guidelines to prevent and check custodial violence and death and also suggest for that purpose suitable amendments in the Police Manual of the State and also submit comprehensive scheme for police accountability of human rights abuse;

(ii) The said committee is directed to submit its report to the State Government within three months of its constitution;

(iii) The State Government is directed to take effective steps in implementing the measures and guidelines suggested by the committee in preventing and checking the custodial violence immediately after submission of report by the said committee.

(iv) The State Government is directed to issue immediately necessary instructions to all police officials of the State concerned that in every case after arrest and before detainee is taken to the Magistrate, he/she should be medically examined and the details of his medical report should be noted in the Station House Diary of police station and should be forwarded to the Magistrate at the time of production of the detainee;

(v) The State Government should also issue instructions to all police officials concerned in the State that even after the police remand is ordered by the concerned Magistrate for any period, every third day, the detainee should be medically examined and such medical reports should be entered in the Station House Diary;

(vi) The State Government is further directed to provide a complaint box duly locked in every police lock-up and keys of the complaint box should be kept by the officer-in-charge of the police station. The officer-in-charge of the concerned police station should provide paper and pen to the detainee if so demanded for writing complaints and the officer in charge of the concerned police station should open the complaint box every morning and, if any complaint is found in the complaint box, the officer- in-charge of the police station should produce such complaining detainee to the Magistrate immediately along with his complaint and the concerned Magistrate would pass appropriate orders in the light of the complaint made for medical examination, treatment, aid or assistance, as the case may warrant;

(vii) The State Government should issue instructions immediately in unequivocal and unambiguous terms to all concerned that no female person shall be detained or arrested without the presence of a lady constable and in no case, after sun-set and before sun-rise.

(viii) The State Government should make proper provision for female detainees in separate lock-ups.

The Government of Maharashtra preferred an appeal against these directions issued by the Bombay High Court. The Supreme Court in its recent judgement in *State of Maharashtra v. C.C.W. Council of India*[10] noticed the said mandate issued by the High Court prohibiting the arrest of a lady without the presence of the lady constable and also after sunset and before sunrise under any circumstances. The Supreme Court while agreeing with the object behind the directions issued by the Bombay High Court[11] opined that strict compliance of the said directions in given circumstances, would cause practical difficulties to the investigating agency and might even give room for evading the process of law by unscrupulous accused. Further, the Supreme Court held that "the object will be served if a direction is issued to the Arresting Authority that while arresting a female person, all efforts should be made to keep a lady constable present but in circumstances where the Arresting Officer is reasonably satisfied that such presence of a lady constable is not available or possible and/or the delay in arresting caused by securing the presence of a lady constable would impede the course of investigation, such Arresting Officer for reasons to be recorded either before the arrest or immediately after the arrest be permitted to arrest a female person for lawful reasons at any time of the day or night depending on the circumstances of the case even without the presence of a lady constable".

This new ruling of the Supreme Court has eroded the rights of women to a large extent. Since then the Cr.P.C. was amended to prevent the arrest of women after sun set and before sunrise.

In 1997, the Executive Chairman, Legal Aid Services, West Bengal addressed a letter to the Chief Justice of India drawing his attention to certain news items published in various newspapers relating to custodial violence. The letter was treated as a writ application under Art. 32 of the Constitution and the case[12] was treated as a public interest litigation. The Supreme Court issued notice to all the State Governments and also the Law Commission of India calling upon them to file affidavits with regard to the steps to be taken to check and prevent custodial violence by the law enforcement agencies. On consideration of these affidavits and on hearing the submissions of all concerned, the Supreme Court has given the following directions:

1. The police personnel carrying out the arrest and handling the interrogation of the arrestee should bear accurate, visible and clear identification and name tags with their designations. The particulars of all such police personnel who handle interrogation of the arrestee must be recorded in a register.

2. The police officer carrying out the arrest of the arrestee shall prepare a memo of arrest at the time of arrest and such memo shall be attested by at least one witness who may be either a member of the family of the arrestee or a respectable person of the locality from where the arrest is made. It shall also be countersigned by the arrestee and shall contain the time and date of the arrest.

3. A person who has been arrested or detained and is being held in custody in a police station or interrogation centre or other lock-up shall be entitled to have one friend or relative or other person known to him or having interest in his welfare being informed, as soon as practicable, that he has been arrested and is being detained at the particular place, unless the attesting witness of the memo of arrest is himself such a friend or a relative of the arrestee.

4. The time, place of arrest and venue of custody of an arrestee must be notified by the police where the next friend or relative of the arrestee lives outside the district or town through the Legal Aid Organisation in the district and the police station of the area concerned telegraphically within a period of 8 to 12 hours after the arrest.

5. The person arrested must be made aware of this right to have someone informed of his arrest or detention as soon as he is put under arrest or is detained.

6. An entry must be made in the diary at the place of detention regarding the arrest of the person which shall also disclose the name of the next friend of the person who has been informed of the arrest and the names and particulars of the police officials in whose custody the arrestee is.

7. The arrestee should, where he so requests, be also examined, at the time of his arrest and major and minor injuries, if any, present on his/her body, must be recorded at the time. The "Inspection memo" must be signed both by the arrestee and the police officer effecting the arrest and its copy provided to the arrestee.

8. The arrestee should be subjected to medical examination by a trained doctor every 48 hours during

his detention in custody by a doctor on the panel of approved doctors appointed by the Director, Health Services of the concerned State or Union territory. The Director, Health Services should prepare such a panel for all tehsils and districts as well.

9. Copies of all documents including the memo of arrest referred to above should be sent to the *'illaqa'* (area) Magistrate for his record.

10. The arrestee may be permitted to meet his lawyer during interrogation though not throughout the interrogation.

11. A police control room should be provided at all district and State headquarters, where information regarding the arrest and the place of custody of the arrestee shall be communicated by the officer causing the arrest, within 12 hours of effecting the arrest and at the police control room it should be displayed on a conspicuous notice board. Failure to comply with the requirements herein above mentioned shall, apart from rendering the concerned official liable to departmental action, also render him liable to be punished for contempt of court and the proceedings for contempt of court may be instituted in any High Court of the country, having territorial jurisdiction over the matter.

NHRC, in its annual report for the year 1996-97 referred to the directions of the Supreme Court in the case of *Joginder Singh v. State of Uttar Pradesh and others.*[13] Additionally, it had highlighted,[14] the detailed instructions of the Supreme Court in a subsequent order and felt that it is of utmost importance that serious attention should be paid by the Central as well as State Governments to the instructions of the Supreme Court in D.K. Basu's case.[15]

Compensation to the victims of police custody

The Supreme Court has taken the lead in awarding of monetary compensation for the contravention of human rights and fundamental freedoms as guaranteed in the Constitution. In *common cause, A Registered Society v. Union of India*,[16] the Supreme Court has reiterated the theory of awarding compensation in public law field when the right of a citizen is infringed because of the State's act or omission and/or negligence.

In *Nilabati Behera (Smt.) v. State of Orissa*,[17] the Supreme Court while ordering compensation of Rs. 1.5 lakh by the State to the petitioner for custodial death of her son aged 22 years, reiterated that compensation for contravention of human rights and fundamental freedoms as guaranteed in the Constitution, is an acknowledged remedy for enforcement and protection of such rights.

In *Arvinder Singh Bagga v. State of U.P.*[18], the Supreme Court has deprecated the highhandedness and, illegal detention of a female witness in custody and the State of Uttar Pradesh was directed to take immediate steps to launch a criminal prosecution against all the police officials involved in the illegal detention and also compensate the victim.

In the case of *Indersingh v. State of Punjab*[19], seven persons were abducted by the police on the suspicion of their involvement in the abduction of the brother of a police official. Those seven persons, when subsequently remained untraced, the police were held guilty and compensation awarded.

In *Mrs. Anganmal v. State of Tamilnadu*,[20] a woman was summoned to the police station for enquiry in connection with a non-cognizable offence. This incident led to social humiliation and the woman committed suicide.

The action of the police officer was held irregular and compensation was awarded.

When an accused died in police custody,[21] the Supreme Court first satisfied with the facts after enquiry, concluded that the death of the accused was because of the torture in police custody and then awarded compensation.

The list of the cases where compensation was awarded for custodial death are many.[22]

Thus, the Supreme Court took an active role and responded to the situation. It not only gave general instructions regarding the treatment of people in their custody but also directed the State Government to take legal action against the erring police personnel. Wherever the victims of illegal arrests, illegal detentions, torture in custody approached the court, they were awarded suitable compensation.

(ii) Judicial Contribution to Judicial Custody

After the arrest of a person and his initial detention in police custody for a mandatory period, he / she will be automatically transferred to judicial custody, of course, through the order of a Magistrate. The treatment meted out to the prisoner under judicial custody is also a subject of intense judicial scrutiny. The justice through law has shaped over the years to meet the needs of women prisoners.

The issues concerning undertrial prisoners such as handcuffing, provisions and ways and means of sanctioning the bail, access to the legal services have drawn the attention of the Supreme Court. The court's comments, directions and suggestions on these issues are evident in the landmark cases discussed hereunder.

Handcuffs

The issue of handcuffing the prisoner was dealt with in *Prem Shankar Shukla v. Delhi Administration.*[23] The undertrial prisoners in transit from court to jail and jail to court are handcuffed, not as a rule, but basing on the perception of the escort party. Sometimes the handcuffs are imposed to humiliate an undertrial prisoner. While disposing the petition of Prem Shankar Shukla, the Supreme Court had upheld the contention of the petitioner that the distinction between the ordinary and better class prisoners for the purpose of handcuffing as provided in Punjab Police Rules was violative of the fundamental rights guaranteed in Articles 14, 19 and 21 of the Constitution. The court also held that even in extreme circumstances, the authority must record its reasons for handcuffing and get the approval from the presiding judge. The handcuffs should be removed once the court directed to do so.

The issue of handcuffings once again came up before the Supreme Court in *Sunil Gupta v. State of Madhya Pradesh.*[24] In this case, the social workers under judicial custody were taken from jail to court and back in handcuffs. There was hardly any possibility of such people running away. So the Supreme Court held that the act of handcuffing of the prisoner is against human dignity and violative of Art.21.

In the same year, an undertrial prisoner was handcuffed and paraded in streets in a procession by the police and the Supreme Court took up the issue and came down heavily on the government and directed the State Government to pay compensation.[25] The Supreme Court further directed that no prisoner should be handcuffed without the orders of the Magistrate.

In *Khedat Mazdoor Chetna Sanghathan v. State of Madhya Pradesh,*[26] the Supreme Court held again that handcuffing was illegal and unconstitutional. In *Citizens for Democracy* through its *President v. State of Assam*,[27] the Supreme Court had lamented over the failure of the police and jail authorities in following the law laid down by the Apex Court in the matter of handcuffing the prisoners. To enforce the law laid down by the Supreme Court meticulously, the Supreme Court stated that any violation of directions issued by it by any official with regard to the use of handcuffs shall be punishable under the Contempt of the Courts Act.

The Supreme Court had laid down the following guidelines for the protection of the arrested persons:

(i) As a rule handcuffs or other fetters shall not be forced on prisoners convicted or undertrial – while lodged in a jail anywhere in the country or while transporting or in transit from one jail to another or from jail to court and back. The police and jail authorities, on their own, shall have no authority to direct the handcuffing of any inmate of a jail in the country or during transport from one jail to another or from jail to court or back.

(ii) Where the police or the jail authorities have well grounded basis for drawing a strong inference that a particular prisoner is likely to jump jail or brake out of the custody, then the said prisoner be produced before the Magistrate concerned and a prayer for permission to handcuff the prisoner be made before the said Magistrate. Save in rare cases of concrete proof regarding proneness of the prisoner to violence, his tendency to escape, he being too dangerous/desperate and finding that no other practical way of forbidding escape is available, the Magistrate may grant permission to handcuff the prisoner.

(iii) In all the cases where a person arrested by a police is produced before the Magistrate and remand – judicial or non-judicial - is given by the Magistrate, the person concerned shall not be handcuffed unless special order in that respect is obtained from the Magistrate at the time of the grant of the remand.

(iv) When the police arrests a person in execution of a warrant of arrest obtained from the Magistrate, the person arrested shall not be handcuffed unless the police has also obtained orders from the Magistrate for the handcuffing of the person to be so arrested.

(v) Where a person is arrested by the police without warrant, the police officer concerned may, if he is satisfied, on the basis of the guidelines given by the Supreme Court, that it is necessary to handcuff such person, he may do so till the time he is taken to the police station and thereafter his production before the Magistrate. Further use of fetters thereafter can only be under the orders of the Magistrate as already indicated by the Supreme Court in *Prem Shankar Sukla case*.[28]

These guidelines along with a copy of the judgment have been sent to the Government of India, to all States and Union Territories for strict compliance.

Legal aid

Access to law and legal aid facility is one of the important rights of the accused. In India, over 75% of prison population are reportedly undertrails whose trial is yet to commence and therefore the significance of the right of access to law and legal facility is obvious. The right to have a lawyer of one's choice[29] and legal aid[30] are provided both in the Constitution and the Cr.P.C.

Nandini Satpathy (Smt.) v. P.L.Dani [31] is a landmark ruling on the topic that an accused has a right to counsel at the time of interrogation by the police.

"Lawyer's presence" is a constitutional claim in the context of Art.20(3).[32] It is an assurance of awareness and observation of the right to silence. Art.20(3) and Art.22(1), in a way, telescoped by making it prudent for the police to permit the advocate of the accused. Over-reaching Art.20(3) and Sec.161(2)[33] Cr.P.C. will be obviated by this requirement. However, the court has not laid down that the police must secure the services of a lawyer as it felt that it will lead to an abusive 'Police-Station-Lawyer' system, which may breed other vices, in the long run. The court clarified that an accused person if expressed the wish to have his lawyer by his side when his examination is on, the facility shall not be denied.

The court remarked that a lawyer's presence is not a panacea for all problems of involuntary self-incrimination, for he cannot supply answers or whisper hints or otherwise interfere with the course of questioning except to intercept where intimidatory tactics are tried, caution his client where incrimination is attempted and insist on questions and answers being noted where objections are not otherwise fully appreciated. The lawyer cannot harangue the police but may help his client and complain on his behalf, although his very presence, as per the court, will ordinarily remove the implicit menace of a hostile police station atmosphere.

The problem of the undertrial prisoner's access to law was dealt at length by the Supreme Court in *M.H. Hoskot v. State of Maharashtra*.[34] In the instant case, the petitioner was found guilty of an attempt to cheat by forging. In the appeal made by the State, the High Court enhanced the sentence to three years. The petitioner approached the Supreme Court both against the conviction by lower court and the enhancement of the sentence by the High Court. He claimed the non-receipt of the judgment copy of the High Court from the prison authorities. The Supreme Court observed that free legal service was implicit in Art.21 of the

Constitution. The court accepted that free legal aid is an essential ingredient of reasonable, fair and just procedure and also as a constitutional right of the accused who is indigent to engage a lawyer.

The Court has laid down the following principles.

(i) The court shall forthwith furnish a free transcript of the judgment when it sentences a person to a prison term.

(ii) In the event of any such copy being sent to the jail authorities for delivery to the prisoner by the appellate, revisional or other court, the official concerned shall with quick despatch, get it delivered to the sentencee and obtain an acknowledgement thereof from him.

(iii) Where the prisoner seeks to file an appeal or revision, every facility for exercise of that right shall be made available by the jail administration.

(iv) Where the prisoner is disabled from engaging a lawyer, on reasonable grounds such as indigence or incommunicado situation, the court shall, if the circumstances of the case, the gravity of the sentence, and the ends of justice so require, assign a competent counsel for the prisoner's defence, provided the party does not object to that lawyer.

(v) The State which prosecuted the prisoner and set in motion the process which deprived him of his liberty shall pay to the assigned counsel such sum as the court may equitably fix.

Subsequently in *Hussainara Khatoon (II) v. Home Secretary, State of Bihar,*[35] the Supreme Court held that "a procedure which does not make available legal services to an accused person who is too poor to afford a lawyer and who would, therefore, have to go through the trial without legal assistance, cannot possibly be regarded as 'just, fair and reasonable'. It is an essential ingredient of just, fair and reasonable procedure to a prisoner who is to seek his liberation through the court process that he should have legal services available to him".

Further, the Supreme Court held that the State cannot avoid its constitutional obligation to provide speedy trial to the accused by pleading financial or administrative inability. Thus it is the constitutional right of every accused person who is unable to engage a lawyer and secure legal services on account of reasons such as poverty, indigence or incommunicado situation, to have free legal services provided to him by the State.

In *Francis Coralie Mullin v. Union Territory, Delhi,*[36] the Supreme Court held that a prisoner has a right to have a lawyer and reasonable access to him, without undue interference from the prison staff. A prison regulation cannot prescribe any unreasonable and arbitrary procedure to regulate the interviews between the detenue and the legal advisors.

In *Suk Das v. Union Territory of Arunachal Pradesh,*[37] the Supreme Court held that the right of a poor person to have legal aid exists even if it is not demanded by him. Failure to inform and provide legal aid to an accused vitiates the trial. It is the duty of the presiding officer to inform the accused of his right.

Further, the Supreme Court in *Triveniben v. State of Gujarat*[38] observed that a person sentenced to death is also entitled to procedural fairness till his last breath of life. Art. 21 of the Constitution says that any procedure which takes away the life and liberty of such person must be reasonable, just and fair.

The Supreme Court has consistently upheld the rights of the accused for legal assistance, the right to obtain bail and also a trial which is fair and just. It went a step further and asked the police to inform the accused of his right to silence against self incrimination. The Supreme Court had thus taken several steps, through its interventions, to protect the accused at every stage of his/her custody.

The Supreme Court issued separate directions relating to legal services to women in police and prison custody. It reiterated that the legal assistance to a poor and indignant accused as a constitutional imperative mandated not only by Art. 39A but also by Articles 14 and 21 of Indian Constitution. It reasoned in the judgment,[39] . . ."injustice is likely to result and undeniably every act of injustice corrodes the foundations of democracy and rule of law, because nothing rankles more in the human heart than a feeling of injustice and those who suffer and cannot get justice because they are priced out of the legal system, lose faith in the legal process and a feeling begins to overtake them that democracy and rule of law are merely slogans or myths intended to perpetuate the domination of the rich and the powerful and to protect the establishment and the vested interests. Imagine the helpless condition of a prisoner who is lodged in a jail who does not know to whom he can turn for help in order to vindicate his innocence or defend his constitutional or legal rights or to protect himself against torture and ill-treatment or oppression and harassment at the hands of his custodians. It is also possible that he or the members of his family may have other problems where legal assistance is required, but by reason of his being incarcerated, it may be difficult, if not impossible, for him or the members of his family to obtain proper legal advice or aid. It is therefore absolutely essential that legal assistance must be made available to prisoners in jail whether they be under-trial or convicted prisoners."

"It follows that one of the major commandments of the Constitution is the organisation of a practical project to reach the know-how of law to the women victims in custody. Currently, there is an iron curtain between the detainees and legal remedies. Lawyer power must respond to distress signals from the women in lock-ups and flexible functional legal services must enter prison portals to salvage women behind bars. The State under Art.39A read with Art.14 has this affirmative duty."

"The lawyers must positively reach out to those sections of humanity who are poor, illiterate and ignorant and who, when they are placed in a crisis such as an accusation of crime or arrest or imprisonment, do not know what to do or where to go or to whom to turn".[40]

In the *Sheela Barse* ruling[41], certain directions to the Inspector General of Prisons were given which it is worthwhile to reproduce:

1) "to send a list of all under-trial prisoners to the Legal Aid Committee of the district in which the jail is situated giving particulars of the date of entry of the under-trial prisoners in the jail and to the extent possible, of the offences with which they are charged and showing separately male prisoners and female prisoners;

2) to furnish to the concerned District Legal Aid Committee a list giving particulars of the persons arrested on suspicion under Section 41 of the Code of Criminal Procedure who have been in jail beyond a period of 15 days;

3) to provide facilities to the lawyers nominated by the concerned District Legal Aid Committee to enter the jail and to interview the prisoners who have expressed their desire to have their assistance;

4) to furnish to the lawyers nominated by the concerned District Legal Aid Committee whatever information is required by them in regard to the prisoners in jail;

5) to put up notices at prominent places in the jail that the lawyers nominated by the concerned District Legal Aid Committee would be visiting the jail on particular days and that any prisoner who desires to have their assistance can meet them and avail of their counselling services; and

6) to allow any prisoner who desires to meet the lawyers nominated by the concerned District Legal Aid Committee to interview and meet such lawyers regarding any matter for which he requires legal assistance and such interview should be within sight but out of hearing of any jail official."

The court further observed: "We would also direct that in order to effectively carry out these directions which are being given by us to Inspector General of Prisons, the Maharashtra State Board of Legal Aid and Advice will instruct the District Legal Aid Committee of the districts in which jails are situated to nominate a couple of selected lawyers practising in the District Court to visit the jail or jails in the district atleast once in a fortnight with a view to ascertaining whether the law laid down by the Supreme Court and High Court of Maharashtra in regard to the rights of prisoners including the right to apply for bail and the right to legal aid is being properly and effectively implemented and to interview the prisoners who have expressed their desire to obtain legal assistance and to provide them such legal assistance as may be necessary for the purpose of applying for release on bail or parole and ensuring them adequate legal representation in courts, including filing or preparation of appeals or revision applications against convictions and legal aid and advice in regard to any other problems which may be facing them or the members of their families. The Maharashtra State Board of Legal Aid and Advice will call for periodic reports from the District Legal Aid Committees with a view to ensuring that these directions given by us are being properly carried out. We would also direct the Maharashtra State Board of Legal Aid and Advice to pay an honorarium of Rs.25 per lawyer for every visit to the jail together with reasonable travelling expenses from the court house to jail and back ... We may point out that this procedure is being followed with immense benefit of the prisoners in jails by the Tamil Nadu State Legal Aid and Advice Board.[42]

"The High Court in each State has to take steps in nominating legal bodies to assist the poor. Law schools can also be used as resources in clinical legal education by conducting free legal service camps".

Though this judgment and directions pertain to the State of Maharashtra, the court said that all State Governments should issue circulars to the police and the prison officials in their States as directed by the court.

Bail

In India, provision to furnish monetary security acts as a hindrance in enjoyment of liberty even if bail is granted. In *Kashmir Singh v. State of Punjab*[43], Justice Bhagawati observed that it would be travesty of justice to keep a person in jail for a period of five to six years for an offence which is ultimately found not to have been committed by him.

In *Moti Ram v. State of M.P.,*[44] Justice Krishna Iyer observed that the demand of huge amount as bail or the sureties of the like amount sounds like a culture of bonded labour. In a country like India, many of the accused are poor and illiterate. They are not only ignorant of their rights but also unable to furnish a bail. In such cases, they must be released on personal bond or bond of his family members.

Through this case, the Supreme Court for the first time rejected the myth of suretyship as a *'Sine qua non'* of pre-trial release. It opined that the poor, especially women, suffer jail life as undertrials as no one comes forward to offer bail. Women rarely breach their bonds to show up in court. The Supreme Court after a lengthy survey of the problem and its constitutional implication observed that women are weak categories and courts should be liberal in releasing them on their own recognisances with whatever reasonable conditions it may impose. The Supreme Court expressed its dissatisfaction over the money-oriented system of bail.

Speedy investigation and trial

Art.21 of the Constitution guarantees speedy investigation and trial of the accused persons. If the investigation is unduly delayed, the trial would automatically be delayed violating Art. 21. Such delayed investigations are liable to be quashed by the courts and the accused is entitled to be set free if the accused (undertrial prisoner) has been in jail for a period longer than the maximum term for which he could have been sentenced, if convicted.

Mrs. K. Hingorani, an Advocate, brought to the notice of the Supreme Court some paper cuttings of an English daily *Indian Express* dated 8th & 9th January, 1979, which disclosed that an alarmingly large number of men and women including children were behind prison bars for 5 to 10 years without commencement of trial in the State of Bihar.

The Supreme Court treated the news paper report as a writ application[45] and held that the procedure which keeps such a large number of people behind bars without trial for long periods cannot be regarded as just, fair and reasonable as to be in conformity with the Art.21 of the Constitution.

The Supreme Court drew inspiration from Art.3 of European Convention on Human Rights (E.C.H.R.) which provides that "every one arrested or detained shall be entitled to trial within a reasonable time or to release pending trial."

If a person is deprived of his liberty under a procedure which is not just, fair and reasonable, such deprivation would be violative of his fundamental right guaranteed under Art. 21. The procedure prescribed by law for depriving a person of his liberty cannot be reasonable, fair or just, unless it ensures speedy trial for determination of the guilt of the person. Accordingly speedy trial i.e., reasonably expeditious trial is an integral and essential part of the fundamental right to life and liberty enshrined in Art.21 of the Constitution.

In *Kadra Pahadiya v. State of Bihar*,[46] four persons were confined in a sub jail without trial for 8 years. Bhagawati J., observed: "There is something wrong with the entire system. A judicial system which keeps a person in jail for 8 years without trial is too cruel. A prisoner has a right for a speedy trial as an essential part of fundamental right enshrined in Article 21 of the Constitution".

Further, the Supreme Court in *Sheela Barse v. Union of India*[47] affirmed that the right to speedy trial is a fundamental right implicit in Art. 21 of the Constitution. The court also observed that the consequences of violation of the fundamental right to speedy trial would be that the prosecution itself would be liable to be quashed on the ground that it is a breach of the fundamental right. The court also directed that in a case involving juvenile offenders, the investigation should be completed within three months of the lodge of a complaint and trial should be completed within six months from the filing of the charge sheet.

Thus the Supreme Court recognized the speedy investigation and trial of criminal cases as fundamental rights enshrined in Article 21 of the Constitution and issued certain directions for speedy trial of the cases in subsequent cases.[48]

(iii) Judicial contribution to prison custody

Prisoners in general are a neglected lot. There is a general complaint that their condition within the four walls of jail is pathetic. Denied of freedom and communication, the prisoners suffered at the hands of cruel prison staff. The jail staff treated prisoners as the slaves of the state. No one cared to study the conditions of prisoners till two decades back. The judiciary felt that its role ended the moment sentence was pronounced. The jail administration, the courts felt, is outside its jurisdiction. That even the prisoners are having constitutional rights is a fact recognised very belatedly.

The conditions of prisoners in independent India came to the notice of the law-makers in mid seventies. In June 1975, Mrs. Indira Gandhi, as Prime Minister, imposed internal emergency and placed all the politicians of all the political parties opposed to her in detention. From district jails to all the central jails in the country – all were brimming with politicians at that time. The law-makers thus had the first hand information on the treatment meted out to the detenues as well as convicts. Thus a political act of the then Central Government helped in drawing the attention of the Nation to the inhuman conditions prevailing in jails and the treatment given to the prisoners.[49]

Subsequently, courts have started interventions into the constitutional rights of prisoners. During the last twenty years or so, the courts have issued directions on a wide range of prison matters like conditions of prisons, treatment of prisoners, health and sanitary conditions, prisoner wages and other related rights of prisoners.

Whenever the jail authorities failed to provide safe and humane conditions within the jail premises, the courts exercised their constitutional powers and intervened and issued necessary directions to the prison staff to follow.

The judicial intervention on prison reforms was based on the fundamental principles of the Indian Constitution. Though the Constitution has not provided any specific rights relating to prisoners, the courts have based their intervention following Articles of 14 (Right to Equality), 19 (Right to freedom of speech etc.), 21 (Right to life and personal and liberty), 22 (Protection against arrest and detention) of the Constitution.

In a series of landmark judgements, the Apex Court has laid down the constitutional dimensions and rights available to the prisoners and the approaches to be adopted in dealing with the various aspects of custodial justice and administration. It invoked Art. 21 to protect and shield prisoners from deteriorating prison conditions.

Some such judicial interventions which played a major role in resetting the meaning of prison and improved the condition of prisoners are presented and discussed.

It is a universally accepted fact that a convict does not forfeit his/her basic rights, even when he/she is in jail, as he/she does not cease to be a human being. The Covenant on Civil and Political Rights also proclaims that all persons deprived of their liberty shall be treated with humanity but the prison administrations are more known for the violation of human rights than their adherence. This fact was recognised by Supreme Court in various judgments.

A major breakthrough in prisoners' rights came in 1974 in *D.B.M. Patnaik v. State of A.P.*[50] The Supreme Court asserted that mere detention does not deprive the convicts of all the fundamental rights they otherwise possess. The court ruled that "Convicts are not, by mere reason of conviction, denuded of all fundamental rights which they otherwise possess. A compulsion under the authority of law, following upon a conviction, to live in a prison-house entitles by its own force the deprivation of fundamental freedom like the right to move freely throughout the territory of India, or the right to practise a 'profession'. A man of profession would thus stand stripped of his right to hold consultations while serving out his sentence. But the Constitution guarantees other freedoms under Articles 19 and 21".

Through this decision the court extended its jurisdiction from the function of sentencing an accused to safeguarding the interests of the convicts. Since then the courts have started suggesting measures to reform the criminal justice system and started acting as a bulwark against executive onslaughts, wherever they occurred. The courts have felt that they have a role of follow-up, till the final release of the persons they have convicted.

Fetters

The next important issue decided by the Supreme Court was regarding the safe custody of the prisoners and keeping the prisoners in fetters. In some instances, fetters are imposed on the prisoners on the alleged safe custody of the prisoner. This situation came up before the Supreme Court in *Charles Sobhraj v. Superintendent, Central Jail, Tihar, New Delhi.*[51] The petitioner in this case was a foreigner sentenced to a long term of imprisonment. Bar-fetters were imposed on him. Sobhraj challenged the action of jail administration in the Supreme Court. The Supreme Court recognized that "right to life is more than mere animal existence. Even in prison a person is required to be treated with dignity. A prisoner enjoys all the rights specified in Articles 19 and 21." The court prohibited inhuman treatment and regarded it as a violation of right to life, guaranteed under Art.21. It recognized the putting of bar fetters only in those cases where absolute necessity demanded them.

Solitary confinement

A person once lodged in a jail loses all his contacts with the outside world. The question whether he could further be isolated from his fellow prisoners by putting him into separate and solitary cell came up before the Supreme Court in *Sunil Batra v. Delhi Administration.*[52] In this case, Sunil Batra was sentenced to death on charges of gruesome murder and robbery and was kept in solitary confinement. This solitary confinement was challenged as vilolation of Art. 21 of the Constitution of India and the court pointed out that it was indeed violative of the fundamental right to impose solitary confinement on a prisoner under sentence of death, not as a consequence of violation of prison discipline but on the sole ground that he was a prisoner under sentence of death. Further the Apex Court held that solitary confinement means harsh isolation of a prisoner from the safety of fellow prisoners by cellular detention. Secs. 29[53] and 30[54] of the Prisons Act, 1894 are penal in character and so must be imposed only in accordance with the procedure which is fair, just and reasonable, in the absence of which the confinement would be violative of Art.21 of the Constitution. In view of the severity and harshness of solitary confinement, the framers of the Code (IPC) have specifically provided that in no case the sentence of solitary confinement may be imposed for more than a period of 14 days at a time, and it must be imposed only at intervals.[55]

In *Kishore Singh Ravinder Dev v. State of Rajasthan*[56], the Supreme Court had observed that solitary confinement offends the spirit of the Constitution, if applied without any judicial control to inflict heavy punishment on prisoners, on flimsy grounds like 'loitering', behaving insolently and in an uncivilised manner, tearing of his history ticket and like instances, without giving the prisoner concerned a reasonable opportunity of being heard, and it cannot be regarded as 'fair, just and reasonable', within the meaning of Art. 21 of the Indian Constitution. The court issued directions to the State that the police and prison officials should be educated regarding the high values of humanity and they should respect the Constitution and human beings.

Freedom of expression and communication

The freedom of expression and communication of the prisoners was also brought before the Supreme Court in different cases. The question of right to publish a book by a prisoner was upheld by the Supreme Court in *State of Maharashtra v. Prabhakar Panduranga Sanzgiri.*[57] In this case, the respondent was detained under the Defence of India Rules, 1962. While in detention the respondent wrote a scientific book, but was not allowed to publish it by the prison authority. When the Bombay High Court allowed the publication of the book, the Government of Maharashtra preferred an appeal in the Supreme Court and contended that freedom to publish was only a component part of speech and expression and as the detenue ceased to be free, he could not exercise his freedom to publish the book.

Dismissing the appeal, the Supreme Court held that by way of imprisonment the prisoner loses only those rights which are incidental to detention. The court also found that the petitioner's right to expression was available and further held that the book being a scientific work could not in any case be detrimental to public interest or safety as envisaged under the Defence of India Rules, 1962 and therefore allowed the publication of the book. This decision was a turning point in effecting an extension of prisoners' rights and the subsequent years witnessed an active Supreme Court extending prisoners' rights further.

The right of the Press to interview the prisoner as a part of investigative journalism was decided in *Prabha Dutt v. Union of India*.[58] In this case, a newspaper correspondent filed a petition to interview Ranga and Billa, two condemned prisoners. She was not accorded permission by the Superintendent of Tihar Jail, Delhi. On appeal, the court allowed the interview holding that the Press is entitled to interview the prisoners unless some weighty reasons to the contrary existed. The court cited the relevant rules of the Jail Manual to support the rights of prisoners to communicate and have interviews with relatives, friends and legal advisers and also the Press, people not specifically included in the rules.

Freedom to meet friends and relatives

The prisoner's freedom to meet his/her friends and the family members came before the Supreme Court in *Francis Coralie Mullin v. Administrator, U.T. of Delhi*.[59] Mullin was a British national, a detenue under Sec. 3 of the Conservation of Foreign Exchange and Prevention of Smuggling Activities Act, 1974 (COFEPOSA); while under preventive detention, she experienced considerable difficulty in having interview with her lawyer and her family members. She was allowed to meet her five year old daughter and sister only once in a month, while the undertrial prisoners and convicts were allowed to have interview with their relatives and friends twice a week. The restrictions imposed on her interview under Sec. 5 of

COFEPOSA[60] were challenged as violative of Articles 14 and 21 of the Constitution.

It was held by the Supreme Court that the right to life includes the right to live with human dignity and all that goes along with it, viz., the bare necessities of life such as adequate nutrition, clothing and shelter over the head and facilities for reading, writing and expressing oneself in diverse forms, freely moving about and mixing with fellow human beings. The magnitude and content of the components of this right could depend upon the extent of the economic development of the country. Any form of torture, or cruel, inhuman or degrading treatment would be offensive to human dignity and constitutes an inroad into this right to live and it would be prohibited by Art. 21, unless it is in accordance with the procedure which is just, fair and reasonable.

The Supreme Court drew inspiration from Art.5[61] of the Universal Declaration of Human Rights, 1948 and Art.7[62] of the International Covenant on Civil and Political Rights, 1966 which enunciate the right to protection against inhuman or degrading treatment.

It was held by the Supreme Court that the right to protection against inhuman or degrading treatment is implicit in Art.21. It is true that the prisoner or detenue cannot move about freely by going outside the prison walls, nor can he/she socialise at his/her free will with persons outside the jail, but as a part of the right to live with human dignity the detenue would be entitled to have interviews with the members of his/her family and friends and the prison regulations imposing unreasonable restrictions on such interviews of the detenue must be struck down for violation of Articles 14 and 21 of the Constitution of India.

Thus the legislative gaps in providing human rights to prisoners have been filled by the judiciary through the extension of constitutional rights by way of interpretation of the Constitution. As a result of this, the development of a new concept of prison jurisprudence has evolved.

Prison labour

Prison labour in India was always viewed as a mode of punishment. The judiciary reacted towards elimination of unpaid labour practices in jails. In *Mohammad Giasuddin v. State of Andhra Pradesh*,[63] the appellant was a Government employee. He was convicted for the offence of cheating and was sentenced to three years rigorous imprisonment. The appellant was 28 years old; and had two university degrees. He lost his job consequent to conviction. The parents and sisters were his dependents. On these facts, the Supreme Court reduced the sentence from three years to eighteen months imprisonment and ordered that suitable mental-cum-manual work should be provided to the prisoner. Regarding wages, the court held that unpaid labour was "bonded labour and humiliating".

Prison labour should be meaningful and it should be helpful to earn livelihood to the prisoner on release. The Supreme Court emphasised the philosophy of reformation and rehabilitation of the prisoner through vocational training in *Dharambir v. State of U.P.*[64] The Supreme Court in this case held that the prisoners are entitled to fair wages for the work done by them. The court analyzed the scope of Sec. 53 of the I.P.C.[65] and said that the Section speaks about "hard labour" but not "free labour" in rigorous imprisonment.

Again in 1998, the issue of the scope of Sec. 53 of the I.P.C. came up for consideration before the Supreme Court in *State of Gujarat v. Hon'ble High Court of Gujarat.*[66] The issue was whether prisoners, who are required to do labour as a part of their punishment, should necessarily be paid minimum wages for such work.

The Supreme Court noted that the mandate of Sec. 53(4)[67] clearly stipulated that in the event rigorous imprisonment was awarded, then such punishment included the obligation to put in labour or work on the part of the prisoner. Thus, the jail authorities are enjoined by law and mandated by court to impose hard labour on prisoners sentenced to rigorous imprisonment. By so compelling, the jail officials could not be said to be committing offences under Sec. 374, IPC (unlawful compulsory labour). However, this would not apply to prisoners sentenced to simple imprisonment, or detention laws under various preventive detention or even undertrial prisoners.

After a detailed consideration of the law, the Supreme Court evolved the following guidelines:

(1) "It is lawful to employ the prisoners sentenced to rigorous imprisonment to do hard labour whether he consents to do it or not;

(2) It is open to the jail officials to permit other prisoners also to do any work which they choose to do, provided such prisoners make a request for that purpose.

(3) It is imperative that the prisoners should be paid equitable wages for the work done by them. In order to determine the quantum of equitable wages payable to prisoners, the State concerned shall constitute a wage fixation body for making recommendations. We direct each State to do so as early as possible.

(4) Until the State Government takes any decision on such recommendations, every prisoner must be paid wages for the work done by him/her at such rates or revised rates as the government concerned fixes, in the light of the observation made above."[68]

(5) We recommend to the State concerned to make law for setting apart a portion of the wages earned by the prisoners to be paid as compensation to deserving victims of the offence, the compensation of which entailed the sentence of imprisonment to the prisoner, either directly or through a common fund to be created for this purpose or in any other feasible mode".[69]

The above judgment sets at rest the issue of whether prisoners sentenced to hard labour, because of the fact that they were sentenced to rigorous imprisonment, should be paid wages.

Compensation for illegal detention or death in prison custody

The judiciary has not hesitated in awarding monetary compensation to the victims of illegal detention. The Supreme Court has considered this right as an aspect of personal liberty under Art. 21 of the Constitution. The first case in which the court awarded monetary compensation for illegal detention in jail was the Bihar Blinding case,[70] popularly known as the Bhagalpur Blinding case. It depicted a very sad picture of undertrials. The police blinded these prisoners in a very crude and barbaric manner. Their modus operandi was to puncture the eye balls of the prisoners with bicycle spokes and then administer acid into their eyes till only the sockets remained. The right to compensation for illegal detention found its recognition in *Rudul Shah v. State of Bihar*.[71] In this case, the petitioner was released from jail after 14 years of acquittal by the court. Rudal Shah filed a petition in the Supreme Court claiming compensation for his illegal detention. The Supreme Court ordered the State to pay to the petitioner a sum of Rs.30,000/- as compensation.

In *Kewal Pati v. State of U.P.*,[72] the Supreme Court awarded compensation to the wife and children of the deceased, who was killed by a co-convict while serving out his sentence under Sec. 302 of the I.P.C., in central jail, Varanasi. The Supreme Court held that though the deceased was a convict and was serving his sentence, yet the authorities were not absolved of their responsibility to ensure his life and safety in jail. Further, the Supreme Court held that the prisoners are entitled to constitutional rights and protection except to the extent deprived of it in accordance with law. But the death of the convict resulted in deprivation of his life contrary to law and in utter violation of the provisions of Art. 21 of the Constitution. Accordingly, the State of Uttar Pradesh was directed to pay Rs.1 lakh to the legal heirs of the deceased convict within a period of three months from the date of the order.

The Supreme Court had again reiterated the position in *State of Andhra Pradesh v. Challa Rama Krishna Reddy* case.[73] In this case, the deceased father of the claimant, and the claimant were involved in a criminal case. They were remanded to judicial custody in a sub-jail. The deceased and his son apprehended danger and requested protection. But their requests were not heeded by the authorities. As apprehended by them, a bomb was thrown at them. This caused the death of the father and injuries to his son. The Supreme Court held that a prisoner, be a convict or undertrial or detenue, even when lodged in jail continues to enjoy all his fundamental rights including right to life. Even the State has no authority to violate that right. This right cannot be defeated by a pleading of sovereign immunity.

The Supreme Court also awarded compensation when an undertrial committed suicide[74] while in custody, as the court felt that the authorities are duty bound to prevent or take reasonable care to prevent such action.

(iv) Judicial Contribution to Social Welfare Custody

Protective homes and Human rights

In *Upendra Baxi and Others v. State of U.P.*[75], the Supreme Court issued detailed instructions to enforce human rights even within Nari Niketans (women's protective homes).[76] It is important to remember that the court in similar situations can issue benign mandates to defend the dignity of women behind bars. The court in this case with regard to the construction of Nari Niketans and conditions therein ordered as follows:

1) The approach to the new building (Nari Niketan) shall be made into a pucca or semi-pucca road so that it does not get blocked or water-logged by rain. This shall be done within 3 months from today.

2) The big hall as also the three rooms used as class-rooms and kitchen shall be provided with cross ventilation by putting up a sufficient number of windows so as to ensure passage of air in and out of the rooms. The District Judge or the Additional District Judge nominated by him shall determine how many windows are necessary to be constructed for this purpose.

3) Exhaust fans shall be provided in the big hall, three class rooms, kitchen and offices.

4) The State Government shall provide police protection throughout day and night for the inmates of the protective home in the new building.

5) The State Government shall either provide accommodation to the staff of the protective home in or near the new building or provide conveyance to the members of the staff for coming to the protective home and going back to their respective homes unless

public transport is available in the immediate vicinity of the protective home.

6) The State Government shall immediately take steps to provide mosquito nets to each and every inmate and member of the staff staying in the protective home.

7) The State Government shall provide conveyance for taking the inmates to the court and bringing them back to the protective home and, similarly, conveyance shall also be provided to the District Judge or Additional District Judge inspecting the protective home.

8) The District Manager (Telephones) Agra shall immediately shift the telephone to the new building and whatever steps are necessary for this purpose shall be taken by the State Government without any delay.

9) The State Government shall immediately provide cooking gas in the kitchen so that it is not necessary to use wood for cooking which may exit a lot of smoke and lead to discomfort and suffocation on account of lack of ventilation.

10) The State Government shall immediately proceed to carry out rewiring as also to install the electric meter in a safe place where there is no dampness .... the State Government shall without any undue delay proceed to take the necessary steps to install a generator so that the safety of the inmates is not jeopardised".

Further, the Supreme Court felt disappointed to know the non-observance of its order in the implementation of Rule 40 of the Rules made under the Suppression of Immoral Traffic in Women and Girls Act, 1956.[77] So the court directed the State Government to set up a Board of Visitors within a fortnight. This showed the importance and urgency attached to the safety of the women by the court in social welfare custody. The Supreme Court also took the lead in prescribing the composition of the Board of Visitors.

The court directed that there should be three social activists working in the field of women welfare, particularly in the welfare of the sex workers besides two persons who are nominees of the District Judge concerned.[78]

The Supreme Court in the same order prevented the Superintendent of protective home from accepting any girl or woman as inmate without the due authority and process of law. The District Judges are directed to make a monthly visit to the protective homes, inspect the conditions of the inmates and take steps to realise or repatriate unauthorised inmates, if found any.[79]

The District Judge was directed by the Supreme Court to appoint two socially committed advocates to visit the protective home in Agra by turns in a fortnight to enquire about the needs and requirements of the inmates and to provide them legal aid and assistance, when required.[80]

The Supreme Court also took note of the absence of the effective rehabilitation programmes to the inmates of the protective home. The Supreme Court stressed the need for such programmes so that the inmates could look after themselves and did not slide into prostitution as and when they are released. It directed the State Government to submit detailed rehabilitative programmes which are already in existence or those proposed. The Supreme Court also suggested the consideration of the possible wedding of the inmates with proper persons after obtaining the consent of the inmates and also proper enquiry into the antecedents of the would-be bride groom so as to ensure that the inmates are not dragged once again into prostitution.[81]

Similarly in *Chinnama Sivadas v. State of Delhi Administration*,[82] the Supreme Court issued commands based upon panel recommendations. These pertain to the safe custody, fair treatment and legal assistance to the women in social welfare custody.

The Supreme Court ordered that though there are several inmates housed in Nari Niketan who are not admitted under the provisions of the Suppression of Immoral Traffic in Women and Girls Act, 1956[83] (referred as SITA), all of them should be provided basic amenities such as food, clothing, health check-up, etc., in accordance with the rules made by the Delhi Administration under SITA as Nari Niketan was declared as protection homes under SITA.

The Supreme Court also directed that free legal aid and advice should be extended to all the inmates of Nari Niketan since it was mandated by several decisions of the Supreme Court to extend free legal aid and advice to all those who are unable to afford it, since in the absence of such aid and advice the poor are likely to be priced out of the legal system. So the court directed the Secretary of the Legal Aid and Advice Board to make a weekly visit to the protective homes to interview the inmates and record any grievances, if any, and sort them out through the legal system.

The Supreme Court ordered the closure of mental ward within Nari Niketan (Protective Home in Delhi) as such a ward in the Home is a gross violation of Indian Lunacy Act[84] and directed the authorities to shift the chronic mental patients to a mental hospital.

The Supreme Court further suggested the classification of the inmates based on their problems and specifically deal with each category of inmates differently for vocational guidance, rehabilitation and social adaptation.

Provision for recreational facilities for the inmates was also considered by the court and accordingly directed the authorities to provide a Radio, T.V. and some indoor games for the recreation of the inmates.

The prospect of marriage of the inmates is a part of rehabilitation, the court felt, but such marriages should be performed only after obtaining the prior permission of the court, so that the court can verify the bona fides of the would-be bridegroom.

The Supreme Court in *Hussainara Khatoon v. State of Bihar*[85] has censured the Bihar Government for keeping a few women in jails in the name of "Protective Custody" without even being accused of any offence and described such imprisonment as a "blatant violation" of personal liberty guaranteed under the Constitution. In its order passed on an affidavit filed by the State of Bihar giving details of the undertrial prisoners in 17 jails in the State, the Supreme Court observed that the particulars given in the affidavit made "very distressing" reading. "Protective Custody" for women kept in jails merely because they happened to be victims of an offence or they were required for the purpose of giving evidence, the court observed, is a euphemism calculated to disguise what is really and in truth nothing but imprisonment. "It is an expression intended to appease the conscience". Observing that the court was not aware of any provision of law under which a woman could be kept in jail by way of protective custody, the judges directed the Bihar Government to release all women and children who were in jail in the State under "Protective Custody". All of them should be taken forthwith to welfare homes or rescue homes and should be kept there and properly looked after.

Rehabilitation of prostitutes and their children

Further, the Supreme Court issued directions pertaining to the rescue and rehabilitation of prostitutes and their children in *Gaurav Jain v. Union of Inida*.[86]

The Immoral Traffic (Prevention) Act, 1956 is not a penal legislation but a social welfare legislation which aims at the rehabilitation of the female and child offenders indulging in prostitution. The summary of the guidelines laid down by the court is as follows:

1) Counselling, cajoling and coercion are necessary to effectively enforce the provisions of the Immoral Traffic (Prevention) Act and Juvenile Justice Act.

2) It is the duty of the State and all voluntary non-government organisations and public-spirited persons to come to the aid of the prostitutes to retrieve them from prostitution, rehabilitate them by lending them a helping hand to make them lead a life with dignity self-employment through provision of education and financial support.

3) Women found in the flesh trade should be viewed more as victims of adverse socio-economic circumstances rather than as offenders in our society. The commercial exploitation of sex may be regarded as a crime but those trapped in custom-oriented prostitution and gender-oriented prostitution should be viewed as victims of gender-oriented vulnerability.

4) The customary initiation of women in the practice of Devadasi, Jogins and Venkatasins, prevalent in Andhra Pradesh, Karnataka and Maharashtra areas and the resultant practice of prostitution is a crime against humanity, violation of human rights and obnoxious to the Constitution and the Human Rights Act. They are void under Article 13 of the Constitution of India and are punishable under the law and the children of fallen women and also child prostitutes should be rescued and rehabilitated.

In fact, the Supreme Court has exercised its extra-ordinary rule-making power under Art.142 & Art.145 to lay down a comprehensive scheme to rescue and rehabilitate the victims of sexual exploitation due to societal conditions and the children. The Apex Court deserves accolades for such an initiative, which in fact should have been taken by the political branches of the Government i.e. legislative and executive.

Eradication of child prostitution

Child prostitution and directions relating to the eradication of prostitution drew the attention of the Supreme Court in *Vishal Jeet v. Union of India*[87]. The Supreme Court has taken note of the fact that many poverty-stricken children and girls in the prime of youth are taken to "Flesh Market" and forcibly pushed into the flesh trade which is being carried on in utter violation of all canons of morality, decency and dignity of human kind and suggested the following measures for the purpose of eradicating the evil of prostitution.

1) "All the State Governments and the Governments of Union Territories should direct their concerned law enforcing authorities to take appropriate and speedy action under the existing laws in eradicating child prostitution without giving room for any complaint of remissness or culpable indifference.

2) The State Governments and Governments of Union Territories should set up a separate Advisory Committee within their respective zones consisting of the Secretary of the Social Welfare Department or Board, the Secretary of the Law Department, Sociologists, Criminologists, members of women's organisations, members of the Indian Council of Child Welfare and the Indian Council of Social Welfare as well the members of various voluntary social

organisations and associations, etc., the main objects of the Advisory Committee being to make suggestions of:

(a) the measures to be taken in eradicating the child prostitutes, and

(b) the social welfare programmes to be implemented for the care, protection, treatment, development and rehabilitation of the young fallen victims namely the children and girls rescued either from the brothel houses or from the vices of prostitution.

(3) All the State Governments and Governments of Union Territories should take steps in providing adequate and rehabilitative homes manned by well-qualified trained social workers, psychiatrists and doctors.

(4) The Union Government should set up a committee of its own on the lines we have suggested under direction No.(2), the main object of which is to evolve welfare programmes to be implemented on the national level for the care, protection, rehabilitation, etc., of the young fallen victims namely the children and girls and to make suggestions of amendments to the existing laws or for enactment of any new law, if so warranted, for the prevention of sexual exploitation of children.

(5) The Central Government and the Governments of States and Union territories should devise a machinery of its own for ensuring the proper implementation of the suggestions that would be made by the respective committees; and

(6) The Advisory Committee can also go deep into the Devadasi system and Jogin tradition and give their valuable advice and suggestions as to what best the government could do in that regard".

(v) Judicial Contribution to Mental Health Custody

Mental asylums and Human rights

The court's oversight into the human side and habilitative aspect of rescue homes and mental hospitals is also borne out by some rulings of the highest court. In *Rakesh Chand Narain v. State of Bihar*[88], the following order was made:

1) "In respect of each patient in the Ranchi Mansik Arogya Shala (mental hospital), the daily allocation for diet will be increased from the existing inadequate figure of only Rs.3.50 to Rs.10/- per day per patient and directory articles of that value shall be supplied to each patient.

2) Arrangements should be made forthwith to supply adequate quantity of pure drinking water to the hospital, if necessary, by engaging water tankers to transport potable water from outside.

3) Immediate arrangements should be made for the restoration of proper sanitary conditions in the lavatories and bathrooms of the hospitals.

4) All patients in the hospitals who are not at present having mattresses and blankets should be immediately supplied with the same within 15 days from today. Such of the patients as have not been given cots should also be provided cots within 6 weeks from today so that no patient shall be thereafter without a cot.

5) This ceiling limit at present in vogue in respect of cost of medicines allowable for each patient will stand removed with immediate effect and the patients will be supplied medicines according to the prescription made by the doctors irrespective of the cost.

6) The State Government shall forthwith take steps to appoint a qualified psychiatrist and a Medical Superintendent for the hospital and they should be posted and take charge in the Institution within six weeks from today.

7) The Chief Judicial Magistrate, Ranchi, to whom a copy of this order would be forwarded by the Registry shall visit the hospital once in 3 weeks and submit quarterly reports to this court as to whether the aforesaid directions given by the court are being complied with."

Scrutiny of management's functions

The management of the mental hospitals and protective homes, where women are detained, came under the scrutiny of the Supreme Court through a series of writ petitions. First, the court ordered[89] a number of steps to be taken for improving the infrastructural facilities and professional services and also their day-to-day management. The Supreme Court also directed the steps to be taken to make these institutions autonomous.

The Supreme Court through its order dated 11 November, 1997 has also involved the National Human Rights Commission (NHRC) in protecting the rights of the women in custody.[90] The court felt that custodial offences mostly pertain to the human rights violation and the NHRC which gained statutory powers through Protection of Human Rights Act, 1993 is primarily meant for curbing such violations. So the Supreme Court requested the NHRC, in *Rakesh Chandra Narain* case, to involve itself in the supervision of the functioning of the Agra, Gwalior and Ranchi mental hospitals, Agra Protective Home, etc.[91]

As per the order of the Supreme Court, the NHRC paid a visit to the Agra Protective Home, Ranchi Institute of

Neuro-Psychiatry and Allied Sciences (formerly Ranchi Manasik Arogyasala) and prepared a report on the conditions therein and the areas that needed attention for further improvement.[92]

The above catena of cases briefly sum up the rights of persons in prisons, police lock-ups, mental hospitals and rescue homes. This is a growing jurisprudence, but the direction of expansion is progressive and clear from the pronouncements summed up above. In the matter of personal liberties and other freedoms the Constitution is the creative receptacle. People are governed by the Constitution but the Constitution is what the judges say it is.[93]

Following the intervention of the Supreme Court there has been some improvement in many areas of the functioning of these institutes.[94]

The NHRC, on the suggestion of the Supreme Court, decided to monitor closely, on a regular basis, all aspects of the situation in regard to the conditions in protective homes and mental hospitals.[95]

In fact the fear of the visits of NHRC was visible in the words and deeds of the people who are in charge of the mental hospitals at Hyderabad, the jail authorities at Chanchalguda, Hyderabad.

The Supreme Court has succeeded in creating a sense of responsibility in the authorities and fixing accountability on the people who are directly dealing with women in custody. The custodial offences, though not totally eliminated, became less frequent. There were no complaints of violence against them from the inmates regarding the treatment either in State Jails for Women or mental hospitals in Andhra Pradesh. The judicial intervention in custodial justice has a direct impact on the treatment of women in custody.

However, in a recent ruling,[96] the Supreme Court has totally departed from its earlier progressive directions. All through the last two decades the Supreme Court was caring for the safety and fair treatment of those in custody in general and women in particular. In the landmark *Sheela Barse*[97] case, the Supreme Court insisted on the presence of women constables at the time of interrogation in the police stations, creation of separate lock-ups for women etc. The Supreme Court on many earlier occasions made adverse comments and expressed utmost concern on the behaviour of the police with the offenders. But the Supreme Court suddenly took a totally different view in arresting the women by permitting the police to arrest the women offenders even during night and in the absence of women constable, of course, in exceptional circumstances.

References

1. Report of National Expert Committee on Women Prisoners (1986-87), Vol. I, p.111.
2. (1986) 3 SCJ 291; 1986 SCC (Cri) 381.
3. AIR 1983 SC 378; (1983) 2 SCC 96; 1983 CriLJ 642.
4. (1986) Scale 739 Ref in Report of National Expert Committee on Women Prisoners, Vol. II, p.55.
5. *Nandini Satpathy v. P.L. Dani*, AIR 1978 SC 1025.
   Kishore Singh v. State of Rajasthan, AIR 1981 SC 625.
   State of U.P. v. Ram Sagar Yadav, AIR 1985 SC 416.
   SAHELI v. Commissioner of Police, Delhi AIR 1990 SC 513.
   Smt. Nilabati Behera v. State of Orissa, AIR 1993 SC 1960.
   Arvinder Singh Bagga v. State of U.P., AIR 1995 SC 117.
6. *Sunil Batra v. Delhi Administration*, AIR 1978 SC 1675; 1978 CriLJ 1741; (1978) 4 SCC 494.
   Prem Shankar Sukla v. Delhi Administration, AIR 1980 SC 1535.
   Sunil Gupta v. State of M.P., (1990) 3 SCC 119;
   State of Maharashtra v. Ravikant S. Patil, (1991) 2 SCC 373.

Citizen for Democracy v. State of Assam, AIR 1996 SC 2193; (1995) 3 SCC 743; 1996 CriLJ 3247.

7. AIR 1983 SC 378; 1983 CriLJ 642; (1983) 2 SCC 96.
8. AIR 1994 SC 1349: (1994) 4 SCC 260: 1994 CriLJ 1981.
9. 1995 CriLJ 4223.
10. 2004 CriLJ 14 (SC).
11. in Cl.(vii) of operative part of its judgement.
12. *D.K.Basu v. State of West Bengal*, AIR 1997 SC 610: 1997 CriLJ 743: (1997) 1 SCC 416.
13. AIR 1994 SC 1349: (1994) 4 SCC 260: 1994 CriLJ 1981.
14. NHRC – Annual Report (1997-98) Para 3.12, p.12.
15. *D.K.Basu v. State of West Bengal* 1997 CriLJ 743: AIR 1997 SC 610: (1997) 1 SCC 416.
16. (1999) 6 SCC 667: AIR 1999 SC 2979.
17. AIR 1993 SC 1960: (1993) 2 SCC 746: 1993 CriLJ 2899.
18. AIR 1995 SC 117: (1994) 6 SCC 565: (1995) 1 SCJ 173: *Bhim Singh v. State of Jammu & Kashmir*, AIR 1986 SC 494: (1985) 4 SCC 677: 1986 CriLJ 192.
19. (1995) 3 SCC 702: 1995 CriLJ 3235.
20. 2003 CriLJ 806.
21. *Nilabati Behera v. State of Orissa* AIR 1993 SC 1960: (1993) 2 SCC 746: 1993 CriLJ 2899: *D.K. Basu v. State of West Bengal* (1997) 1 SCC 416: 1997 CriLJ 743. *Harbans Kaur v. Union of India* (1995) 1 SCC 623.
22. Some of them are: *State of M.P. v. Shyam Sunder Trivedi* (1995) 4 SCC 262. *People's Union for Civil Liberties v. Union of India* AIR 1997 SC 1203: (1997) 3 SCC 433. *Solgabai Sunil Pawar v. State of Maharashtra* 1998 CriLJ 1505 (Bom). *Savitri Behera v. State of Orissa* 1998 CriLJ 4716 (Ori). *D.K. Basu v. State of West Bengal* 1997 CriLJ 743: AIR 1997 SC 610: (1997) 1 SCC 416. *Geeta (Smt.) v. Lt. Governor* 1999 CriLJ 1099 (Del). *D.B.M. Patnaik v. State of A.P.* AIR 1974 SC 2092. *Chandbai Yadav v. State of M.P.* 1997 CriLJ 3844. *Dharmishtaben Narendrashin Zala v. State of Gujarat* 1997 CriLJ 3866. *Jagruti v. S.G.Chaudhari* 1998 CriLJ 3251 (Guj). *Samji Ladha v. State of Gujarat* 1998 CriLJ 2746 (Guj). *Praful Kumar Sinha v. State of Bihar* 1994 SCC (Cri) 1666. *Kamini Bala Talukdar (Smt.) v. State of Assam* 1997 CriLJ 874 (Gau). *Supreme Court Legal Aid Committee v. State of Bihar* (1991) 3 SCC 482.

Jacob George (Dr.) v. State of Kerala (1994) 3 SCC 430: 1994 CriLJ 3851. *Paschim Banga Khet Mazdoor Samity v. State of West Bengal* AIR 1996 SC 2426. *Manju Bhatia (Mrs.) v. New Delhi, Municipal Corporation* AIR 1998 SC 223: (1997) 6 SCC 370. *Soubhagya (Smt.) v. Chief Secretary, State of Karnataka* 2001 CriLJ 238 (Kant). *Shyama Devi v. National Capital of Delhi* AIR 1999 Del 264. *Lawyers Forum for Human Rights, Calcutta v. State of West Bengal* 1997 CriLJ 1762. *Kamala Devi (Smt.) v. Govt. of National Capital Territory of Delhi* 2000 CriLJ 4867 (Del) (DB). *Kewal Pati v. State of U.P.* 1995 CriLJ 2920. *Dhanno (Smt.) v. Union of India* 2001 CriLJ 4119 (Del). *Murti Devi v. State of Delhi* (1998) 9 SCC 604. *Chandania v. State of U.P.* 2001 CriLJ 2090 (All) (FB). *Anguri (Smt.) v. State* 2001 CriLJ 3697 (Del) (DB). *T. Joicy (Smt.) v. Union of India* 2000 CriLJ 764 (Gau) (DB). *Suguna (Smt.) v. State of Karnataka* 2000 CriLJ 4408 (Kant). *Madina (Mst) v. State of Rajasthan* 2000 CriLJ 4484 (Raj). *Fattuji v. Superintendent of Police*, Akola 2002 CriLJ 914. *Bheemma v. Station House Officer*, Hyderabad 2002 CriLJ 694. *P. Viswanathan v. A.K. Burman* 2003 CriLJ 949 (Cal). *Samata Vedika v. State of Karnataka* 2003 CriLJ 1003.

23. (1980) 3 SCC 526; 1980 CriLJ 930: AIR 1980 SC 1535.
24. (1990) 3 SCC 119.
25. *State of Maharashtra v. Ravikant S. Patil* (1991) 2 SCC 373.
26. (1994) 6 SCC 260: AIR 1995 SC 31: 1995 CriLJ 508.
27. AIR 1996 SC 2193: (1995) 3 SCC 743: 1996 CriLJ 3247.
28. AIR 1980 SC 1535.
29. Sec.303, Cr.P.C. 1973, Art.22(1), Indian Constitution.
30. Sec.304, *Ibid*.
31. AIR 1978 SC 1025: (1978) 2 SCC 424: 1978 CriLJ 968 (SC).
32. Art.20(3) provides that no person accused of any offence shall be compelled to be a witness against himself.
33. Sec. 161 Cr.P.C.: Examination of witnesses by police:
    (1) Any police officer making an investigation . . . may examine orally any person supposed to be acquainted with the facts and circumstances of the case.
    (2) Such person shall be bound to answer truly all questions relating to such case put to him by such officer, other

than the questions the answers to which would have a tendency to expose him to a criminal charge or to a penalty or forfeiture.

34. AIR 1978 SC 1548: (1978) 3 SCC 544: 1978 CriLJ 1678.
35. AIR 1979 SC 1369: 1979 CriLJ 1045: (1980) 1 SCC 98.
36. AIR 1981 SC 746: (1981) 1 SCC 608: 1981 CriLJ 306 (SC).
37. (1986) 2 SCC 401: AIR 1986 SC 991: 1986 CriLJ 1084.
38. AIR 1989 SC 142: (1988) 4 SCC 574: 1989 CriLJ 870.
39. *Sheela Barse v. State of Maharashtra*, AIR 1983 SC 378 at page 380.
40. *Sheela Barse v. State of Maharashtra*, AIR 1983 SC 378, pp.380-382.
41. *Ibid*.
42. AIR 1983 SC 378 at p.381.
43. AIR 1977 SC 2147: (1977) 4 SCC 291: 1977 CriLJ 1746.
44. AIR 1978 SC 1594: (1978) 4 SCC 47: 1978 CriLJ 1703.
45. *Hussainara Khatoon v. Home Secretary, State of Bihar*, AIR 1979 SC 1360: 1979 CriLJ 1036: (1980) 1 SCC 81.
46. AIR 1981 SC 939.
47. AIR 1986 SC 1773: (1986) SCC 632: 1986 CriLJ 1736.
48. *A.R. Antulay v. R.S. Nayak* (1992) 1 SCC 225 *Common cause v. Union of India* (1996) 4 SCC 33: *Rajdeo Sharma v. State of Bihar* AIR 1998 SC 3281: (1998) 7 SCC 507: 1998 CriLJ 4546.
49. L.K. Advani, "Prisoners Scrap Book (1978) Arnold Associates, New Delhi. Kuldip Nayar, "The Judgement", (1977), Vikas Publishing House Pvt. Ltd., New Delhi.
50. AIR 1974 SC 2092: (1975) 3 SCC 185: 1975 CriLJ 556.
51. AIR 1978 SC 1514: (1978) 4 SCC 104: 1978 CriLJ 1534.
52. AIR 1978 SC 1675: 1978 CriLJ 1741: (1978) 4 SCC 494.
53. Sec. 29 of Prisons Act, 1894 reads: "No cell shall be used for solitary confinement unless it is furnished with the means of enabling the prisoner to communicate at any time with an officer of the prison, and every prisoner so confined in a cell for more than twenty-four hours, whether as a punishment or otherwise, shall be visited at least once a day by the Medical Officer or Medical subordinate.

54. Sec.30(2) of Prisons Act, 1894 reads: Every such prisoner shall be confined in a cell apart from all other prisoners, and shall be placed by day and by night under the charge of a guard.

55. Sec.74 IPC reads: In executing a sentence of solitary confinement, such confinement shall in no case exceed 14 days at a time, with intervals between the periods, of solitary confinement of not less duration than such periods, and when the imprisonment awarded shall exceed 3 months, the solitary confinement shall not exceed 7 days in any one month of the whole imprisonment awarded, with intervals between the periods of solitary confinement of not less duration than such periods.

56. AIR 1981 SC 625: (1981) 1 SCC 503: 1981 CriLJ 17.

57. AIR 1966 SC 424: 1966 CriLJ 311.

58. (1982) 1 SCC 1: 1982 SCC (Cri) 41: AIR 1982 SC 6: 1982 CriLJ 148.

59. AIR 1981 SC 746: 1981 CriLJ 306.

60. Sec.5 of COFEPOSA: Every person in respect of whom a detention order has been made shall be liable–

    (a) to be detained in such place under such conditions including conditions as to maintenance, interviews or communication with others, discipline and punishment for breaches of discipline, as the appropriate Government may by general or special order, specify; and

    (b) to be removed from one place of detention to another place of detention, whether within the same State or in another State by order of the appropriate Government.

    Provided that no order shall be made by a State Government under clause (b) for the removal of a person from one State to another State except with the convenience of the Government of that other State.

61. Art.5, Universal Declaration of Human Rights, 1948 – No one shall be subjected to torture or to cruel, inhuman or degrading treatment or punishment.

62. Art.7, International Covenant on Civil and Political Rights, 1966 – No one shall be subjected to torture or to cruel, inhuman or degrading treatment or punishment. In particular, no one shall be subjected without his free consent to medical or

scientific experimentation – B.L. Bansal, "The Law relating to Human Rights – The Protection of Human Rights Act, 1993" 2000 Edn., Capital Law House, Delhi, p.117.

63. AIR 1977 SC 1926: (1977) 3 SCC 287: 1977 CriLJ 1557.
64. (1979) 3 SCC 645: 1979 SCC (Cri) 862.
65. Sec.53 of the IPC, 1860 reads – The punishments to which offenders are liable under the provisions of this Code are:-

    Firstly – Death

    Secondly – Imprisonment for life

    Thirdly – (Repealed by Act 17 of 1949)

    Fourthly – Imprisonment, which is of two descriptions, namely:

    (1) Rigorous, that is, with hard labour,

    (2) Simple

    Fifthly – Forfeiture of property

    Sixthly – fine.
66. AIR 1998 SC 3164: 1998 CriLJ 4561.
67. S.53(4) of IPC reads: Imprisonment, which is of two descriptions, namely:-

    (1) Rigorous, that is, with hard labour; (2) Simple.
68. Six weeks time (from date of judgement i.e., 24 September, 1998) was given to State Government; to fix the interim wages.
69. 1998 CriLJ 4561 at pp. 4572-73.
70. *Khatri v. State of Bihar*, AIR 1981 SC 928: (1981) 1 SCC 635.
71. AIR 1983 SC 1086: (1983) 4 SCC 141: 1983 CriLJ 1644.
72. (1995) 3 SCC 600: 1995 CriLJ 2920: (1995) 2 SCJ 540.
73. AIR 2000 SC 2083: (2000) 5 SCC 712.
74. *Puppala Seetaramaiah v. Superintendent: Sub-Jail, Bapatla* 2003 CriLJ 2978.
75. (1986) 3 SCJ 291: AIR 1987 SC 191: (1986) 4 SCC 106.
76. "Hindi" terminology for protection homes.
77. Later renamed as Immoral Traffic (Prevention) Act, 1956.
78. *Upendra Baxi v. State of U.P.*, (1986) 4 SCC 106 at Para 5, p.114.
79. *Ibid.*, Para 6, pp.114-115.
80. *Ibid.*, Para 7, p.115.

81. *Ibid*., Para 8, p.115.
82. Writ Petition No.2526 of 1981 Order dt.14-9-1981 as cited in the Report of National Expert Committee on Women Prisoners, Vol. II, p. 58.
83. Now it is called Immoral Traffic (Prevention) Act, 1956.
84. This Act is now replaced by Mental Health Act, 1987.
85. AIR 1979 SC 1369: 1979 CriLJ 1045: (1980) 1 SCC 98.
86. (1997) 8 SCC 114: AIR 1997 SC 3021.
87. AIR 1990 SC 1412: 1990 CriLJ 1469: (1990) 3 SCC 318.
88. (1986) Scale 739 – cited in Report of National Expert Committee on Women Prisoners (1986-87), Vol. II, p.55.
89. S.C. Order dated 8 Sept. 1994 – NHRC Annual Report 1997-98, Para 8.6, p.30.
90. NHRC – Annual Report 1997-98, Para 8.1, p.30.
91. *Ibid*., Para 8.4, p.30.
92. NHRC – Annual Report 1997-98, Para 8.8, p.31.
93. Report of National Expert Committee on Women Prisoners (1986-87), Vol. II, p. 89.
94. NHRC – Annual Report 1997-98, Para 8.10, p.31.
95. *Ibid*., Para 8.11, p.31.
96. *State of Maharashtra v. C.C.W. Council of India*, 2004 CriLJ 14.
97. AIR 1983 SC 378: 1983 CriLJ 642: (1983) 2 SCC 96.

7

Conditions of Women Prisoners in Different Custodies in Andhra Pradesh, India

Any one irrespective of gender can commit crimes. However, due to the different social status of women in our society, prison conditions and the rules applicable to women prisoners deserve special consideration. Contrary to this in the penal thinking and literature women have figured less significantly. The substantive and procedural laws, as they existed also contained very few provisions for women criminals.

But the social changes of the last century, more so after the Industrial Revolution, the roles of women have undergone a change. The social and political freedom gained not only made them equal to the men in status but also equal partners in crime. So the number of women in custody is also on the rise.

Woman as such is vulnerable and when the custodian is a man her vulnerability and unequal status are more strongly reflected. A woman requires a different type of handling in various criminal justice processes. Hence, the emphasis on gender justice during the last two decades.

Despite the recommendations made for special procedures for handling women in detention, the treatment of women offenders in police lock-up and penal and correctional institutions by various committees and separate guidelines issued by the Supreme Court, the ill-treatment of women in custody is reported quite often.

To understand the actual treatment meted out to women who are presently under judicial custody and prison custody, a research methodology is designed. Following that method, women prisoners held under penal and non-penal custodies were personally interviewed and their custodial experiences were recorded. The information thus obtained and gleaned is presented in this chapter under different headings. The interviews were conducted with the women prisoners mainly to find out whether the statutory provisions, the rules contained in the Jail Manual and the directions of the courts with regard to women prisoners are being implemented.

(i) Research Procedure

In the different stages of the criminal justice system, women criminals will experience the custody of police at the first instance followed by the production before the Magistrate, then as remand prisoner for sometime and finally the jail custody, if convicted. Sometimes women may also be placed in the custody of social welfare and mental health institutions.

It is difficult to identify the women in police custody and interview them as the police very rarely allow a stranger into the police station and permit an interview with those in the lock-up. Even the study at the time of the production before a Magistrate can't be carried out for obvious reasons. So the only place where information can be elicited from the experiences of women in custody is the prison. The convict prisoner has already undergone the police, judicial custody and she could narrate her experience vis-à-vis the safety provisions available in the law.

So an empirical study is planned by visiting the central jails in the state where women are lodged in separate enclosures. Since all the women convicted for over a month are lodged only in the State Jails for Women either at Rajahmundry or Hyderabad, the study was focussed on the inmates of these two jails though visits were also made to other central jails at Visakhapatnam, Warangal to see the physical conditions.

Visit to jails

The study of criminals is always beset with some problems. Jails are out of bounds for others as none is allowed inside, more so in case of women jails. A special and specific permission is required from the Director General of Prisons (D.G. of P.) who is the competent authority to issue such permission. The D.G. of Prisons, after going through the abstract of the proposed work and on the production of authorisation from University authorities and establishing the identity of the researcher issued necessary permission to interview the convicts subject to certain restrictions.

The State Jails for Women both at Rajahmundry and Hyderabad are administered by a female jail Superintendent, one Jailer, one Deputy Jailor, one Welfare Officer and female Matrons. The investigator was allowed to take down all the information of the female convicts and remand prisoners available in the jail records. A Matron was entrusted with the job of assisting the researcher. In Rajahmundry, the Deputy Jailor herself accompanied the researcher.

In both the jails, the researcher was allowed to stay from 9 a.m. to 4.30 p.m. and conduct interviews with the convicts. The inmates were asked to appear before the researcher and answer her questions. The inmates initially questioned the motive, relevance and usefulness of the study of their conditions. The convicts, as was revealed later, had answered the questions of many social scientists and social organisations earlier and couldn't benefit any from such studies. Some of them didn't like to reveal their identity and family background to a stranger. So initially the inmates were either not answering or not properly answering the questions.

It took some time to explain to them the purpose of the research and its usefulness, if not immediately but at a later date. It was explained to them how the jail conditions have improved over a period of time and how the research works of this kind directly and indirectly helped the convicts. It was difficult for those illiterate prisoners to understand the need and purpose of this research work. They would not easily believe that a total stranger unrelated to any one of the inmates, without any personal gain could take all the pain of visiting them and recording their custodial experience. The persistent question they put was, "can you help us in any way in meeting our children?". When the researcher explained the purpose of the study and the limitations in helping them, some of the prisoners serving long term sentence could understand the position. Some of the remand prisoners who are educated tried to convince the convicts to open up and talked about the need to cooperate with the researcher. The Deputy Jailor at Rajahmundry who has the confidence of prisoners made a lot of difference in completing the task with little resistance.

It is the experience of the researcher that when interviewed individually the inmate's way of answering was slow. When questioned about their experience in police custody, the majority of the prisoners were reluctant to share their experiences. They were not even willing to accept the suggestive answers of the researcher.

Hence, in order to elicit the information a more or less natural conversational style was planned. The inmates were made into groups and conversation was started with issues unconnected with the research. Thus after gaining their confidence the conversation was turned on to the specific issue of their crime, mode of arrest, treatment given by the police, production before a Magistrate, etc. By and large, this procedure turned out to be useful and rewarding. However, it should be mentioned that in the absence of ways and means to check and counter-check their statements the researcher had to believe in the narration of the inmates. In the process, the researcher was made to listen to them patiently, whether it was relevant for study or not, for it was only by this behaviour that one could win the confidence of the inmates. It is believed that the more relaxed prisoners were more reliable in their response and information.

Each jail has remand prisoners along with convicts. This study covered both. But the interview with the remand prisoners proved to be a different experience. Normally, it is believed that it is difficult to interact with undertrials as they are busy with court cases, preparing their own defence, meeting their lawyers and not having either time or mood to talk freely and frankly. Since the charges levelled against them are not confirmed by the court, they were opposed to label them as criminals. Moreover, they reportedly fear that they may spill something out during interview which may turn against them at the trial.

This general belief is found to be untrue by the researcher. All the remand prisoners were ready to narrate their experiences in the police custody and the experience of their very first appearance before the Magistrate. Each remand prisoner requested the researcher to note her experience in the police lock-up and publicise it.

The researcher had the chance of observing and noting down the admission process of the prisoner and interview them immediately as seven of them were admitted into Hyderabad jail on the day of the study. Out of them, one was a convict and while three were arrested on charges of prostitution, two for shop-lifting and one for theft. The physical examination process done on them at the time of admission was also observed. Marks of beating were noted on the bodies of the remand prisoners. So the next day they were specifically selected for interview as their police custody experience was fresh in their memory. Those women undertrials gave a graphic account of the beatings they received from the police. They even narrated the way the Magistrates acted towards them.

Visit to rescue home

As part of the research study, an attempt is made to study the conditions and experiences of the women criminals under social welfare custody. Oral permission from the Women & Child Welfare Officer, Hyderabad, was obtained to visit the rescue home located at Malakpet area of the city.

In the home, on the day of the visit, there were no rescued women. So, the Superintendent of the home was interviewed and information from the records was obtained. It is observed that very rarely prostitutes are referred to that home. Some of the sex workers who stayed there for a few days obtained bail and moved out. In a rare incident, one of the prostitutes who was willing to reform was married to a progressive thinking man at the State expense.

Except this, there is nothing to present regarding the conditions and experiences of women under social welfare custody.

Visit to mental health hospital

To understand the status of women prisoners under mental health custody, both the mental health hospitals located at Visakhapatnam and Hyderabad were visited. The Superintendents of both the hospitals extended all the help to meet the women in custody. A staff member of the hospital escorted the researcher through the women enclosures, wards, kitchen, etc., of the hospital.

There is only one woman prisoner each in Hyderabad and Visakhapatnam. Both are under remand on a murder charge. Though they were presented before the researcher, and encouraged to speak they failed to communicate properly. Their mental illness prevented them from speaking in a coherent manner. They couldn't understand the questions put to them. Their answers were irrelevant. They spoke only what they wanted. So the details of the conditions of mental custody patients were obtained by observation and interviewing the doctor who is treating them and the staff who are looking after them.

The mental condition of those destitute mental patients placed in hospital on the orders of the court was found to be no different. They were found to be totally ignorant of their parents, native village, etc. So the attempt to obtain information from them became abortive.

The method of personal observation and interview with staff was followed here too.

Separate profiles of convicts and undertrial prisoners are presented. The researcher has interviewed all the prisoners available on the date of the interview. Thus 158 convicts and 147 undertrial prisoners are interviewed and the details are presented hereunder.

(ii) Convicts Profiles

Literacy among convicts

The total number of women convicts lodged in the State Jail for Women, at Hyderabad and Rajahmundry put together, as in May 2003, comes to158. Out of these, a huge 133 or 84% are illiterate. The remaining 25 women convicts are literate. This yields the conclusion that more illiterate women, who are not aware of the legal consequences of crimes are prone to commit crimes.

Table 1

Literacy Among Convicts

Literacy level	Total	Percentage
Illiterates	133	84.17
Literates	25	15.78
Grand Total	**158**	**99.95**

Details of Literate Convicts

The total literate convicts are 25 in number. Out of them, two are graduates and five have completed the secondary level of education while two each completed IX, VIII, VII; six convicts have completed V Standard and 4 of them completed Class IV. Of the remaining two, one has studied only Class I, while others went up to third class. The figures are shown in the table and graph. This shows that even among the literates only 22% of them have reasonably average education; even among the literates 78% of the convicts just know only to read and write the vernacular.

Table 2
Details of Literacy Level Among Convicts

Literacy Level (Out of total 158)	**Total**	**Percentage**
Graduates	2	1.26
Class X & above	5	3.16
Class IX	2	1.26
Class VIII	2	1.26
Class VII	2	1.26
Class V	6	3.79
Class IV	4	2.53
Class III	1	0.63
Class I	1	0.63
Grand Total	**25**	**15.78**

Religious identity of convicts

The large percentage of women convicts hailed from Hindu religion. They formed 87.34% of the total convicts. There are 17 Muslims forming 10.75% and only 3 Christians making them 1.89% of the total convicts. It may be noted that these percentages broadly represent their actual population percentages.

Table 3
Religion of Convicts

Religion	**Total**	**Percentage**
Hindus	138	87.34
Muslims	17	10.75
Christians	3	1.89
Total	**158**	**99.98**

Caste division of Hindu convicts

The castewise data of the Hindu convicts is presented in this Table and Graph. Out of the 138 Hindu convicts, 42 are from the forward castes (O.C.) followed by 35 from Scheduled Tribes, 33 from Backward Classes (B.C.) and 28 from Scheduled Castes. Their corresponding percentages are 30.43%, 25.36%, 23.91% and 20.28%. These percentages show that the Scheduled Caste (S.C.) and Scheduled Tribe (S.T.) convicts are more than their actual population percentage i.e. 15 and 6. This yields the conclusion that more number of convicts i.e., about 4.6% are from S.C. and S.T. who are considered as the most backward sections of society both socially and economically.

Table 4

Caste Division of Hindu Convicts

Caste	Total	Percentage
O.C.	42	30.43
B.C.	33	23.91
S.C.	28	20.28
S.T.	35	25.36
Total	**138**	**99.98**

Occupation of convicts

The occupation of the women convicts is also recorded. Out of the 158 convicts, 96 constituting 60.75% are housewives. 56 of them i.e., 35.44% are manual labourers. There is only one self-employed person. Out of the remaining five, one is agriculturist, another is a private employee and one more is a Government employee. There are two convicts who are Naxalites. This may be taken as an indication that more housewies having no other extra family occupations are involved in crimes.

Table 5

Occupational Details of Convicts

Occupation	Total	Percentage
Housewives	96	60.75
Manual labour	56	35.44
Govt. employee	1	0.63
Private employee	1	0.63
Agriculturists	1	0.63
Naxalites	2	1.26
Self-employed	1	0.63
Total	**158**	**99.97**

Sentence of convicts

Basing on the sentence they are serving, the convicts are classified into four categories. The first one is life convicts. Their number is 84 forming 53.16%. 7 prisoners are serving a sentence of 10 years or above. 38 of them are imprisoned for periods between 1 and 7 years. The remaining 29 are serving a sentence of less than 1 year.

Table 6

Sentences of Convicts

Term of Sentence	Total	Percentage
Life	84	53.16
10 year & above	7	4.43
Above 1 year and below 7 years	38	24.05
Below 1 year	29	18.35
Total	**158**	**99.99**

Details of sentences

Those who are serving above 10 years are further classified. 4 of them are serving 20 years, while 3 are serving a 10 year period. Those who are serving between 1 and 7 years are further classified. 7 of them are serving 7 years while there is only one who is sentenced for 6 years. 2, 6 and 9 of them are serving 5 years, 3 years and 2 years sentences respectively. 13 are sentenced for 1 year in the Jail, while the remaining 29 are behind bars for less than a year.

Table 7

Details of Sentences Being Served by Convicts

Sentence	Total	Percentage
Life	84	53.16
20 years	4	2.53
10 years	3	1.89
7 years	7	4.43
6 years	1	0.63
5 years	2	1.26
3 years	6	3.79
2 years	9	5.69
1 year	13	8.22
Less than year	29	18.35
Total	**158**	**99.95**

The total number of the prisoners convicted under different sections of I.P.C. and other laws are shown in Table 8.

Table 8

Women Convicts – Their Offences

Sl. No.	Name of the Offence / Act	Section	No. of Convicts
1	Abettor present when offence is committed	114	1
2	Criminal conspiracy	120-B	2
3	Rioting armed with deadly weapons	148	2
4	Every member of unlawful assembly guilty of offence committed in prosecution of common object	149	2
5	Causing disappearance of evidence of offence, or giving false information to screen offender	201	13
6	Altering appearance of coin with intent to pass it as coin of different description	248	2
7	Murder	302	83
8	Culpable homicide not amounting to murder	304	4
9	Dowry death	304B	14
10	Abetment to suicide	306	3
11	Attempt to murder	307	1
12	Voluntarily causing hurt	323	2
13	Voluntarily causing hurt with dangerous weapons	324	6
14	Voluntarily causing grievous hurt	325	1
15	Voluntarily causing grievous hurt by dangerous weapon or means	326	1

Sl. No.	Name of the Offence / Act	Section	No. of Convicts
16	Causing hurt by means of poison, etc., with intent to commit an offence	328	1
17	Wrongful confinement for ten or more days	344	1
18	Punishment for kidnapping	363	8
19	Kidnapping or abducting in order to murder	364	3
20	Kidnapping for ransom	364A	2
21	Theft	379	7
22	Dishonest misappropriation of property possessed by deceased person at the time of his death	404	1
23	Dishonestly receiving stolen property	411	4
24	Dishonestly receiving property stolen in the commission of decoity	412	7
25	Cheating	420	2
26	Dishonest or fraudulent removal or concealment of property to prevent distribution among creditors	421	1
27	House tresspass	448	1
28	Forgery for the purpose of cheating	468	1
29	Cruelty by husband or relatives of husband	498A	33
30	Jumping out the bail		1
31	Andhra Pradesh Prohibition Act	57 & 58	16
32	Dowry Prohibition Act, 1961	53 & 54	4
33	Immoral Traffic (Prevention) Act, 1956	—	1
34	Negotiable Instrument Act	—	1
35	Passport Act	—	1

Note:- Some of the convicted persons were prosecuted and convicted for more than one offence.

The data recorded above about the details of the sentences reveal that about 65% of the convicts (83 for murder and 14 for dowry death) had committed serious offences most of which relate to internal family problems resulting in the murder of daughters-in-law. Similarly about 22% of the convicts (33) were involved in the crime of "harassment by husband and husband's relatives" (498-A). On the whole 87% of the convicts were involved in crimes related to family disputes, in particular between the victim and the in-laws in the family.

(iii) Undertrial Prisoners Profile

Literacy among undertrial prisoners

Only 17% of the 144 undertrials are literate. About 83% of the remand prisoners are illiterate. This nearly corresponds to 87% of illiterate convicts. The same is nearly the percentage of literate convicts, i.e. 15.78%.

Table 9

Literacy Among Undertrial Prisoners

Literacy level	Total Nos.	Percentage
Illiterate	122	82.90
Literate	25	17.00
Total	**147**	**99.99**

Details of literate among undertrial prisoners

The details of the literates and their level of education is shown in Table 10. Out of the 25 literates one is a postgraduate, six are graduates, one completed her pre-university, 8 of them studied upto school final, one dropped out at class IX, 6 of them studied up to class V, while 2 studied only up to class IV.

Table 10

Details of Literacy Level Among Undertrial Prisoners

Literacy level	Total Nos.	Percentage
Post-graduate	1	0.68
Graduates	6	4.08
P.U.C.	1	0.68
Class X	8	5.44
Class IX	1	0.68
Class V	6	4.08
Class IV	2	1.36
Total	**25**	**17.00**

Religious identity of undertrial prisoners

A large number of undertrial women are Hindus. Out of the total 147 undertrial prisoners 137 or over 93% are from Hindu community. There are 7 Muslim women and 3 Christian women. They formed 4.76% and 2.04% respectively.

Table 11

Religion of Undertrial Prisoners

Religion	Total Nos.	Percentage
Hindus	137	93.19
Muslims	7	4.76
Christians	3	2.04
Total	**147**	**99.99**

Caste division of Hindu undertrial prisoners

The caste analysis of the Hindu undertrial women has shown that 61 or 44.5% and 47 or 34.30% hailed from forward and backward castes respectively. There are 21 S.Cs forming 15.32% of undertrials while S.Ts. are 8 in number or 5.83%. These percentages roughly represent their proportion in the actual population of Andhra Pradesh.

Table 12

Caste Division of Hindu Undertrial Prisoners

Caste category	Total Nos.	Percentage
O.C.	61	44.52
B.C.	47	34.30
S.C.	21	15.32
S.T.	8	5.83
Total	**137**	**99.97**

Occupation of undertrial prisoners

Occupation-wise, the larger prison population is from the unorganised sector. i.e. 61 or 41.49% are daily wage earners. 57 or 38.77% are housewives, without any income of their own. 18 of them or 12.24% are engaged in petty businesses like running grocery shops, tea stalls, etc. Two are unmarried major girls without any specific employment, while two are beggars. Of the remaining seven, one each is a domestic servant, an agriculturalist owning some land, an elected Panchayat member, a government employee, a former bank manager and a director of a private bank. The last one is a Naxalite undertrial.

Table 13

Occupational Details of Undertrial Prisoners

Occupation-wise	Total Number	Percentage
Housewives	57	38.77
Coolies	61	41.49
Business	18	12.24
Beggars	2	1.36
Agriculturalist	1	0.68
Maid servant	1	0.68
Government employee	1	0.68
Panchayat member	1	0.68
Bank Manager	1	0.68
Bank Director	1	0.68
Naxals	1	0.68
Unspecified/Unmarried	2	1.36
Total	**147**	**99.98**

The total number of undertrial women prisoners held under various Sections of the Indian Penal Code and other laws are shown in this table.

Table 14
Undertrial Prisoners Held Under Different Offences

S. No.	Name of the Offence/ Act	Section	No. of Prisoners charged
1	Abettor present when offence is committed	114	2
2	Criminal conspiracy	120-B	1
3	Rioting armed with deadly weapons	148	1
4	Affray	160	1
5	Causing disappearance of evidence of offence or giving false information to screen offender	201	2
6	Offering gift or restoration of property in consideration of screening offender	234	1
7	Murder	302	24
8	Culpable homicide not amounting to murder	304	2
9	Dowry death	304B	10
10	Abetment to suicide	306	9
11	Attempt to murder	307	12
12	Voluntarily causing hurt with dangerous weapons	324	3
13	Voluntarily causing grievous hurt with dangerous weapons	326	1
14	Causing hurt by means of poison, etc., with intent to commit an offence	328	2
15	Kidnapping or abducting or inducing woman to compel her marriage	366	1

Contd...

S. No.	Name of the Offence/ Act	Section	No. of Prisoners charged
16	Abetment to commit rape	109/376	2
17	Theft	379	18
18	Theft in dwelling house	380	7
19	Theft by clerk or servant of property in possession of master	381	1
20	Robbery	392	1
21	Dacoity	395	3
22	Criminal misappropriation	403	1
23	Dishonestly receiving stolen property	411	2
24	Assisting in concealment of stolen property	414	1
25	Cheating	417	1
26	Cheating by personation	419	1
27	Cheating and dishonestly inducing delivery of property	420	6
28	Dishonest or fraudulent removal or concealment of property to prevent distribution among creditors	421	1
29	Dishonestly or fraudulently preventing debt being available for creditors	422	1
30	Mischief by fire or explosive substance with intent to destroy house, etc.,	436	1
31	House-trespass	448	2
32	Lurking house, trespass or house breaking after preparation for hurt assault, wrongful restraint	454	3
33	Lurking house, trespass or house breaking by night in order to commit offence punishable with imprisonment	457	4

Contd...

S. No.	Name of the Offence/ Act	Section	No. of Prisoners charged
34	Dishonestly breaking open receptacle containing property	461	1
35	Cohabitation caused by a man deceitfully inducing a belief of lawful marriage	493	1
36	Cruelty by husband or relatives of husband	498A	33
37	Criminal intimidation	506	1
38	Andhra Pradesh Prohibition Act	31	
39	Immoral Traffic (Prevention) Act	5	
40	Narcotics Act	1	
41	Not mention	10	

Note: Some of the undertrials are facing charges for more than one offence.

It may be noted that a total of 36 are facing charges of murder, dowry death or attempt to murder, and 133 are facing trial u/s 498-A "harassment by husband and relatives of husband". This pattern conforms to the percentage of convicts for similar offences.

(iv) Police Custody

During the interview with women prisoners it was revealed that none of them were produced before the Magistrate within 24 hours of their arrest as stipulated in law. They said that they were produced before the Magistrate as soon as they confessed to their crime. The period of illegal detention by the police ranged from 48 hours to 30 days. One of the life convicts, aged 60, lodged in Rajahmundry State Jail for Women said that she was held by the police for almost a month in illegal detention. Most of them said they were in police custody for a minimum of two days. Many women said that they were not informed of the reasons for their arrest. A few women said that they were arrested late in the night and the information of their arrest was not given to their relatives.

After their arrest, as per the prisoners, they were not handcuffed, and kept in the police station verandah or a hall but not in the lock-up. The absence of separate female toilets and facilities for taking a bath are the major discomforts faced by them during their stay in the police lock-up, they said. As per the observation of the women prisoners no women constables guarded them, even in some police stations where there are women constables they stayed with them only during the day. "Interrogation was conducted by men officers and no women constable stayed with us during the interrogation" , said the prisoners.

The prisoners said that they were not offered the bail and the available legal provisions are not explained to them. None from the free legal aid committee visited them while in detention. Prisoners said that no medical examination facility was offered to them.

In conclusion, it may be said that the police custody is the most feared custody. The inmates gave a graphic account of their experience in the police lock-up. It was always the men police who handled the women prisoners. The women police though present couldn't take charge of the arrested women.

The police were allegedly using a highly abusive and foul language. Assault, threat to break the limbs, etc., formed part of the ill-treatment. This allegation is supported by the darkened parts of the body and the bruises found on the body of some of the remand prisoners who were admitted into jail on the very day the researcher visited the jail. On enquiry, the prisoners revealed that the police were not ill-treating arrested persons if they confessed to the crime.

Those women who refused to confess were even reportedly threatened of 'rape' by the police. The woman in custody, the study revealed, is safe only when she is ready to confess to whatever the police ordered her to do so. Otherwise, the women are subjected to prolonged illegal stay in the lock-up, torture, starvation, etc. The police custody continues to be dangerous for the women arrestee.

(v) Judicial Custody

An arrested person is produced before the Magistrate having jurisdiction over the place where the crime was allegedly committed. When such production is made, the Magistrate shall follow the obligation imposed on him by the Supreme Court through the Sheela Barse case.[1] The Magistrate shall enquire into the treatment given by the police during her custody. If there is an instance of maltreatment or torture, the arrestee should be informed of her right for medical examination.[2]

But the survey revealed that no accused person was asked any question by the Magistrate about the treatment by the police. All the prisoners said that they were remanded to custody within minutes of their production before the Magistrate. Several of them said that they couldn't open their mouths, though they wanted to do so, because of the stern warnings given by the escort police. The escort police force is found to be a consistent threat to the arrested women.

Another obligation imposed by the Supreme Court on the Magistrates and Sessions Judges is to inform the accused that she is entitled to free legal services, if she is unable to engage such services on her own due to poverty. This right to legal services, as per the Supreme Court[3] is available to the arrestee even at the time of her very first appearance before the Magistrate. In Andhra Pradesh, the Legal Services Authority is providing legal assistance to S.Cs., S.Ts.,

B.Cs., Women and Children for the last several years as shown in the Table.

Table 15

A.P. State Legal Services Authority Statement Relating to Legal Aid Beneficiaries from 1996-97 to 30-4-2003

Year	S.Ts.	S.Cs.	B.Cs.	Women	Children	Others	Total
1996-97	107	191	301	95	0	788	1,482
1997-98	120	155	233	239	0	862	1,609
1998-99	123	145	231	267	0	350	1,116
1999-2000	84	151	286	258	0	290	1,069
2000-01	85	110	NIL	301	0	424	920
2001-02	138	99	189	320	0	236	982
2002-03	136	179	218	277	0	214	1,024
2003-04 (upto April, 03)	10	14	17	11	0	10	62
Total	**803**	**1,044**	**1,475**	**1,768**	**0**	**3,174**	**8,264**

The arrested persons, once remanded have to be produced before the Magistrate once in every fifteen days.[4] In Andhra Pradesh Jails for women nearly 75% of the prisoners are remand prisoners.[5] Some of them are languishing in jail, though they were granted bail, because of their inability to produce money or sureties. For them, attending to court at fortnightly intervals is proving to be the most difficult time. Sometimes, the prisoners couldn't be taken to court because sufficient escort police are not available.

Absence of vehicles is also one of the factors resulting in the delay of production of remand prisoners in the court. Women, when taken out, are carried in the same vehicle along with the hardened, habitual male criminals causing a lot of embarrassment. The remand women prisoners are forced to wait in the court premises from morning till evening. In the absence of toilet facilities in the court premises, the women prisoners are found to be suffering a lot.

(vi) Prison Custody

Andhra Pradesh has seven central prisons, nine district jails, two open prisons and one semi-open prison, one borstal school, 147 sub-jails and two State prisons for women. As on 31st October, 2002,[6] the total number of prisoners held in all these jails put together were 13,555. The average number of women prisoners held in the State, as per the records, ranged from 500 to 600 at any given time. It is to be noted that 76.6% of the women prisoners are undertrial (see Table 16). The details of the capacity of the prisons and the number of prisoners as on 31st October, 2002 are presented in the Table.

Table 16

Authorised Capacity and Details of Number of Prisoners in Andhra Pradesh as on 31st October, 2002

	Male	Female	Total
Capacity	**10,454**	**818**	**11,272**
Convicts	4,610	153	4,763
Remand prisoners	8,269	501	8,770
Others	22	—	22
Total	**12,901**	**654**	**13,555**

In Andhra Pradesh, all the remand women prisoners are referred to the district jails or central jails for reasons of administration. As per the direction of the Supreme Court,[7] the female remand prisoners should be guarded by female guards or in the absence of women police by some other women specially engaged for that purpose. Till last year, women were engaged on a daily wage basis by all sub-jails, where women sentry are not available and during periods women were in custody. Since the State Government has abolished the employment on daily wages, all the sub-jails refer the female remand prisoners to the nearest district jails or to central jails where there are separate enclosures for women or to the State Jails for Women.

The women sentenced to imprisonment not exceeding one month are lodged in women enclosures at the central jails in Visakhapatnam, Rajahmundry, Warangal or Cuddapah. Women from Coastal and Rayalaseema areas sentenced for over a month are lodged in State Jail for Women, Rajahmundry, while those from Telangana are lodged in State Jail for Women, Hyderabad. At the time of the visit, there were no women convicts at central prisons of Visakhapatnam, Warangal and Cuddapah. So the present study is made with reference to the women prisoners lodged in State Jails for Women at Rajahmundry and Hyderabad.

Accommodation

There are two exclusive jails for women in the State located at Rajahmundry and Hyderabad. The authorized capacity and the number of prisoners lodged in these jails at the time of the study are presented below:

Table 17

Authorised Capacity and Details of Number of Women Prisoners in State Jails for Women in Andhra Pradesh as on May 2003

Sl. No.	Name of the Prison	Authorised capacity	No. of convicts	No. of under-trials	No. of children of women prisoners	Total
1	State Jail for Women, Rajahmundry	200	65	56	09	130
2	State Jail for Women, Hyderabad	120	93	91	05	189
	Total	**320**	**158**	**147**	**14**	**319**

Andhra Pradesh has a separate State Jail for Women at Rajahmundry even at the time of drafting of the A.P. Jail Manual in 1979. But that jail was under the administrative control of the Superintendent of Central Prison, Rajahmundry. However, based on the recommendation of the National Expert Committee on Women Prisoners for full autonomy to the prisons for women managed by women Superintendents issued G.O. Ms.No.647, dated 12-9-1994, creating a State Jail for Women at Hyderabad. Both the Jails are made autonomous with the appointment of women Superintendents.

The State Jail for Women at Rajahmundry has an authorized accommodation for 200 prisoners. It is spread over 2 acres with three barracks in the jail. The State Jail for Women at Hyderabad has an area of 2.5 acres having both barracks and cells and accommodates 120 prisoners. Whereas the number of prisoners in Rajahmundry jail were

130 against the capacity of 200, in Hyderabad jail there were 189 prisoners against the capacity of only 120. This clearly shows that there is overcrowding in Hyderabad jail resulting in inconvenience to the inmates. Therefore, there is need for one more jail for women at Hyderabad.

In other central jails in the State separate women enclosures have been established to segregate women prisoners from male prisoners as per Sec.27(1) of the Prisons Act of 1894.

Classification

As per the Jail Manual, there should be strict separation of convicts and remand prisoners, but in both the jails for women there was no such separation except during lock-up time. In normal circumstances, all of them are allowed to mix freely. However, in the evening before locking them up the convicts and remand prisoners are segregated and attendance taken separately. All the life convicts are placed in one barrack, other convicts serving short term sentences are placed in a separate barrack. The separation of prisoners based on the socio-economic status of the convicts as suggested in the Jail Manual didn't arise in these two jails as all women convicts lodged there are from the same low economic and social background without much formal education.

All the remand prisoners are grouped together in a single barrack in Rajahmundry but in Hyderabad they are using cells to lodge them. In each cell about 8 to 9 remand prisoners are placed giving an impression of overcrowding. Most of the remand prisoners in both jails are poor, illiterate and hail from rural areas and as such deserve 'C' class prisoner's status. So there was no demand for the classification based on the status. Very few educated undertrials are kept separately in cells on their request.

While the Jail Manual mentions about the separation of prostitutes from others, there was neither facility to separate them nor inclination to keep them separately. No formal complaint for such separation was made by the inmates to jail authorities except that of their inconvenience to an occasional visitor, though they were afraid of infectious diseases spreading because of the mixed prison population.

Admission of women prisoners

A woman remand prisoner or convict as soon as handed over to the jail authorities was taken into the search room where the body search was made by a female Warden with due regard to the privacy and decency of the women.

The women convicts or remand prisoners were dispossessed of their personal belongings, such as ornaments, cash, etc., and they are carefully documented and kept in a separate container. Medical examination was conducted on every prisoner by the prison doctor and the health condition of the prisoners before actual entry into the jail was recorded. That includes the height and weight of the prisoners and they are also examined for infectious diseases, if any, and recorded in the prison register as per the need.

In Rajahmundry jail, married women prisoners were found wearing *'mangala sutra'*. On enquiry, it was learnt that they were wearing this after obtaining permission of the jail authority. The jail staff said that they were permitting that to honour the sentiment of Indian women's attachment to the *'mangala sutra'*. But such a consideration was not shown by the jail authorities at Hyderabad and so the women prisoners in the State Jail for Women, Hyderabad, are without *'mangala sutras'*.

Restrictions on women prisoners

In no way can the women prisoners move away from the enclosed area of the jail. Their movements are restricted up to the inner gate of the jails. They are allowed to move out of the gate only for the attendance in the court, transfer or under the order of the Superintendent of the jail for a specific legitimate purpose. The Superintendents of both the jails for women are very strict in this regard. No male member is allowed entry into the prison unless he has a legitimate duty to attend to within the premises. Even such legitimate entry is prohibited after the sunset unless an emergency demanded such entry. Even such entries are permitted only after obtaining the necessary permission from the Superintendent and accompanied by a female staff of the jail. A female staff of the jail accompanied the man till he finished his job and reached the gate. Even escorts to the lady visitors and officials are also not allowed to go inside the jail.

Staff: The jail for women both at Rajahmundry and Hyderabad are exclusively manned by women staff. From Superintendent at the top to the Matron including the clerical and medical staff are all females.

Hospital: A full-fledged hospital headed by a lady Medical Officer, female Staff Nurse are found in operation in both the jails. The immediate medical attention is available for the sick prisoners within the jail. There is an inpatient ward in the hospital. They are treated for normal ailments, but in case of serious sickness they are referred to the prison ward of the Government headquarter hospitals for specialised treatment. As per jail authorities, pregnant prisoners were sent to the headquarter hospital for the delivery. In Hyderabad a Naxalite prisoner, who was pregnant at the time of arrest, delivered a baby in Government headquarter hospital and on discharge was shifted to jail. All the arrangements are made for the baby's comfort including a craddle within the jail hospital room. The hospital doctor has performed the naming ceremony for the baby in the presence of the jail inmates and jail staff. The entire cost of the treatment was borne by the Government. Before discharging a prisoner either on bail or parole or furlough, a medical examination is conducted and the same is repeated on readmission into the jail.

Prisoners suffering from contagious diseases are kept separately and if necessary transferred to the medical care centre. In Hyderabad prison, provision is also made for counselling and treatment to the prisoners suffering from STD/HIV related diseases. Prisoners who are in need of mental health care are sent either to the mental health care hospital, Visakhapatnam or Hyderabad. A lady escort is provided for their journey as well as during their stay in the mental hospital.

Dietary: The Government of Andhra Pradesh has laid down a dietary scale for prisoners keeping the calorification requirements as per the medical norms. The diet is in tune with the prevailing dietary preference of the prisoners as well as the geographical area where the prison is located.

In Andhra Pradesh, the women prisoners are provided with nutritious diet as laid down in the Andhra Pradesh Jail Manual. The timings are also prescribed. The dietary schedule includes a cup of tea in the morning; breakfast (kichidi) at about 7.30 a.m. followed by lunch at 10.30 a.m. with rice, dhal and rasam. Dinner at 4.30 p.m. in the evening includes rice with curry and rasam. In between lunch and dinner, tea is served. In Rajahmundry jail, the breakfast is varied with idly or upma. There was a provision to alter the diet scale either temporarily or permanently. Non-vegetarian food is served on Sundays. Yellow rice and occasional sweets are served on festive days and on days of national importance. Special diet for female prisoners and their children will be provided on medical advice. Special consideration in the diet is shown for the pregnant and nursing female prisoners. Milk, bread, coconut water, eggs and glucose are given to them. Similarly sick prisoners and old age prisoners are also served with special diet as per medical advice. Low salt content curries and chapathis are served for prisoners suffering from hypertension or diabetes, respectively.

The kitchen of both the jails are equipped with modern amenities like gas stoves, grinders etc. A separate dining hall is found only in Rajahmundry jail. In both the jails, the convicts as a rule perform the duty of cooking by rotation as per the instructions of the authorities. It is observed that while the Government is straining to provide nutritional food to prisoners, a good percentage of food is going waste for several reasons. One of the reasons mentioned by the prisoners is the badly timed lunch. There is little time gap between breakfast, served at 7.30 a.m., and lunch at 10.30 a.m. in the morning. This difficulty was expressed only by the inmates of Hyderabad jail. In Rajahmundry Jail, the lunch is served at 10.30 a.m. for those who are to be produced at the court, while the rest of the inmates are served at 12.30 p.m. in the afternoon. The jail authorities serve red gram, green gram or bengal gram twice a week which is not relished by the prisoners. This is also the reason for the wastage as they throw away this unrelished dhal into the drains.

The following is the official dietary scale which is prominently displayed in the jail premises, per prisoner per day (Table 18).

Clothing: The Jail authorities provide clothing and bedding material for the women prisoners in accordance with the local climate at the rate of two pairs a year. Extra clothing is provided on medical grounds for a specific period or during a specific season of a year as per the suggestion of the Medical Officer. Old and infirm prisoners are also provided extra warm clothing by the authorities.

Education: All eligible and willing illiterate prisoners are taught the basic education within the jail. In Hyderabad jail, the responsibility of teaching is entrusted to the educated remand prisoners who are paid for the services. However, it is observed that in this jail the prisoners are not enthusiastic to learn. In Rajahmundry Jail, a small room is designated as a school. A teacher appointed for the specific purpose of teaching the prisoners works from 9 a.m. to 5 p.m. The prisoners attend the classes on a shift basis during the working hours of the school.

Besides this, Government sponsored *'Akshara Jyothi'* programme is also implemented in the jail. For those who are in a position to appear for the Open University degree courses, part-time teachers are available to coach them for the entrance test as well as degree examinations. There are very few women prisoners who are inclined to take up this opportunity.

Table 18

Official Dietary Scale for Women Prisoners in Andhra Pradesh

Sl. No.	Name of the Dietary Article	Labouring Quantity	Non-labouring Quantity
1	a. Rice diet – Rice	700 gms	600 gms
	b. Wheat diet – Wheat	700 gms	600 gms
	c. Mixed diet – Jawar or Bajra flour and Rice	700 gms	600 gms
2	Dhall (not to be issued on Sundays)	100 gms	100 gms

Sl. No.	Name of the Dietary Article	Labouring Quantity	Non-labouring Quantity
3	Vegetables	250 gms	250 gms
4	Groundnut oil or any other substitute	30 gms	30 gms
5	Tamarind	20 gms	20 gms
6	Fuel (firewood or any other suitable substitute)	700 gms	700 gms
7	Salt	35 gms	35 gms
8	Mutton with bones or any other non-vegetarian dish like fish, beef, etc. once a week	175 gms	175 gms
9	Onions (to be issued on Sundays only)	15 gms	15 gms
10	Chillies	10 gms	10 gms
11	Turmeric	2 gms	2 gms
12	Garlic	4 gms	4 gms
13	Coriander	4 gms	4 gms
14	Chillies to be issued on Sundays (Extra, besides the usual quantity of 10 gms)	5 gms	5 gms
15	Milk (to be converted into buttermilk or Curd)	70 ml	70 ml

Moderate library facility is available in both the jails where a few newspapers, magazines and some books are kept. However, there was no interest among the women prisoners to visit the library as 84.0% of convicts and 83% of remand prisoners are illiterate.[8]

All the prisoners are counselled to meditate for half an hour every morning. Yoga training is imparted to those willing. Moral and religious activities are encouraged. Religious groups are permitted once a week to address the prisoners on religion and the need for morality. Scriptures are distributed among prisoners free of cost.

Amenities: The women prisoners are encouraged to maintain personal hygiene by providing washing soap and bathing soap every month. Combs are also supplied. Each barrack is provided with a mirror. The following items are supplied (as per the prison authorities) to the prisoners.

a. Sanitary napkins: All the women prisoners are provided with sanitary napkins as per their requirement.

b. 8 gms of coconut oil – per day

c. 15 gms soap nut power – per day

d. 1 washing and 1 toilet soap – per month

e. 80 gms of washing soda – per week

f. tooth powder, comb, kum-kum.

Sanitary facilities: All the barracks/cells are provided with flush out toilets for night use while separate toilets are provided for day time use of the prisoners. Both of them have running water facility and are maintained clean and dry.

Recreation facilities: Television is the only recreation facility available inside the barrack. They show one cinema a week through a video recorder. Prisoners are allowed to play indoor games like carroms, chess, etc. But being illiterate, the women prisoners do not engage themselves in such games. Prisoners are found playing their own native games. The occasional cultural programmes are the other means of recreation. They are very few and are mainly presented at the time of religious festivals.

Interview facilities: Special attention is paid for the maintenance and improvement of relations between a woman prisoner and her family. They are allowed to meet their relatives and friends. The convicts are also permitted to meet their lawyers and friends for preparing an appeal or revision in the higher courts. The women prisoners maintain the contacts with the family through the two permitted interviews per month. However in practice they are allowed to meet the family members more frequently. Prisoners are encouraged and assisted in writing letters to their relatives. They are allowed to receive letters from relatives and friends after necessary scrutiny as per the rules.

Women prisoners are allowed to meet the male members of their family if they are also lodged in the central jail located in the same city. This is permitted once a month. Women prisoners are also allowed to meet their relatives lodged in other central jails in the State after obtaining the necessary permission from the authorities concerned.

Work/ Labour: All the convicted prisoners except those who are prohibited on medical advice are engaged in some work or other. Cooking, cleaning and gardening are allotted on rotational basis. Some amount of bias is shown by the Matrons in the allotment of works. Some prisoners are forced to over work while some favoured lot are not allotted any work. This complaint was made in Hyderabad jail but not in Rajahmundry jail.

Vocational training: The women prisoners in Hyderabad are imparted vocational training in the manufacture of tooth powder, chalk pieces, tailoring, knitting, etc. In Rajahmundry, they are trained in tailoring, knitting, coir products, laces and envelopes-making. The prisoners are categorised into skilled and unskilled workers and are paid Rs.15/- and Rs.10/- per day respectively. The money earned is deposited in the individual prisoner's account and withdrawn partly as and when the prisoner makes a request. Such withdrawn money shall be spent within the jail to purchase some items of their choice. The other part of their earning is handed over to the women prisoner at the time of her release. The illiterate prisoners are found to be ignorant of their account and the money available therein.

Premature release of lifers and long term prisoners

The prison rules are liberal for the premature release of women prisoners in the State. While a male prisoner serving a life sentence is considered for early release after serving a minimum of seven years, the woman prisoner's case is considered for release after five years of her stay in the jail. Such premature releases mostly coincide with some important occasion either at State level or national level. A special G.O. is issued for all such premature releases.

The details of women prisoners released prematurely during the last two decades is presented in Table 19.

Table 19

Details of Premature Release of Lifers and Non-lifers

Sl.No.	Year	Lifers		Non-Lifers	
		Hydera-bad	Rajah-mundry	Hydera-bad	Rajah-mundry
1	1995	2	4	4	4
2	1997	2	2	6	14
3	2000	12	6	—	—
4	2003	—	—	—	—

Release on Parole and Furlough: The parole[9] and the furlough[10] are the provisions incorporated for the temporary freedom of the convicts. They are aimed at maintaining hormonious family ties. During the survey, it was found that the women convicts did not know about these provisions. The illiteracy of the prisoners is the prime reason. Those few who know about them are also not enjoying the facility for various reasons. The sanction of parole requires a lot of paper work. The consent of the police officials from where the prisoner hails has to be obtained. The District Superintendents of Police concerned, it is believed, do not clear their applications. Such a clearance and permission from the Superintendent of Police concerned, being mandatory, the prisoners are released on parole very rarely. During the last three years, only one woman convict used the parole while eight went out of jail on furlough.

Children of prisoners

Following the Rule 828(2) of Andhra Pradesh Prisons Rules, 1979, the children of the women prisoners are allowed to stay with the mothers till they complete 5 years of age. After that, children are handed over to their blood relatives or other guardians who are willing to take care of them. Besides this, the State of Andhra Pradesh has started some innovative schemes for the welfare of the children of the prisoners. A creche was established within the jail where a balwadi teacher was entrusted with the responsibility of the children. Children above 5 years who have no guardian are admitted into the State-run residential educational institutions.[11] From the records, it is clear that some of the voluntary organisations are playing a role, besides the jail authorities, in educating children outside the jail. Arrangements are made to send children below the age of five years to nearby schools and bring them back to the jail every day. The idea behind this is not to make the children suffer for the fault of the mother. The children are also exposed to normal and healthy surroundings outside the prison walls. All the children who are staying with their mothers are given extra milk and bread. The Women and Child Development Department of Andhra Pradesh provide a nutritious food to those children in the form of biscuits and peanuts.

Discipline and punishment to women prisoners in jail

All the women prisoners move about freely from 6 a.m. to 5 p.m. No fetters or handcuffs were found on any of the female inmates. As per the records of the jail, no woman prisoner has violated any rule or committed any offence within the prison. The jail authorities vouchsafe for the discipline and good behaviour of the convicts. During the interview of the women prisoners in Hyderabad jail, some of the new entrants complained about mild ragging by the prisoners who have been staying there for a long time.

Social activities: Various NGOs are involved in the social activities of the jail inmates in Andhra Pradesh. The names of the organisations which regularly visit the jail and undertake some useful activities include:

1. Penal Reform And Justice Association (PRAJA)
2. Prison Ministry
3. Prison Fellowship of India
4. Freedom Foundation
5. Asmitha Resource Centre
6. Ladies Circle of Round Table
7. Good Samaritan Reformatory Association
8. Lioness Club
9. Rotary Club
10. Bala Rakshana Samithi

These organisations organise medical camps, moral lectures, cultural programmes, prayers and bhajans throughout the year. Some of these organisations help the family members of the prisoners in education and economic affairs.[12]

Welfare activities: In each jail, a woman welfare officer looks after the welfare needs of the women prisoners. This department helps in drafting the appeal petitions and pursues the court cases. It counsels the newly admitted prisoners and encourages them to lead undisturbed life during their stay in the jail. The welfare officer also functions as a link between the prisoners and their family back in the village.

Legal aid: The women in custody receive free legal aid from the Andhra Pradesh Legal Services Authority subject to certain conditions like the annual income of the accused. As per the prison records, 58 prisoners, including convicts and remand prisoners, received the legal aid in the State Jails for women in Andhra Pradesh.

The establishment of separate enclosures for women prisoners in all central jails and the establishment of two separate State jails for women prisoners have totally changed the atmosphere of the jails. These enclosures and jails are totally administered by the female staff. This gives the necessary privacy needed for the women prisoners. The prisoners are allowed to move freely within the premises and interact with the female staff and as such there is a sort of comradeship between the prisoners and the staff. The women prisoners found the women staff more accessible, caring and compassionate whereby they are open their hearts freely and express their problems in life and seek solutions. The women staff on their part treat the women prisoners not as criminals but as those who did something wrong at a momentary loss of judgment. The sensitivity of the women staff is reflected in the good words of the prisoners during the interview. The women prisoners felt that they are safe in the hands of the women staff and there is not even an iota of corruption which is normally said to be associated with the jail administration. There are no restrictions whatsoever on the movements within the jail or during the interviews of the prisoner with her friends or relatives.

The concept of prison has undergone a sea change over the years. Prison life, in earlier times, meant life in a dark, unventilated cell coupled with hard labour and substandard food. At that time, it was meant for punishing the criminal and the reformative part was totally ignored. Now the emphasis is on the reformation of the criminal. So the jail structure and function has totally changed in tune with the new concepts. Andhra Pradesh is in the forefront in undertaking reforms in jail administration. Even before the Justice Krishna Iyer Committee made the recommendations for the treatment of women prisoners on a separate scale, the Jail Department of Andhra Pradesh was implementing them on their own. It is heartening to note that out of the 44 recommendations[13] made by the Justice Krishna Iyer Committee 38 recommendations have been implemented in the prisons of Andhra Pradesh. Proposals for the implementation of recommendation Nos. 14[14] and 19[15] have been submitted to the Government of Andhra Pradesh, while the recommendation Nos. 28[16] and 44[17] are under examination for implementation. Recommendation Nos.38[18] and 39[19] are outside the scope of jail department and hence referred to the Women and Child Welfare Department for implementation.[20]

The jail authorities in Andhra Pradesh have started many innovative measures and programmes to improve the quality of life in jail in general and of women prisoners in particular. To study the problems of the women during their incarceration and to improve their mental health, a special research project was undertaken in the year 2000 on 'mental health and care of women and children in prison' in association with PRAJA (Penal Reform And Justice Association). In each jail, the DIG/Superintendents take new initiatives to make the life in jail more meaningful and some such initiatives are described hereunder.

In all the central jails, health camps are arranged at regular intervals. The prisoners are examined and free medicines and free spectacles are distributed through the efforts of superior officers. Adult education programmes are conducted under the 'Sarva Siksha Abhayan' programme of the Human Resources Department of the Central Government and 'Akshara Jyothi' programme of State Government. Slates, books and writing materials are distributed. Under the clean and green programme of the State Government, the prisoners are encouraged to plant trees and take care of them. Religious festivals are celebrated in the jail. Women prisoners are encouraged to do *pujas* on such festive days. There is a temple within each jail where inmates can offer their prayers.

The highlight of the sensitivity of a superior officer is evident in the Visakhapatnam Central Jail. When a pregnant remand prisoner delivered a female baby, the authorities had arranged everything for the naming ceremony of the baby. The function was attended by all the women prisoners and social workers from outside. The Regional Passport Officer was the chief guest of the function and she named the baby as 'Arundhathi Krishna Vani'.

In Hyderabad jail, a special programme for teaching 'Annamacharya Sankeerthanas' was arranged in February 2003. A well-known exponent of Annamacharya Kirthanas, Mrs. Kondaveeti Jyotirmayee, has trained the prisoners for a week. This was the part of the closing ceremony of 500 years of 'Annamayya Aradhanostavam'. More than 100 women prisoners attended the music camp.

The International Women's Day and World Mother Tongue Day are also organised besides the Independence day, Republic day, State Formation day and Mahatma

Gandhi's Birthday. During all these days, people from outside are invited to address and interact with the prisoners.

The Government of Andhra Pradesh has recently introduced an annual jail week during which the gates of the jails are kept open for the general public. Various articles produced by the inmates are exhibited and sold to the public.

Innovative Initiatives in Prison Administration in Andhra Pradesh

The Department of Prisons and Correctional Services in Andhra Pradesh is a progressive looking department and perhaps few other States have taken so many initiatives in the jail administration. The first initiative in the penal reform is the establishment of the State Institute of Correctional Administration (SICA) to sensitise the jail staff through training. The department has provided video linkage between jails and courts for the speedy disposal of remand prisoners. The proposed new initiatives are the community service as an alternative to jail sentence and classification of prisoners for better security arrangements and jail administration. The formation of Prison Development Board for improving the physical facilities in jails and improve jail administration is another such initiative.

State Institute of Correctional Administration (SICA)

This Institute was established in 1984 at the State capital of Hyderabad. Andhra Pradesh has the distinction of being the first to establish such an institution in South India. This pioneer institute is headed by the Superintendent of Jails.[21] During the 20 years of its existence, SICA has been imparting basic induction training to the newly recruited jail staff. Special training to the inservice jail staff, both middle level and lower level, is imparted through refresher courses and crash courses. During the training the staff are encouraged, besides outdoor training, to participate in case studies, panel discussions, group discussions covering the major and minor Criminal Acts, Criminology & Penology, Human Rights, etc. Basic computer training is also provided. Experts in the field of jail administration are engaged to interact with the trainees.

The Department has made the training mandatory for all its staff. The staff manning different jails are made to attend one training programme of seven days every year. 'Transparency in the work sphere' is the major theme for recent training classes. The ministerial and executive officers of the jails in the State are trained to meet any challenge posed in the field of security and treatment of prisoners.

Video-Linkage of Prison and Court

This new initiative in penal reform was introduced by the Andhra Pradesh jail authorities, to solve the problem of the large number of poor men, distressed women and unfortunate children lodged behind prison bars awaiting trials for long periods. As per Sec.167(2)(a) and (b) of Criminal Procedure Code, 1973, the accused person once remanded have to be produced before the Magistrate once in every fifteen days. The production of the accused before the Magistrate is necessary for the extension of the remand.

In India, nearly 75% of the prison population is remand prisoners. The production of them before the court is a daunting task. The main problem involved in producing the remand prisoner before the court is the requirement of a large police force to complete the elaborate procedure of checking the prisoner before and after the production. Besides the escort duty, the police are involved in several other duties. As a result, many a time, the police fail to perform escort duty and could not produce the accused before the Magistrate at the end of the remand period.

The other problem, as per the authorities, is transport. A number of vehicles are required for transporting the prisoners. The absence of sufficient vehicles is also stated as one of the reasons for non-production of remand prisoners before the Magistrate. Because of the shortage of vehicles, the female remand prisoners are carried with the habitual and hardcore male criminals in the same crowded vehicles causing a lot of inconvenience to the women prisoners.

The women prisoners are invariably forced to wait in the court till the evening as the same vehicle is used to carry all the remand prisoners back to the prison. The long stay in the court premises, coupled with the absence of toilet facilities in courts tells on the female prisoner's health. Besides all these, the expenditure involved in producing remand prisoners is huge as per a departmental study[22] made by the prison authorities in Andhra Pradesh. The study revealed that a monthly expenditure of Rs.6,45,000/- is incurred for escort duty for one prison (Table 20). So one can imagine the total billing in Andhra Pradesh, where there are 7 central prisons, 2 State jails for women, 9 district jails, 147 sub-jails and 1 borstal school. Obviously it runs into crores.

To overcome all these problems and also to administer speedy justice to remand prisoners, the prison department of Andhra Pradesh has proposed a new initiative in penal reforms by providing a video-linkage between prison and courts.

Table 20

Expenditure and Savings on Utilization Of Video Linkage Between Prisons and Courts in Central Prison, Hyderabad

Daily average production of prisoners	50
No. of police men required for escort	75
Average salary per month for one police man	Rs. 8,000
Average salary per month for 75 police men	Rs.8,000 x 75 = Rs.6,00,000/-
Fuel per vehicle for 25 working days	25 x 20 Liters x Rs.15/- = Rs.7,500/-
Fuel per 6 vehicles	Rs.7,500 x 6 = Rs.45,000/-
Total cost of production of prisoners per month at an average of 50 prisoners per day and fuel charges	Rs.6,00,000 + Rs.45,000 = Rs.6,45,000/-
Rent for Video-Linkage at each end Rs.80,000/-	
Rent for Video-Linkage at two ends (-) Rs.1,60,000/-	= Rs.1,60,000/-
Net saving per month (-)	= Rs.4,85,000/-
Net saving per annum	Rs.4,85,000 x 12 = **Rs.58,20,000/ -**

The Government of Andhra Pradesh which is in the forefront in utilizing the Information Technology in administration has immediately responded to the proposal and amended the Criminal Procedure Code, 1973.[23] With the amendment to Section 167(2) of the Code, prisoners can now be produced before a Magistrate through electronic video-linkage.

The following amendment was made to Sec. 167 of Cr.P.C., 1973. "In the Code of Criminal Procedure, 1973, in Section 167, in its application to the State of Andhra Pradesh, in sub-section (2) . . . . .

(i) to clause (b), the following shall be added at the end, namely:-

"either in person or through the medium of electronic video linkage".

(ii) In the Explanation thereunder, for the words "an accused person was produced", the words "an accused person was produced in person or as the case may be, through the medium of electronic video-linkage", shall be substituted.

Following the amendment, studios have been set up in both the State jails for women and the court. On each working day at a specified hour the video linkage is activated and the remand female prisoner is presented before the camera within the jail premises. The Magistrate at the other end can see and listen to the prisoner and take a decision on the extension of remand or otherwise.

This innovative penal reform has many advantages:

- The expenditure involved on deploying the police force for checking and as escorts to the remand prisoners is saved.
- The investment on video linkage is one time investment and it is hardly one third of the monthly expenditure incurred by a central jail on the personal production of remand prisoner before courts.

- The remand prisoners are now assured of their production before the Magistrate at the appointed time and day.
- The women prisoners are saved from their inconvenience involved in the travel and stay in the court premises for long hours.
- The judiciary can dispose of the cases of remand prisoners in a short time and can concentrate on the trial cases.

This initiative of penal reform is in tune with the reformative process and ensures speedy trial and removes the hardships of remand prisoners.

Prison Development Board

Most of the jails in Andhra Pradesh are old, ill-ventilated, overcrowded and situated in unhygienic locations. The need to improve the existing jails by arranging proper ventilation, protected water supply, good security measures to prevent escape etc., was recognised by the department. Besides maintainance of jails and custodial justice also became an expensive one and it is becoming increasingly difficult to provide productive work to all inmates.

In these circumstances, Prison Development Board was established in 2001[24] in Andhra Pradesh with the following members:

(a) Chief Minister .. Chairman

(b) Minister for Prisons .. .. Vice-Chairman

(c) Registrar General of the High Court of Andhra Pradesh .. .. Ex-officio Director

(d) Principal Secretary to Government in

	Home (Prisons) Department	Ex-officio Director
(e)	Principal Secretary to Government, Finance Department	Ex-officio Director
(f)	Principal Secretary to Government, Revenue Department	Ex-officio Director
(g)	Secretary to Government, Law Department	Ex-officio Director
(h)	Director General and Inspector General of Police	Ex-officio Director
(i)	Director of Prosecutions	Ex-officio Director

The main functions of the Board are:

(a) to examine the living conditions of the prisoners with specific reference to their basic needs and provision of facilities compatible with their dignity;

(b) to look after the prisoners with humanity and help them lead law abiding and useful lives after their release;

(c) to endeavour to reform and reassimilate the prisoners in the social milieu by giving them appropriate correctional treatment;

(d) to see that the prisoners are provided sufficient accommodation, hygienic surroundings, sufficient water supply, sun light, ventilation and adequate medical attention, if necessary by repairing or altering the existing jails;

(e) to build new prisons, where the existing prisons are not in a satisfactory condition or beyond repair;

(f) to review the programmes of treatment of prisoners, education, vocational training, industry, manufacturing activities, agriculture, poultry, dairying, horticulture and such other occupational activities being carried on in prisons with a view to developing prisons as correctional centres; and

(g) to efficiently manage the prisons, if necessary, by acquiring properties, whether movable or immovable, including computers, communication facilities, gadgets, vehicles, security or surveillance equipment, electronic video linkage system, etc.[25]

Community Service

The other innovative penal reform proposed by the Andhra Pradesh jail authorities is community service in place of jail sentence.[26] This will be the most innovative experiment, as and when implemented, in regard to non-custodial measures of dealing with offenders. Though such community service as an alternative was in vogue in different countries, India has not yet decided on this. Andhra Pradesh has taken a lead in this regard.

It is a new form of sentence under which an offender is required to perform unpaid work to benefit the community under the supervision of the probation officer. He shall also provide rehabilitative counselling and guidance to the offender. The order is punitive and the offender is required to use his leisure time to perform community service as reparation to the harm he has done to the community. It imposes restriction on the freedom of the convict.

The jail authorities in Andhra Pradesh have identified the following as the advantages of the proposed community service.

1. A community service order scheme is less costly than custodial measure. The cost to the State of keeping an offender on community service order scheme is much less than keeping him in prison. It costs little to administer and is also inexpensive in terms of human and social cost. It avoids the expenses of providing food, clothing, shelter, medical care and other necessities in prisons.

2. It relieves the pressure on the prison system by reducing the prison population and thus helps prevent overcrowding of prisons.

3. The community will benefit through the work performed, which could not otherwise be carried out, such as assisting social institutions.

4. It enables the offenders to live with their families in the community thereby maintaining family ties. The dependents are saved from interruption of family life including the loss of bread winner.

5. The offender may benefit from diverting energy from anti-social to socially acceptable activities. Because of the offender's direct involvement with the community agencies, he/she may be positively influenced by the good example of those working with him/her.

6. The offender is saved from the dangerous effects of contamination from other offenders and the effects of prisonisation.

7. The re-entry crisis (from prison to community) is avoided. The offender will not suffer great changes in employment and family situation that go with incarceration.

The A.P. prison authorities also prpared the features of the proposed community service programme. They are the following:

(i) The offender must be aged 18 and above.

(ii) The offence must be one which is punishable by imprisonment.

(iii) The court must be satisfied that the offender is a suitable person and that arrangements can be made for him to carry out the obligation – which is described thus: "To perform unpaid work" for a specified number of hours. The court must specify the number of hours.

(iv) The minimum number of hours for a community service order is forty and the maximum a thousand hours.

(v) A social enquiry report is a pre-requisite. The court needs to be assured that the offender is "A suitable person to perform work under such an order".

(vi) Probation Officers should be made responsible for the community service order scheme in the area concerned. The social enquiry report is the responsibility of the District Probation Officer.

(vii) The offender must consent to the making of the order.

(viii) The court must explain the measure of the order to the offender in ordinary language and supply him with a copy of the order.

(ix) No order can be made which conflicts with the offender's religious beliefs or times of normal work or school attendance.

(x) A community service order can be made for a breach of probation order.

(xi) Breach of community service order is, like probation, finable, or the order may be revoked and the offender dealt with for original sentence.

(xii) The offender is bound, (1) to report and notify the change of address, and (2) to work as directed to the satisfaction of the supervising officer.

Classification of Prisoners

The classification of prisoners on the basis of security perception is another penal reform attempted by Andhra Pradesh jail administration.[27] At present, the confinement of prisoners in jails is on territorial basis and also on the length of the sentence. Remand prisoners are confined among various prisons based on the place of offence and proximity of the jail. In the absence of a proper and scientific way of classifying prisoners based on security risk, most of the times dangerous prisoners and ordinary prisoners are mixed up in many jails. The level of the security imposed is the same for ordinary prisoners and dangerous prisoners. Therefore, the Andhra Pradesh Prison Department felt that there is a need to classify the prisoners on the basis of the risk they pose to the society. The number of escapes would also come down and the man-power which is now being wasted on ordinary prisoners can be put to better use and improve the security.

Feeling the need for introducing classification of prisoners on the basis of security and to prevent the escape of dangerous prisoners, the following is the classification:

Security Category-1 (S.1)	:	Naxalites, radicals, extremists and terrorists (High Security Prisoners)
Security Category-2 (S.2)	:	Dacoits, Robbers, drug peddlers, Hired assassins and other escape-prone prisoners including previous escapes (Dangerous prisoners)

Security Category-3 (S.3)	:	All types of offenders who do not pose any threat to the society even if they were to escape like ordinary murderers, offenders involved in attempt to murder, grievous hurt, simple hurt, traffic offenders, excise offenders, railway offenders and other offenders.
Security Category-4 (S.4)	:	Prisoners who are eligible for open air prisons

If all the prisoners are classified according to the above system, the appropriate level of security can be provided to them.

(vii) Social Welfare Custody

The Women Development and Child Welfare (WD & CW) Department, Government of Andhra Pradesh, is primarily concerned with the administration of the following major enactments in the State.[28]

1. Suppression of Immoral Traffic in Women and Girls Act, 1956, [Immoral Traffic (Prevention) Act, 1956].
2. Dowry Prohibition Act, 1961
3. Orphanages and other Charitable Homes (Supervision and Control) Act, 1960
4. The Women's and Children's Institutions (Licensing) Act, 1956.
5. The Andhra Pradesh Women's Commission Act, 1998.

Suppression of Immoral Traffic in Women and Girls Act, 1956[29]

This Act is mainly intended to curb the habit of immoral traffic among women and girls in the State. Under Sec.17 of this Act, the Magistrate, subject to provisions of this Act, makes an order that such a girl may be detained for such a period as may be specified in the order, in a protective home or such other custody as he, for reasons to be recorded in writing, shall consider suitable.

According to Sec.19 of the said Act, 'A woman or girl who is carrying on, or is being made to carry on prostitution, may make an application to the Magistrate within the local limits of whose jurisdiction she is carrying on, or is being made to carry on, prostitution, for an order that she may be kept in a protective home. If after hearing the applicant and making such inquiry as he may consider necessary, the Magistrate is satisfied that an order should be made under this Section, then he shall make an order, for reasons to be recorded, that the applicant be kept in a protective home for such period as may be specified in the order'.

Such women and girls who are ordered to be kept in the protective homes, also known as 'rescue homes', which are under the control of the Women Development and Child Welfare Department, will be kept under the supervision of the Superintendent of the rescue homes for the entire period of conviction. It is the duty of the Superintendent to see that the convicted persons are lodged in the homes to ensure their protection and to look after their well-being. Except this, the Department has no other responsibility in administering the said Act.[30]

The Women's and Children's Institutions (Licensing) Act, 1956[31]

This Act is intended to provide for the licensing of institutions for women and children and for mothers incidental thereto. According to Sec. 2 of the said Act, 'Child' means a boy or girl who has not completed the age of 18 years. Licensing authority means the State Government or such officer or authority, as may be prescribed. Sec.10 of the said Act indicates that hostels, or boarding houses attached to, or controlled or recognised by educational institutions, or any protective home established under the Suppression of Immoral Traffic in Women and Girls Act, 1956 (ITPA), are also covered under this Act. The issue of making rules under this Act is still under consideration of the Government of Andhra Pradesh. Unless the rules are made, the role to be played by the functionaries of the Department in issuing licenses for maintenance of such homes or the homes maintained by this Department will not be known.[32]

Keeping in view the above Acts, the Social Welfare Department has established a rescue home to protect the inmates and also to rehabilitate them for their well being.

Rescue Home

Only one rescue home was established by the Government of Andhra Pradesh for the entire State and is located in the capital city of Hyderabad, for 'court committed cases' under the provisions of the 'Immoral Traffic (Prevention) Act of 1956', and the convicted women are kept during their period of conviction in this home.

At present, the rescue home has no building of its own and it is running in a private building at a monthly rent of Rs.8,000/-. It is not designed to house the rescued women and as such it suffers from the lack of minimum facilities like ventilation, sanitation and other amenities. The living conditions are much below the desirable standard. The inmates are not provided with cots but the rescue home is equipped with running water, electricity and fans.

Safety measures: The height of the compound wall is much similar to the normal residential homes and no special protection is provided on the compound wall. At present, there are no trained security personnel guarding the said home. As per the Government record a police constable was posted at the entrance earlier but for some unknown reasons that security post was not only withdrawn but totally abolished. Only an attender was keeping watch during day time while the night security is entrusted to the night watchman.

Staff: The home is headed by a Superintendent and she is assisted by a Matron. A post of craft instructor is sanctioned to train the inmates in vocational courses. There are two posts of night watchman and the post of attender to look after the day-to-day needs of the inmates and to provide security.

Education: There are no facilities to educate the inmates. The Superintendent in-charge of the home observed that the inmates are not interested in pursuing education. There are library facilities where newspapers and some books were provided.

Diet: The Government sanctions Rs.330/- per month for each inmate to meet their nutritional and sanitary requirements.

On Sundays, the inmates are served a special lunch which includes a non-vegetarian dish or eggs. Similarly on Saturdays, fruits are given as supplement. The sick inmates are provided with special diet on medical advice. The inmates cook their own food and as such there are no complainants to complain on the quality of the food served. The kitchens are provided with cooking gas cylinders and stoves.

The daily diet includes:

Table 21

Dietary Chart in Rescue Home, Hyderabad

Sl.No.	Detail of Diet	Time	Items
1.	Breakfast	7.30 a.m.	Tiffin like Idly, Upma with cup of Tea
2.	Lunch	12.30 p.m.	Rice, Dhal, Rasam, Buttermilk
3.	Evening Snack	3.00 p.m.	Light snacks like Biscuits, fried corns, etc., with Tea
4.	Dinner	7.30 p.m.	Rice, Curry, Rasam, Buttermilk

Amenities: The inmates are supplied with soap, oil, soapnut, comb, etc.

Clothing: Each inmate is provided with two pairs of clothing including undergarments. A carpet and a bed sheet are provided at the State expense and the inmates are allowed to buy the goods of their choice, if they can afford to do so.

Segregation of inmates: There is a special provision to segregate the inmates who suffer from infectious and contagious diseases.

Hospital facilities: There is no medical personnel to attend on them within the home. Either they are taken to the nearby private medical practitioner or referred to the Government General Hospital depending upon the severity of the disease and also based on the medical advice. The whole medical expenses are borne by the State.

Recreational facilities: The only recreational facilities available are a tape recorder and a television.

Separation of inmates: The home is meant for keeping prostitutes, rescued girls, victims of rape, etc., under the court orders. They have to be necessarily kept in separate enclosures. But such facilities are not available in this home.

Vocational courses: Vocational training in tailoring and embroidery is imparted to the inmates. A craft teacher works there on a permanent basis. Wages are paid by the State. The money earned by the inmates, if any, is paid at the time of their release from the home.

Labour: No special labour work is imposed on any inmates. They have to clean their premises, wash their clothes and cook for themselves. The inmates are neither asked to do some work nor paid any amount as wages.

Release: The inmates are kept in the home as per the direction of the court for a period specified in the order, subject to the maximum period of three years. Subsequently they are released. If they wish so, they are shifted to the State home for training and rehabilitation. However, beyond the period of 3 years the State takes no responsibility, if they are able bodied.

Legal aid: Free Legal Aid facility is available for the inmates. They are encouraged to approach the A.P. State Legal Services Authority directly or through the advocates appointed by the said Authority.

Counselling: The Women Welfare Department has organisers who visit the homes and do the counselling.

The Superintendent and other staff members have taken the initiative in helping the inmates to move away from the profession and lead a normal life in the society. They are encouraged to take up other means of livelihood. In some cases, when a suitable groom is available, the home conducts the marriages of some of the inmates.

During the study, no prostitute is found staying in the rescue home. As such, all the observations made above are based on the records and also the information provided by the Superintendent of the home.

State Homes

State homes are meant for women who are discharged from correctional institutions and who are unable to protect themselves from adverse social forces and also for those women in the age group of 18-35 years who voluntarily seek shelter. There are at present five such homes in the State of Andhra Pradesh. They are located at Hyderabad, Mahabubnagar, Rajahmundry, Kurnool and Srikakulam. The inmates will stay in the homes for 3-5 years. The capacity of the State homes varied with a maximum capacity of 100 in the Hyderabad home. The homes allow children up to 3 years to stay with their mothers. They are given free boarding and lodging at the rate of Rs.330/- for adults and Rs.230/- for their children.

Those who are interested in studies are provided with teaching material and those women who cleared 10th class are sent for nurse's training.

The home trains them in job-oriented and training-cum-production units like stitching, book binding, beautician, etc. The uneducated women are employed as domestic servants after obtaining an undertaking from the employer and the women. The women who are released after the completion of their term are provided with a sewing machine.

For the entire State of Andhra Pradesh, there is only one rescue home which is located in Hyderabad. The home is in an old rented building not suited for such a home where the segregation of the women held on different offences and women as victims is a necessity. In the absence of such a facility to home them separately, even prostitutes, when lodged, mingle with the other young girls who are likely to be influenced.

A police security which is a must for such a home as per the direction of the Supreme Court[33] is not in place at the rescue home. The sanitary and other living conditions reflect the low budgetary allotments made by the Government for running the rescue home. There is no meaningful infrastructure to train the inmates of the rescue home and provide educational facilities, personal or career counselling or psychiatric treatment.

There are hardly any health camps or legal camps held in the premises of the home.

Any contact between the authorities and those released is non-existent. The N.G.Os. are not encouraged to involve in the activities of the rescue home. As such, the rescue homes are run more or less like the jails, thus defeating the very purpose for which they were established.

(viii) Mental Health Custody

There are two mental health hospitals in Andhra Pradesh located at Hyderabad and Visakhapatnam. At both the places, the hospital buildings are more than 50 years old and are not originally designed as hospitals and as such some of the basic needs cannot could not be maintained properly. The overall sanitary conditions are below normal. However, a new specially designed hospital building is coming up at Visakhapatnam. There is no such proposal at Hyderabad.

In both the hospitals, there are separate enclosures to lodge female patients. The admission into the hospital is based on

1. the request of the relatives;
2. the reception orders of the court; or
3. the report of the jail authorities in case of convicts or remand prisoners.

The prisoners referred to the mental hospitals are sent either to the Hyderabad or Visakhapatnam depending upon the geographical proximity or on the specific reference of the authorities concerned. There is no hard and fast rule of jurisdiction for mental hospitals. In case of mentally ill from the jails located in coastal Andhra and Rayalaseema, the reference is made to the Visakhapatnam Mental Health Hospital while those from Telangana are sent to the Mental Health Hospital, Hyderabad.

The number of mentally ill women prisoners, as per the hospital records, is negligible and they are not kept in the hospital beyond six months. They are shifted back to jail on completion of the treatment and on the certification by the discharge committee. The mentally ill women admitted through court never exceeded ten at any given time.

During the present study, one remand prisoner each was lodged in the Hyderabad and Visakhapatnam Mental Health Hospitals. They were referred to the mental hospital by the Superintendents of the State Jail for Women, Hyderabad and Central Jail, Visakhapatnam respectively. Both of them are charged under Sec. 302 I.P.C. for murder. The woman prisoner in Visakhapatnam hospital is kept in a separate cell while in Hyderabad the prisoner is allowed to stay along with the other inmates. Both of them are guarded by a specially deputed female escort round the clock. The mental condition of both these remand prisoners is such that they could not answer properly the questions put to them. However, the prisoner in Hyderabad Mental Hospital appears to be satisfied with the conditions and the behaviour of the staff but expressed dissatisfaction about the food served and her stay in the hospital. There are nine mentally ill women admitted through court orders to the Visakhapatnam Mental Health Hospital and two such patients to Hyderabad Mental Health Hospital. The majority of them have recovered but they are still in the hospital, as their relatives do not accept their discharge for fear of relapsing. They long to move out of the hospital though they are satisfied with the conditions and the staff in the hospitals. Some of them are destitutes ignorant of their parentage or place of origin. The State may have to consider ways and means to rehabilitate them in a suitable manner.

Separation of mentally ill women from men

In both the hospitals, the mentally ill women are placed in a separate enclosure far away from the normal visibility of the outsiders. Entry is restricted to the female staff only, except for male doctors depending upon the need of the treatment.

Classification of mentally ill women

No cells are earmarked in Hyderabad Mental Health Hospital to lodge the mentally ill women prisoners. They are placed along with the other patients in the same barrack. In this hospital, there is no segregation of patients based either on the mode of admission, or the age, illness, etc. In contrast, in Visakhapatnam mental hospital there are exclusive cells to lodge the mentally ill women prisoners. Except prisoners, all other mentally ill women are kept in the same barrack. There is a provision to keep the seriously ill patients in separate cells. In both the hospitals, the mentally ill prisoners are guarded round the clock by the female escorts.

Staff pattern: The hospitals at Visakhapatnam and Hyderabad have sufficient female doctors and clinical staff to take care of the mentally ill patients. In the case of the women prisoners referred to the mental hospital, a female doctor is specifically designated to treat them.

Restrictions on enclosures: The female enclosures are locked throughout the day to prevent any unauthorised entry. No male member is allowed into the enclosure. The mentally ill women are allowed freely within the barracks during the day but locked after sunset.

Accommodation, cleanliness and sanitation

In Hyderabad, there are wards like in any other general hospital, with cots and beds. The wards are neat and clean. In Visakhapatnam, the building in which the mentally ill-prisoners are lodged is an old dilapidated building. The flooring is uneven, broken and dirty. There is no proper ventilation. The mentally challenged persons deserve better conditions. The cells in which the criminally charged prisoners are placed are no better, except that they are separate, and open for the escort police to have an eye on the inmates. The physical facilities like cots and beds are not sufficient and the sanitary conditions and other facilities like running water, ventilation, etc., are very poor. When questioned about these conditions, the authorities pointed to the new block under construction, where the mentally ill-patients and prisoners are to be shifted to in the near future. The personal cleanliness of the inmates is taken care of by the hospital staff. The hair is cut to maintain the hygiene of the patient.

Clothing: The mentally ill women are supplied with uniform as per the scale laid down by the government. A Dhobi is engaged for washing the clothes of the patients. Bed sheets are washed every alternate day.

Dietary: There are no separate cooking facilities in the female enclosures. Cooking is done in the common kitchen and the food is then carried to the enclosure. The diet is as per the scale prepared by the respective mental hospitals. A dietician oversees the quality and quantity aspect of the diet. While the hospital staff are engaged in cooking in Hyderabad Mental Hospital, the same job is entrusted to a contractor in the Visakhapatnam Mental Hospital. The diet is provided as per the specific quality and quantity and also time schedule and both of them are displayed prominently.

Table 22 is the diet schedule in Visakhapatnam Mental Health Hospital.

In Hyderabad Mental Health Hospital there is no restriction on dietary and the patients are served bananas daily.

The diet scale is periodically reviewed by the committee headed by Superintendent of the hospital. The committee includes two members other than the dietician.

On important occasions like Independence Day, Republic Day, International Women's Day special food is served in the female ward.

Amenities: The mentally ill women are provided with tooth powder, coconut oil, soap and shampoo.

Interviews: The relatives of the patients can meet the inmates after their identity is established and visitors pass is issued by the hospital authorities.

Labour: No work is allotted to the inmates.

Vocational training: No vocational training is imparted to the mentally ill women, but are allowed to make paper covers in order to study their mental conditions. No wages are paid for such work.

Recreational facilities: The hospital has provided a T.V. in the female ward. Inmates are allowed to play caroms. Newspapers and magazines are kept in the wards.

Voluntary organisations: Voluntary organisations are permitted to undertake service activities subject to the rules and guidelines of the Mental Health Hospital. In Visakhapatnam, Sri Satya Sai Organisation visits the hospital on a regular basis and serves the patients. This organisation helps out in cleaning the premises, gives head baths to the inmates, changes the clothes of inmates. Singing *bhajans* and distributing *prasadam* are also part of their activities. Other N.G.Os. like Christian sisters, Mahila Sravanthi are also engaged in helping the inmates. No social organisation is associated with the Hyderabad Mental Health Hospital.

Board of visitors: In both the hospitals, a Board of visitors comprising of two psychiatric doctors and three social workers are in place as per the Mental Health Act, 1987. One of the social worker is a female.

Development Committee: The Development Committee headed by the hospital Superintendent looks after the developmental activities of the hospital.

Legal aid: Some of the local women advocates visit the hospital to help the needy women inmates.

Discharge of inmates: As per Sec. 40 of Mental Health Act, 1987 the power to discharge the mentally ill patients is vested with the medical officer of the hospital. He discharges the patients after obtaining recommendation of two medical practitioners out of which one is a psychiatrist. The medical officer informs the authorities and the authorities in turn refer the matter to the Magistrate under whose orders the mentally ill person was detained.

Table 22

Dietary chart in Visakhapatnam mental hospital

Sl.No.	Name of the diet	Time	Day	Details of item served	
1	Full diet at a cost of Rs.20/- per patient per day	Breakfast	Monday Thursday	3 idlies Chutny Tea	200 gms each 50 gms 200 ml
			Tuesday	Upma (Bansi Ravva) Chutny Tea	3 cups (400 gm) 50 gms 200 ml
			Wednesday Saturday	Upma (Bombay Ravva) Chutny Tea	3 cups 50 gms 200 ml
			Friday	Kichidi Chutny Tea	300 gms 50 gms 200 ml
			Sunday	The breakfast is served by Satya Sai Voluntary Organisation while the tea is served by the Hospital	

Contd...

Sl.No.	Name of the diet	Time	Day	Details of item served	
		Lunch	Everyday	Rice	678 gms
				Vegetable curry	150 gms
				Sambar	200 ml
				Boiled egg	1 each
				Curd	150 ml
		Dinner	Everyday	Rice	675 gm
				Vegetable curry	150 gms
				Sambar	200 ml
				Boiled egg	1 each
				Curd	150 ml
			Monday Thursday & Saturday	Banana	1 No.
2.	C.M.B. diet (Convalesent: Milk, Bread) Rs.15/- per day per patient	Breakfast Lunch Dinner	Everyday	Bread Milk with sugar	200 gms

If there is no response from the authorities or the police station concerned or from the relatives to whom the information was passed on, the hospital authorities send them at their own cost to their last known residential address. In case of refusal by the relatives to accept the discharged women patients, the authorities to counsel them. When all the efforts fail, the discharged persons are entrusted to the care of State homes run by the Department of Women Development and Child Welfare. Since such a State-run home is not available in Visakhapatnam, such patients are admitted into the homes run by reputed voluntary organisations like Prema Samajam, Mother Theresa Institutions, etc.

The Hyderabad Hospital Authorities have taken the lead in accommodating the destitute discharged patients. A separate enclosure is created for them and they are encouraged to do small activities. Some of their cases were referred to the Social Welfare Department of the Government of Andhra Pradesh and got them sanctioned for old age pensions. Some of the patients based on their age are also referred to for old age homes and State homes according to their age.

Mental Health Hospitals in Andhra Pradesh maintain separate female enclosures, wards and are fully staffed with women nurses and doctors to treat them. The female mentally ill-patients, lodged in the hospitals under the orders of the court, are treated on par with other patients. Only the mentally ill prisoners are held separately for reasons of security. In Hyderabad, under the advice of the psychiatrist even the prisoners are allowed to mingle with other mentally ill patients. The sanitary conditions are not sufficiently good. The attitude of the staff towards the patients is positive and wholesome.

There are no avenues or facilities to segregate the patients who respond to the treatment from the partially recovered patients. The training and rehabilitation of such patients are not attempted in right earnest. The attempt to make the family members play a role in the treatment process of the mentally ill patients as has been attempted in the Hyderabad Mental Health Hospital may be extended even to the patients in custody.

References

1. AIR 1983 SC 378; 1983 CriLJ 642.
2. *Ibid*., and Sec. 54, Criminal Procedure Code, 1973.
3. *Khatri v. State of Bihar*, AIR 1981 SC 928; (1981) 1 SCC 635 See also *Suk Das v. Union Territory of Arunachal Pradesh*, AIR 1986 SC 991; (1986) 2 SCC 401; 1986 CriLJ 1084.
4. Sec.167(2), Criminal Procedure Code, 1973.
5. See Table No.16, p. 268.
6. Bharathchandra, A Brief note on Status of Women Prisoners in Andhra Pradesh, Principal Secretary, Home Department, Government of Andhra Pradesh.
7. *Sheela Barse v. State of Maharashtra*, AIR 1983 SC 378; 1983 CriLJ 642.
8. Tables 1 and 9 in pp. 248 and 257 respectively.
9. Chapter LIV. R. 974, A.P. Prisons Rules, 1979.
10. *Ibid*., Rules 967 to 973, *Ibid*.
11. Vide: G.O.Ms.No.38, Education (Prog. I) Department, dated 16-4-2002.
12. Bharathchandra, A Brief Note on Status of Women Prisoners in Andhra Pradesh, Principal Secretary, Home Department, Government of Andhra Pradesh.
13. Report of National Expert Committee on Women Prisoners (1986-87) Vol. I, pp.322-327.
14. Recommendation No.14 : The menial duties in the female prisons or ward shall not be assigned to inmates and no monetary or non-monetary incentive should be given to such work. The prison budget should provide for this function as a routine staff expense.

15. Recommendation No.19 : Female prisoners shall be classified on the basis of the age groups, nature of crime, type and length of sentence, etc., and correctional treatment of prisoner shall be related to her specific problem and situation. For this purpose, treatment personnel trained in correctional approaches shall be appointed.
16. Recommendation No.28 : Women who pose no security risk and meet other suitability criteria may be housed in open jails where work facilities related to their agricultural or other occupational background should be available.
17. Recommendation No. 44 : Visiting Committees to jails should be constituted in consultation with professional bodies and University Departments of Law, Criminology, Social Work and Social Sciences from the neighbouring area. Visitors should be nominated on the basis of merit, public spiritedness, activist record and actual time likely to be made available to the visitorial function.
18. Recommendation No. 38 : Appropriate assistance shall be rendered to every female prisoner on release whether during or after completion of sentence. For this purpose, a centre for assisting released prisoner shall be set to service a cluster of prisons and custodial institutions on an area-wise basis. Even without the centre, the prison authorities shall take necessary steps to arrange the rehabilitation of the released prisoner either through the family, the relief centre or a voluntary organisation.
19. Recommendation No.39 : After-care and short-stay homes for women prisoners may be established in every State to serve prisoners who are homeless or rejected by their families.
20. Bharath Chandra, A Brief Note on Status of Women Prisoners in Andhra Pradesh, Principal Secretary, Home Department, Government of Andhra Pradesh.
21. G.O.Ms.No.132, Home (Prisons) Department, dated 20-2-1984.
22. S.R. Sukumara, "New Initiatives in Penal Reform – Andhra Pradesh", I.P.S., D.G. of Prisons and Correctional Services, Government of Andhra Pradesh, Hyderabad.
23. The Code of Criminal Procedure (Andhra Pradesh Amendment) Act, 2000 with effect on and from 6-12-2000.

24. Act No.12 of 2001. Received the assent of the Governor on 13th April, 2001.
25. Sec.10(1), Andhra Pradesh Prison Development Board Act, 2001.
26. M.R. Ahmed, "Community Service, a new initiative in Penal Reform", D.I.G. of Prisons, Government of Andhra Pradesh.
27. S.R. Sukumara, "New initiatives in Penal reform – Andhra Pradesh", I.P.S., D.G. of Prisons & Correctional Services, Government of Andhra Pradesh.
28. Women Development & Child Welfare, Department Manual – WD & CW 082 – Dr. M.C.R. Human Resource Development Institute of Andhra Pradesh, pp.55-57.
29. Later renamed as Immoral Traffic (Prevention) Act, 1956 by Act No.44 of 1986, w.e.f. 26-1-87.
30. Women Development & Child Welfare – Department Manual. WD & CW 082 – Dr. M.C.R. Human Resource development, Institute of Andhra Pradesh, p.55.
31. Act No.105 of 1956, *Ibid*., p.57.
32. Women Development & Child Welfare – Department Manual – WD & CD 082 – Dr. M.C.R. Human Resource Development Institute of Andhra Pradesh, p.57.
33. *Upendra Baxi v State of U.P.* AIR 1987 SC 191; (1986) 3 SCJ 291; 1986 SCC (Cri) 381.

8

Conclusions and Suggestions

SUMMARY

Rights of Prisoners under National and International Law

International Law

In the international arena there are many Declarations, Conventions and instruments dealing with the rights of people and prisoners. The Universal Declaration of Human Rights of the United Nations, 1948 is the first instrument which provided for preventing the arbitrary arrest, the presumption of innocence till proved guilty, the right to free and public hearing, etc. The prevention of torture, inhuman or degrading treatment and punishment, deprivation of liberty of any person in accordance of the law are the highlights of the European Convention on Human Rights, 1950. The protection of religious beliefs of the prisoners, separation of different categories of prisoners, separation of the male and female prisoners formed part of "The Standard Minimum Rules for the Treatment of Prisoners, 1955".

The International Covenant on Civil and Political Rights, 1966 guaranteed legal assistance, bail provision, fair and prompt trial, etc. The serious issue of torture of the prisoner was dealt with through the Declaration of Protection from Torture, 1975; The Declaration of Medical Ethics for Protection of Prisoners and Detainees against Torture, 1992; and the Convention against Torture of Prisoners, 1994. The protection of prisoners was strengthened by the General Assembly in 1988 with the adoption of 39 principles for protecting all persons under any form of detention or imprisonment. In 1990, the General Assembly adapted 11 point standard the as basic principles for the treatment of prisoners and the Standard Minimum Rules for the Non-Custodial measures. The principles include the employment of women to search women detainees and women police official to supervise the women detainees. All these Declarations and Conventions have an impact on the codes of civilised countries which have started recognising the importance of the reformative aspect of punishment and treating prisoners as human beings.

Indian Constitution

The Indian Constitution has responded to the international opinion and incorporated provisions such as the Right to Equality (Art. 14), the Right to Freedom (Art. 19), the Doctrine of ex-post facto-law (Art. 20(1)), the Doctrine of double jeopardy (Art. 20(2)), the Rule against self-incrimination (Art. 20(3)), the Right to life and personal liberty (Art. 21), the Right to fair trial (Art. 22(1), and the Right of detenues (Art. 22(4) to (7)).

Art. 15(3) permitted the State to make special provisions for the advancement of women and children. Equality of opportunities for all and prohibition of discrimination against women (Art. 16), Prohibition of traffic of human beings (Art. 23), equal pay for equal work (Art. 39), facility for maternity relief (Art. 42), uniform civil code (Art. 44), free legal aid (Art. 39A), prevention of practices derogatory to the dignity of the women (Art. 59A(e)) are some other important provisions.

Despite all these provisions, there are no special safeguards to protect the interests of the women prisoners. The only rights available to the women accused are general in character. The women prisoners, by their very status of gender, need special treatment which was totally ignored by the framers of the Constitution. However, the interests of the women prisoners can be protected through Art. 15(3) of the Constitution; since it permits the State to make special provisions in the existing laws or to make new laws for the benefit of women and children. Laws protecting the interests of the women in various custodies have to be made to enforce this guarantee.

Rights of Women Prisoners in Police and Judicial custody

Police custody

Women prisoners are subjected to inhuman treatment in police custody. Custodial violence involving rape and molestation is on the increase in almost all corners of the country. The Rameeza Bee and Shakila cases in Andhra Pradesh, the rape of Adivasi women in Madhya Pradesh, the Mayatyagi case in Uttar Pradesh, the Mathura case in Maharashtra highlighted the plight of women in police custody. The inadequacy of the law in protecting the women in police custody was plugged by amending the rape law. Sec.376 of I.P.C. was amended in 1983 by revision of the existing laws and inserting new provisions. Thus the person in-charge of custody of women is made responsible not only for the safe custody of women but also any sexual abuse not amounting to rape or rape committed against women.

The custodial victim is entitled to her privacy. So the Cr.P.C. was amended to protect the rape victim from the blaze of media publicity. The trial of the rape case 'in camera' was made mandatory. The printing and publishing of the trial proceedings are prohibited, unless the court permitted to do so. This was all done to prevent further embarrassment to the victims of sexual abuse. The privacy of women is given prominence irrespective of the character of the women. The police officer's action against even a lady of easy virtue was held offensive in *State of Maharashtra v. Madhukar Narain Mardikar.*[1]

The objective of Cr.P.C. is to provide a suitable mechanism and just procedure for the enforcement of criminal law. But special protections given to the women accused, if any, are negligible. The Code, surprisingly does not provide sufficient safeguards to protect the interests of the women under arrest. The Code is unfortunately silent on the police lock-up where there are more chances for the police to commit sexual offences.

Presently, the Cr.P.C. provided for the woman, a practising pardanashin, to withdraw from the place under search and even a police officer is duty bound to announce his arrival for search of the place. As far as the search of the person is concerned, the law insists on the search of a female suspect by a female police officer, with strict regard to decency and privacy.

Sec.53 of the Cr.P.C. imposes an obligation upon the arrested person to undergo a medical examination and in the case of females it should be by a female medical officer. Sec. 54 of the Cr.P.C. impose an obligation on the police officer not to summon either a woman or a child below the age of 15 years to the police station, even when they are suspected of the crime. A duty is cast on the police officer to examine them at the residence of the suspect.

Following the national outcry over the treatment meted out to Mathura in police custody the Union Home Secretary issued a circular[2] on 10-3-1980 to the Chief Secretaries of all States listing the norms to be followed in the matter of arrest, search, detention in police lock-up, police remand of women and also examination of a woman as witness. When these guidelines were ignored by many States, the Supreme Court intervened through *Sheela Barse case*[3] and outlined seven guidelines to protect women in custody. The creation of exclusive police lock-ups, interrogation of female suspects in the presence of women police officers, communication of her arrest to her friends or relatives and also to the nearest free legal aid clinic, right to medical examination on production before a Magistrate and the mandatory enquiry by the

Magistrate regarding the treatment given to her by the police are all now part of the legal process.

The police is the law-enforcing arm of the civil government. The police force is entrusted with the fundamental duty of safeguarding the lives and property, protecting the innocent against deception, the weak against oppression or intimidation and the peaceful against violence and disorder.

But it is a universal phenomenon that the police have been found committing acts which are contrary to the cherished ideals of the police force. The police are condemned for the abuse of the power given to them. Their acts of oppression or intimidation of the weak, use of third degree methods to obtain a confession, torture in the custody are reported in the country at regular frequency. The treatment meted out to the women by the police included sexual harassment and rape.

There are so many incidents of custodial offence, especially rape of women by the police, which led to the judicial enquiries in this country. Despite the stringent condemnation by the judiciary and the conviction of the some offending police officials with severe punishment, such incidents continue to recur.

To curb this, the Expert Committee appointed by the Government of India made several recommendations. Besides the existing rules and the existing provisions aimed at protecting the interests of the people in custody, an exclusive provision is added to protect the women.The legal arrest of the women is restricted to the day time and also the insistence on the presence of a woman police both at the time of arrest and also at the time of interrogation are now part of the law of the country.

But all the protective provisions are more ignored than practised by the police. The treatment meted out to the women prisoners lodged in different jails of Andhra Pradesh was brought out through the present survey. The police, as per the inmates' account, invariably ill-treated, abused and threatened the women when they were in their custody. The lower the level of the police in the hierarchy, the more the objectionable behaviour.

Based on the answers of the female prisoners both remand and convict, the following are the findings on the experiences of the women in custody.

The police continue to arrest women during night irrespective of the gravity of the offence. The women were led to police stations in the darkns. The women were handled by the male police. The women, on arrest were neither informed of the fact of arrest, nor briefed on how long they would be away, where they would be held or the rights available to them like bail, free legal aid, etc., in custody. The news of their arrest was not communicated to their family or friends. They were not allowed to talk to family members or friends. The women were neither permitted to bring their young-children with them nor were aided in making suitable arrangements for them at the time of the arrest. From the account of the prisoners, it is clear that the search of the woman arrestee was made with least regard to the decency and respect to the legal provisions.

The most feared part of the custody is the interrogation by the police and this is of special concern in the Indian context. The suspects were subjected to merciless beatings with lathis, rifle butts and whips. Many were kicked, punched and trampled on the ground. The use of abusive language is quite rampant. The women were threatened with sexual abuse. The presence of the women police, which is mandatory, was not followed. The police collected bribes for every little favour.

Many police stations suffer from the absence of proper physical facilities. There are no separate women enclosures or lock-ups. The arrested females were kept either in the hall or verandah of the police stations. Separate toilets for women in custody are not in existence in the police stations. There are no bathing facilities and space for changing clothes in the police stations. Drainage and ventillation facilities are very poor.

Medical facility is not available. Permission to contact friends, relatives or lawyer is not given by the police. Except in a few police stations in big cities in Andhra Pradesh, no women constables were seen while women were held in custody. The police stations where women constables made their appearance during day time are also not many. Though the women are entitled to the bail immediately, in case of bailable offences, the police have never informed them about the available legal provisions. It appeared that the nearest legal aid committee was not posted with the information of the arrest.

No arrested woman was produced before the Magistrate within the stipulated 24 hours. The illegal detention ranged from a minimum of 48 hours to a maximum of 30 days. One of the convicts, aged over sixty, serving life sentence in Rajahmundry jail was held in illegal police custody for about 30 days. It appears that illegal detention period is directly proportional to the time the arrestee took to confess the crime. Those who confessed to the crime immediately after arrest are produced within 48 hours, but not in 24 hours as required under the law.

The I.P.C. and Cr.P.C. contain several hundreds of provisions dealing with several aspects of the crime and administration of justice. But the provisions which exclusively deal with the protection of the interests of the women in police custody are negligible and they can be counted on one's fingers. As such, the custodial justice for women is a far cry, resulting in crime against the women in the custody. Lack of protective provisions for the women in police custody resulted in the continued violence against the women by the custodians.

Judicial Custody

The role of the judiciary in a democratic country needs no emphasis. It is the only pillar of democratic society on which a citizen can confidently lean, when all other pillars coldshoulder him. The judiciary of this country has the tradition and history of coming to the rescue of the innocent victim. But in modern days the pendency of cases and long delays in the administration of justice are lowering the confidence in the judiciary to a certain extent.

'Justice delayed is justice denied' is a well known proverb. But this proverb is not provoking the judiciary in dealing with the disposal of cases. The judges are required to administer justice not only in accordance with the law but also expeditiously. But in practice, the long inexplicable delay of the criminal justice system is taking frustrating years altogether before one got the final word from the Apex Court.

There were attempts to reform this judicial system through many recommendations by Expert Committees and by the Apex Court itself. There were many recommendations made and guidelines laid down, for reasonable and prompt administration of justice should be rooted in confidence for the survival of the democratic set-up of governance.

While framing the guidelines, the courts have taken the gender factor into consideration though the term 'criminal' has no gender as such. The unequal social status of women, the disadvantageous position they are placed in educational and economic issues in the family and the historical bias against them all made the Apex Court and the Expert Committees to recommend a different treatment of women by the judiciary when they were brought before them. Though the recommendations and suggestions are there on paper, the judicial share of doing injustice to women, as observed by the NEC[5], is continuing till date.

The Supreme Court of India has imposed certain obligations[6] on the lower judiciary, especially when women are produced as accused before them. On the first production, the judicial officer is duty bound to enquire about the treatment meted out to her by the police. The time and mode of arrest, the persons who arrested her, the mode of interrogation are some of the issues on which the judicial Magistrate has to be satisfied before remanding her. The Magistrate, as per the Supreme Court guidelines[7], should offer the facility of medical examination.

All these provisions are not observed in practice, as the present study revealed, because of several reasons. The Magistrates do not treat the women accused as a separate category though they are required to do so. They routinely handle the cases of women. Magistrates show no awareness of women forming a special category especially those with minor children or with bread earning responsibilities in cases of female headed households.

The accused woman's thumb impressions are taken and they are remanded to judicial custody on a routine basis. The women undertrials stated that the Magistrates have not even talked to them directly. The escort police is used as the medium for communicating with the women accused. One is not sure whether the Magistrates are behaving so out of respect for or utter disregard for the females. But in any case, the females are hurriedly sent to jail. The majority of women undertrials are found to be ignorant of the language of the court and do not know their fate till they land in jail. Although, the majority of the women prisoners are apparently first-timers some of whom are arrested for relatively minor offences, their cases are not referred to Probation Officers for pre-sentence investigation.

During the study, it became clear that 84 per cent of the undertrial women prisoners are illiterate, poor and socially backward. Many of them are ignorant of the reason for their presence in jail. Some of the women prisoners who are accused of bailable offences are still in jail because they can't obtain their surety. They are incapable of tackling their problems on their own and are ignorant of the ways and means to come out on bail. Thus many unfortunate women are behind bars, deprived of their liberty, even not sure of the date of commencement of their trial.

The production of undertrial women prisoners at the end of the remand period is delayed because of minor administrative deficiencies such as lack of a female police escort, absence of a transport vehicle, etc. Even when produced, their remand is routinely extended by further 14 days without giving even a thought about to set them out on bail. It is a fact that judicial remand is a protective intervention but in the case of women a wise exercise of remand power is essential. Normally the women are not 'bail jumpers'. There is no record of women prisoners making an escape from prison in Andhra Pradesh. Even when escaped elsewhere in the country, they were very easily traced. They are not dangerous even when outside on bail. So it is suggested that women may liberally be granted bail on personal bonds without any violation of the broad principles of administration of justice.

For this, the judges and Magistrates require a thorough sensitization and orientation for the handling of judicial and legal procedures affecting the women. The psychological needs and the behavioural patterns of women should form part of the training programme of judicial officers. Just as women police are recruited, women police stations and State Jails for Women are formed, it may be considered to have separate women judicial officers to deal with women offenders. Such women judicial officers could understand better the woman offender's responsibilities towards her dependent children and family and minimise the undue damage likely to be caused by the judicial ambivalence.

There is a need to involve the law schools and colleges in the practical legal work as it sensitizes the young minds in understanding their obligation to the weaker sections of the society, particularly the women and children. This sensitization of prospective judicial officers at a very early age will go a long way towards shaping their responsibilities towards the women as and when they assume office.

The women who are not involved in serious offences may be released on probation with supervision rather than imprisoning them for short periods. There are cases where women were held as undertrials for a period longer than the actual sentence they would have served had they been convicted. This is an embarrassment for the functioning of the legal system and also sticks a social stigma on the face of the women. So the agencies involved in the investigation of crime, the police and the judiciary should work in a spirit of co-operation and co-ordination which will ultimately benefit the women in custody.

As things stand the procedural aspects are rather complicated and cumbersome. The court language continues to be English, which is understood by a small fraction of the population.

Prison Custody

The number of Acts relating to prisons and prisoners are many. The Prisoners Act, 1900 consolidated the law relating to the prisoners confined by order of a court and provides for the custody of prisoners. The attendance of the prisoners in courts is covered by the Prisoners (Attendance in Courts) Act, 1955. Transfer of Prisoners Act, 1950 permitted the removal of the prisoners from one State to another. Reference may also be made to the Identification of Prisoners Act, 1920. All these enactments have a significant bearing so far as the women arrestees are concerned. In an emerging situation when custodial justice to the women has assumed more and more significance, a fresh look at all these statutory provisions relating to the prisoners is due.

The Prisons Act, 1894 provides for the regulation of prisoners almost throughout India. This Act defined the duties of the prison officers including medical officers, admissions, removal and discharge of prisoners, discipline of prisoners, food, clothing and bedding and different categories of prisoners as well as the issues relating to their health. But there are hardly any provisions in this Act for safeguarding the interests of the women prisoners. Amendments to this

Act are to be made keeping the interests of the women prisoners in mind.

The maintenance of jails is a State subject. The jails are run in different States on different lines. There is no national policy on prisons. The recommendations of the National Expert Committee on the women prisoners are not implemented by many States. Andhra Pradesh is progressive in jail administration. But still a National Prison policy is desirable in the interest of the prisoners in general and the women prisoners in particular.

Prison sentence damages the mind of a person. It wreaks havoc with the personality of the individuals, more so with the women who are sensitive. With their social, family life gone, their interaction with the outside world curtailed, the women often go into depression. The problems associated with the women prisoners were identified and accordingly some rules and regulations were made in the jail manual.

One such suggestion is the segregation of women prisoners on the basis of their crime. Those held or convicted under Immoral Traffic (Prevention) Act, 1956 and those suffering from contagious or infectious diseases, including the dangerous HIV, are directed to be kept separately. Another categorisation based on the criminological and social assessment of the inmates is also recommended in the jail manual. But, in the State Jails for Women such a separation is not adhered to. Even convicts and undertials are allowed free interaction during the day. They are segregated only during lock-up time. It is necessary for the separation of women convicted for immoral sexual offences, since they are likely to influence young girls and other vulnerable women in the jails.

Further, the classification of the women prisoners, on the basis of age, nature of crime, type and length of sentence, etc., are not followed in the State jails for Women.

Three fourths of the women in jail are undertrials / remand prisoners. Most of them are poor and uneducated. They are ignorant of the bail provisions and legal aid facilities available for them. There is none to guide them. In some cases, the women prisoners couldn't move out of the jail as they didn't have the financial capacity to fulfil the bail conditions stipulated by the court.

Even when released on bail, the social stigma faced by the women are more disastrous than their life in jail. The societal acceptance of such women is rather difficult. If one is an unmarried lady, it will be very difficult to find a suitable groom. If she is a married lady, she is not accepted back by the in-laws. Her parents and children are the worst sufferers.

In case of a convict prisoner life is more miserable for she has to live with the stigma of 'jail bird'. When the sentence she served is long, she loses touch with her family. The husband in most cases acquires a new wife. Her children are either ill-treated or abandoned.

To avoid such tragic social consequences on women, bail should be offered liberally without sending them to judicial custody. The routine way of ordering the 14 day remand has to be abandoned by the Magistrates. Whenever a mother is sent to jail her minor children suffer. The Magistrates concerned should make needed enquiry regarding the children of the women and order suitable custody of those children depending upon the age of the children and the rules of the jail manual.

Probation, parole and other non-institutional modalities of corrective treatment shall widely be considered in the case of women offenders. There are not many habitual offenders in the jails for women. Most of them are first-time offenders and can be corrected very easily. So those women prisoners who pose no security risk may be transferred to open jails where work facilities related to their agricultural or other occupational background are available.

Special consideration can also be shown to women prisoners for their premature release in cases where the women prisoner is the sole bread winner or where no surrogate care is possible for older dependent parents or children. In a case of the prisoner who is pregnant even at the time of her entry into the jail, reduction or suspension of sentence can be considered as far as possible to avoid delivery in jail.

For those for whom confinement is an absolute necessity, there is no substitute for jail term. *But prison is not only a place for punishing them but also a place for reforming them.* Besides their reformation, adequate training and rehabilitation is a necessity.

The vocational training which is presently imparted to the women in jails is not of any serious rehabilitative value. The women prisoners are presently trained in sewing, envelope making, lace making, etc. These training programmes have no relevance to the social or occupational background of the convicts. Most of the convicted women are from agricultural families. The prisoners who are educated, though low in number, have no proper training facilities to suit their requirement.

It is necessary that the prisoner's social background is taken into consideration before assigning a training programme. New agricultural practices like vermi composting, organic farming can be started with the help of people from agriculture department of the Government or Agricultural University. The women inmates can be trained in gardening, lawn laying, horticulture, vegetable growing, etc. The training so provided should be employment-oriented. In other words, it should be directed towards the labour requirements of the market or lead to self-employment. Experts in rehabilitation programmes may be associated in the designing and implementation of the innovative training programmes for the prisoners.

Such training programmes may help the prisoners in the gainful utilisation of the skills and the experiences on their return to the society. A prisoner coming out of the prison should feel that she is now equipped to face the likely challenges in the society both for her honourable living and economic well-being.

The major and recurring worry of the women prisoners was found out to be their concern for their children. In recognition of the woman's responsibility of motherhood and to enable her to discharge that function, the criminal justice system, in an act of sagacity and empathy, has tried to accommodate the young children of the offending mothers in prison. However that concession is restricted to children up to the age of 5 years.

But in all the cases, the children below five years are not automatically allowed into the prison along with the convict mother. In such cases, the convict woman is forced to apply to the court for the admission of the child along with her. This invariably causes delay in the union of the mother and child. To avoid this undue hardship, the jail superintendents should be under a legal duty to allow the children below 5 years to stay with the mother in custody.

Beyond the fifth year children are transferred to the custody of a suitable person of the family and failing that the children are placed in the Government homes. This transfer of children is causing undue physical and emotional distance between the women prisoner and her child. In order to minimise the emotional hardships, the transfer of the child to a local facility may be considered from where visits and contact between the mother and child are made possible and encouraged.

There are other problems with older and other dependent children. Often in the absence of adequate surrogate care arrangements or due to the female prisoner being the sole earner such children face undue hardship.

An alternative to the prison terms should be thought of. Community service is a good alternative and it can be implemented. In this way, a woman offender is not cut off from society. Rather this system helps the woman in getting involved and getting integrated into the society. Her links with the community remain and that is an important factor in controlling the damaging effect of being confined to prison.

The post release phase is found to be a much more difficult period for the woman than the time spent in jail. She is not readily accepted by the family and society. She is rediculed for her criminal record. Sometimes, she is termed as dangerous. In the absence of skills and economic resources coupled with low esteem, life becomes miserable for her.

It is the time when the women require more support and it is here the Government is found wanting. There is no mechanism or machinery to trace the welfare of the former convicts. The government may consider some mechanism either directly or through non-governmental organisations to take care of the women who are released from jail.

Social Welfare Custody

Prostitution is a social malady which couldn't be curbed despite best intended legislations. Reformation rather than punishment should form the intention. One way of doing that is to arrest the women, involved in prostitution, under Immoral Traffic (Prevention) Act, 1956 and not under the Police Act, 1861. Once the arrest takes place under the I.T.(P) Act it becomes mandatory on the part of the Magistrate to hand over the girls to the custody of protective homes. Since it is the practice to book them under Police Act, the prostitutes are released on bail. The bail sureties are invariably the pimps. The brothal organisers double up as parents and receive the girl's custody only to force them to continue in profession.

Sections 13 and 17 of the IT(P) Act suggest useful mechanisms such as the creation of non-official Advisory Boards to advise police officers or a panel of social workers to assist the court in the discharge of its duties. These suggestions which are not implemented so far should be implemented at once.

The reformation of a prostitute is a long process and requires prolonged custodial stay. Sec. 10(A) of IT(P) Act permits a maximum detention of five years. To wean away the girls from prostitution and to equip them with some skills for self-sustenance during the five year custodial stay should be the normal practice. Since reformation of the prostitution is an investment in the improvement of social health, the Government should consider the opening of more rescue homes in different parts of the State. But in the State of Andhra Pradesh, there is no facility of rescue homes at the District headquarters. Only one rescue home has been established at the State capital, that too in a rented home without proper facilities. There is neither proper classification of the inmates nor segregation. The rescue home is not manned by a trained Superintendent. Medical facilities are meagre while psychiatric facilities are not available. Education programmes are also not properly provided. There is no meaningful and motivated programmes of earning. The expenditure alloted for the running of the home is fixed at the very old rate of Rs.3.30 per inmate per day and not revised as per the present cost. Legal aid and counselling on health which are essential are not given to the inmates. Recreation facilities are not in existence. No women group or N.G.O. is involved in playing a watch dog role. The security arrangements for the home are very poor. A single watchman is entrusted with the job of the security while police security is mandatory as per the law.

Mental Health Custody

The treatment of criminal lunatics is presently not fair and humane. They are treated more as criminals rather than lunatics, keeping them in isolation under the care of the jail staff who are untrained in attending to the needs of the mentally ill persons. The I.G. of Prisoners who is equally ignorant of the assessing process of mental status of a lunatic is vested with the overall charge of the lunatic prisoners. The mentally disturbed criminals need to be shifted to mental health centres and be kept under the care of psychiatrists.

Sec. 37 of the Mental Health Act provides for the appointment of visitors to the psychiatric hospitals and the committee of visitors should include two social workers. This Section needs to be amended so as to include at least one woman visitor. Further amendment is necessary to make the Board of visitors powerful to correct, on the spot, any neglect of treatment of the mentally ill-prisoners. The institutions must be made accountable for flouting the guidelines of the board.

The First Class Judicial Magistrate or Metropolitan Magistrate is vested with the power to curtail the liberty of a person and to decide the place of the custody. The criminal court has also jurisdiction to try the mental capacity of the accused vis à vis the offence alleged to have been committed and the ability to plead and answer the charge. An ordinary judicial officer without proper knowledge of psychiatry can't competently discharge his forensic responsibility in a technical field beyond his normal equipment. To assist the Magistrate in cases dealing with the mentally ill prisoners a psychiatric doctor should be designated. Law can't do it alone and medical questions can't be left to legal judges.

There are two mental health hospitals in the State of Andhra Pradesh, where the physical facilities at present are not satisfactory. The Government of Andhra Pradesh has taken up the modernisation of the mental health hospitals following the provisions of the Mental Health Act, 1987 and the directions of the Supreme Court.[8] A new building with modern facilities is coming up at Visakhapatnam, while the facilities are being strengthened at Hyderabad.

There are two women prisoners in the mental hospitals of the State. The main problem, as per the mental health specialists attending on them, is the absence of the family support to the victims which is a pre-requisite in any mental health treatment. The women under depression or mental derailment require understanding, constant companionship to note down the ups and downs of their moods. Such a support is not forthcoming from the family members and the State has no means and personnel to have a 24 hour attendance on them.

Mentally ill persons are disowned by the family. There are virtually no visitors for them. As a result, the institutes of mental health care became custodial institutions rather than therapeutic institutions. The State which has dumped them legally has forgotten the follow-up.

The undertrial prisoners, referred to the mental hospitals, should have been out on bail if they were neither given free legal aid nor their families supported them. Free legal services are virtually the right of the patient and an obligation of the State.[9] Justice through law has relevance to a mentally ill person only if a lawyer qualified in mental health jurisprudence is sent to the institutions. Such an arrangement which is not presently available may be made by the Government to aid the mentally ill-prisoners.

The problems of the mentally ill-prisoners must be identified and persons attending on them should be educated and sensitized in order to elicit their support and help in the inmates treatment. Families should be sensitized to accept the mentally ill-prisoners since their co-operation is a key element in the treatment. Familial ties through visits and even parole and furlough must be facilitated as part of the treatment.

The stigma coupled with 'mental' label makes the family to totally disown them. In one case in Hyderabad, though a lady was cured of mental illness, no relatives cared to take her out. Hence she is languishing in the mental hospital.

Counselling plays an important role and voluntary organisations should be encouraged to work among the mentally ill prisoners. The post-treatment rehabilitation of the mentally ill women is non-existent. The provisions intended to the other physically challenged persons may be extended to the mentally challenged persons and some rehabilitative steps may be initiated.

Testing of Hypotheses

This comprehensive study made through analytical and empirical methods clearly substantiates the following hypotheses formulated for the study.

1. The custodial justice to women suffers from the following drawbacks:

a) mode of arrest

b) absence of women in police force

c) lack of physical facilities in police stations

d) non-adherence to procedures by police

e) cruel treatment meted out

f) judicial apathy

g) non-implementation of recommendations made by various committees

h) delayed trials

i) absence of post release rehabilitative schemes

j) lack of concern for fallen women

k) ill maintained rescue homes and mental hospitals

2. The women suffered in custody due to the following reasons:

a) traditional bias against women

b) police highhandedness

c) non-observance of the prescribed procedure for arrest and production of women by the police

d) the routine manner of remanding of women by judicial officers

e) the ignorance, illiteracy, financial and social backwardness of the women arrestee

f) the absence of availability of free legal aid

g) lack of legal knowledge

3. The prisoners suffered even after their release in the absence of support both from their family and society. This will change only when prisoners are trained in semi-skilled or skilled jobs.

If the above drawbacks are removed by:

(a) increasing the women at various levels of police

(b) provision for separate lock-ups for women

(c) insisting on interrogation by women police

(d) liberal granting of bail

(e) fair and fast trial

(f) better education and training facilities for convict prisoners

(g) post release rehabilitation procedures through the NGOs, then safety and fairness for women while in custody can be ensured.

Findings of the Study

There are two State Jails for women in Andhra Pradesh and both have been visited by the researcher for the collection of information about the women in prison and to find out their experiences in the custody.

The State Jail for women at Rajahmundry has an authorised capacity of 200, while the State Jail for Women at Hyderabad can accommodate only 120. Whereas the number of women prisoners in Rajahmundry jail during the study period (May 2003) are only 130, in Hyderabad jail there are 189 prisoners as against 120 capacity. This clearly shows that there is overcrowding in Hyderabad jail resulting in inconvenience to the inmates.

The profiles of both the convict and undertrial women prisoners were collected.

Convicts: Out of the total 158 women convicts in the State of Andhra Pradesh 133 are illiterates who are not aware of the legal consequences of their acts as well as their rights as prisoners. Even among the literate women prisoners only 22% have reasonably average education while the rest of them just know only to read and write in the vernacular.

Among the women convicts 87.34% are Hindus, 10.75% Muslims and 1.89% Christians, and these percentages broadly represented the actual religious population percentages of India.

The social profile revealed that 46% of women convicts are from the Scheduled Castes (S.Cs.) and Scheduled Tribes (S.Ts.) who are considered most backward, economically and socially, in the Indian society. The percentage of S.Cs. and S.Ts. in prison is far higher than their actual population percentage of 15 and 6 respectively in the society. The social and economic backwardness of the S.Cs. and S.Ts. may be making them crime prone.

Nearly 61% of the women convicts are housewives without any specific job while 35% are manual labourers having seasonal employment. This may be taken as an indication that more women having no specific occupation are involved in crimes.

The data of the details of sentences reveal that about 65% women convicts had committed serious offences, i.e. offences punishable with imprisonment for 5 years and above. Most of the crimes relate to the internal family problems resulting in the murder of daughters-in-law (murder and dowry death u/Ss. 302 & 304-B). Similarly 22% of the convicts are in jail for harassing their daughters-in-law for dowry. On the whole, 87% of the convicts were involved in crimes relating to family disputes.

Undertrial Prisoners: About 83% of the undertrial women prisoners are illiterate and this nearly corresponds to 87% of illiterate convicts. Among the literate only 4% are reasonably educated i.e. graduates. The undertrial population has a very high percentage (93%) of Hindus, followed by 5% Muslim and 2% Christians. Hindu percentage in undertrials is higher and Muslim population is lower when compared to their actual percentage in Indian population.

The undertrial women representing 45% of forward castes, 34% of backward castes, 15% of S.Cs. and 6% of S.Ts. roughtly represents their proportion in the actual population of Andhra Pradesh. The occupational details of the undertrial women revealed that manual labourers formed 41% followed by 39% of housewives, and 12% are from the business community. It may be noted that a total of 36 undertrials (about 25%) are facing charges of murder, dowry death or attempt to murder and 33 are facing trial under section 498-A, which relates to the harassment of daughters-in-law by husband and relatives of husbands. This pattern conforms to the percentage of convicts for similar offences.

Police custody: The present study has revealed that most of the women were arrested at night, kept in illegal detention, and not produced before the Magistrate within the legally stipulated period of 24 hours. They were handled and interrogated by male police officers. The female police rarely interacted with the women in custody. The police custody is a feared custody, with rampant physical and mental abuse. Torture, threat to rape and use of vulgar language are quite common as stated by the women prisoners.

Judicial custody: The judicial officers who are supposed to enquire about the treatment meted out to the women in police custody, offer bail and provide free legal aid have failed in performing these duties as laid down in law. As a result, most women are in jail as undertrials, though the nature of the offence is not that serious. Their illiteracy, ignorance and economic conditions are the reasons for the denial of custodial justice to them. The court language and all the court papers being in English, the women prisoners concerned are ignorant of the whole process.

Prison custody: The prison custody is relatively safe custody. The prison conditions have improved. The video linkage of the jail and court in Andhra Pradesh has further enhanced the chances of women undertrials getting bail. The parole and furlough facilities are not utilised by the prisoners once again for the well established reason of illiteracy. The jail staff are insufficient to discharge all the necessary duties. Even the available staff have no inclination to educate the women prisoners on the latest position of custodial justice.

Social welfare custody: Social welfare custody suffered from the absence of physical facilities. There is only one rescue home for the entire State of Andhra Pradesh. A rented house is designated as a rescue home. There are no proper water supply and ventilation. There are no security arrangements for the house. There is no proper segregation of the inmates. Training and rehabilitation facilities are not provided. Educational facilities are absent while recreational facilities are not proper.

Mental health custody: The mentally ill-prisoners are lodged in mental health custody at Hyderabad and Visakhapatnam. At present, the conditions at Visakhapatnam are not satisfactory. The seriously ill-patients and mentally ill-prisoners are lodged in isolation in cells. The recovery of the inmates is very slow. Even those who have recovered are not received by their family members. So they are suffering in isolation. There are no training and rehabilitative facilities. The physical facilities are being improved at Visakhapatnam through the construction of a new building with modern facilities. The Government of Andhra Pradesh has no special rehabilitation package for the recovered mentally challenged persons.

SUGGESTIONS

The women are held under penal and non-penal custodies and each custodial place has a different environment and conditions which require some changes which are suggested hereunder. It should be noted that some of the suggestions are common to all types of custody, while some suggestions are specific to a specific custody. So the suggestions applicable to all types of custody are made first. These suggestions are in addition to the recommendations already made by the National Expert Committee and the National Commission for Women.

General Suggestions

1. Dishonour and harassment of women prisoners shall be treated as a serious offence.
2. At the time of admission into the custodial premises, the women must be made aware of their rights and duties.
3. The Custodial premises like the police stations, rescue homes and jails should have a secure and therapeutic environment.
4. An obligation should be imposed on the Magistrate to enquire and record a statement on the status of the children of the arrested women and to order the custody of the children below 5 years along with the mother.
5. Proper medical facilities and medical examination of the women inmates on admission and periodically thereafter are to be ensured through the appointment of qualified lady doctors and nurses on a visiting basis.
6. Women suffering from contagious diseases shall be placed in isolated care.
7. Expectant mothers in custody shall be shown special consideration by way of medical and nutritional care.
8. Lack of literacy and self-confidence are the bane of the women in custody. Education for the women in custody

be made compulsory and literate prisoners shall be encouraged to pursue further learning.

9. Women shall be imparted training which suits their qualifications and which makes them economically self-sufficient and capable of functioning independently in the society.

10. Marketability and independent earning potential should form the basis for training of the women in custody. Nursing, gardening, toy-making, fruit preservation, electronics related works may be considered besides the ongoing weaving, tailoring, stationery article making, etc.

11. Drawing, painting, music, etc., may be added to the recreation facilities in the custodial premises.

12. Since the inmates with children require special attention, a suitable order, keeping the interests of both the mother and child, be issued by the magistrate.

13. Even after the attainment of five years, the custodial management shall ensure that the mother-child link is not totally severed.

14. A grievance box may be provided in the custodial premises which shall be opened in the presence of a judicial Magistrate at least once a week and each complaint or request shall be registered and enquired into without delay.

15. Post release rehabilitation is a major challenge and it shall be tackled at once, engaging various government agencies and, if necessary, involving NGOs.

16. A Visitors Board, comprising members from a cross section of the society, be constituted to help improve the prison conditions.

17. Training and sensitization of custodial staff need to be carried out continuously.

18. Alternatives to custody may be thought of by the sociologists, jurists and executives, particularly in case of women offenders.
19. The visits of judicial officers to the custodial premises be made more frequent and more meaningful.
20. The students of legal study should be involved, as a practical legal work, in studying the custodial premises of their area so as to make them understand their obligation to the weaker sections of society.
21. The establishment of socio-legal counselling cells in all custodial institutions to aid the inmates should be considered.
22. Judicial camps can be conducted in the custodial institutions to help the women in getting speedy justice.
23. Legal aid camps shall be organised periodically to educate the inmates.
24. Custodial neglect, abuse or excess shall be dealt with with due severity by making the concerned person solely responsible for compensating the victim.
25. A separate treatise on the custody and treatment of women prisoners needs to be developed.

Police Custody

In addition to the instruction of the Government issued in 1983, the following suggestions are made through the present study.

1. Just as State Jails for Women are created in the State, the Government may consider the establishment of separate women police stations, manned exclusively by women police staff.
2. Where a separate women police station is not justified a separate police lock-up for women, with women police staff may be established in all existing police stations. The

lock-ups for women should ensure privacy. The entry of men in uniform should be restricted into the women enclosures of police stations.

3. Keeping in view the role of women in the family, the authorities may avoid detention of females involved in non-violent and minor offences.

4. Where arrest is warranted and no women police are available, women's submission to custody shall be presumed and handed over to women police staff at the shortest time possible.

5. No woman shall be arrested or remanded to custody without recording the special reasons for the arrest and/or custody. In the absence of any reasons or if the reasons are flimsy, the police officer should be taken to task.

6. Provision regarding bail should be liberalised and bail may be granted liberally to women even in non-bailable offences, unless special circumstances warrant a different course.

7. Basic amenities should be strengthened in the police stations. Those amenities should include separate bathing facilities, facility and privacy for changing clothes, etc., to the women detainees.

8. A lady doctor may be attached to the police station, on a visiting basis, for the referral and medical examination of the inmates.

9. Children should be allowed to stay with the mother in the lock-up in the absence of suitable care and custody for the children outside the police station.

10. To operate effectively, women police stations need to be fully equipped and independent in all operational aspects. The women police must be trained in the use of arms and in controlling violence.

11. During the interrogation, the legal counsel shall be allowed to stay within sight of the women in custody.

12. Facilities for legal assistance, consultancy, guidance and assistance should be given.
13. The Police Act, 1861, which guides all police actions is out moded and is not suited to the changed outlook of criminal justice system. So it has to be replaced or amended incorporating special duties of police force towards women and children.
14. All the custodial offences against women be made non-bailable and persons involved should be arrested immediately so as to prevent the destruction or fabrication of evidence or threatening of the witnesses.
15. The guidelines issued by the Supreme Court in various cases should be followed in letter and spirit while handling women.
16. In improving the performance of the police vis-à-vis the women, police training should include a special sensitization of the trainees towards the females. Gender issues should be included in the training curriculum. Besides the initial training, the police personnel should be sent to periodic refresher courses to deal with sensitive issues.

Judicial Custody

1. Judges should be trained on the new methodology of alternatives to sentences in prison.
2. Except in extreme situations when detention is desirable, the Magistrate shall release the women on her own bond.
3. No judicial remand of the women shall be allowed except into those institutions which are completely under the control of women officials.
4. The Judges and Magistrates require a thorough sensitization and orientation for a more scientific and humane handling of the judicial and legal procedure affecting women.

5. Overcrowding of custodial institutions could be remedied by speedy trials and the constitution of jail Adalats to dispose of simple cases.
6. Imposition of fines can be considered for minor offences, instead of detention.
7. Generally, the women will not make any attempt to escape and, even if they escape, they are not dangerous to society and it is easy to rearrest them. So the women accused can be released on bail liberally.
8. Women may be released on probation with supervision rather than imprisonment for short periods. Community service can be used as an alternative.
9. The judiciary should itself understand better the women offenders' responsibilities towards their dependent children and family and try to minimise the undue damage caused to them through judicial ambivalence.
10. Court procedures need to be simplified and understandable to even illiterate persons.
11. Special courts for women, just like women jails, with women judicial officers should be established.
12. Pre-trial detention and short term prison sentences should, wherever possible, be replaced by non-custodial alternatives.

Prison Custody

1. At least once a month, the female prisoners shall be allowed to go and meet their family members at their own cost.
2. The social welfare schemes of Government may also be linked with the needs of female offenders.
3. Meditations, yoga, etc., may be included in the correctional programmes for women prisoners.
4. Regular counselling and consultancy services are to be provided at least once a week and the treatment to get

away from their psychological or emotional disturbances through experts is to be continued.

5. Women remand prisoners should not be made to travel in the same vehicle along with male prisoners or male wardens.

6. The administration of the prisons be streamlined to ensure that the staff members are not overworked; simultaneously prison staff be made more accountable for their conduct towards the prisoners.

7. The administration of the prisons is a State subject under the Constitution and therefore different States have different laws. There is a need to move the subject of prisons and prisoners from the State list to the Concurrent list. This would enable finances to be provided from the Central Government particularly for the rehabilitation of prisoners, since several States have problems of funding their prisoners welfare programmes. In this context, it is desirable to draft a National Prison Policy.

8. The use of effective pre-release methods should be promoted.

9. The custody and treatment of the women prisoners should be dealt in a separate section or book of the Prison Manual of the State.

10. The classification of prisoners has to be examined afresh in terms of the threat posed to society.

11. Jail visiting committees comprising members of the judiciary, social workers, media personnel and legal academicians shall visit the jails more frequently to interact with the inmates and consider their grievances.

12. Prostitutes and brothel keepers who are likely to have a bad influence on other females, shall be kept separately.

13. Frequent visits by the children of the women prisoners to jails be encouraged as this will have a soothing effect on the minds of the women prisoners and in turn on the prison atmosphere.

14. Parole and other non-institutional modalities of corrective treatment shall be widely used in case of the women offenders.
15. Open jails may be preferred for lodging women convicts, who pose no security risk, where work facilities related to their agricultural or other occupational facilities are made available.
16. As far as possible, the delivery of expectant mothers in jail shall be avoided.

Social Welfare Custody

1. The physical and operational security of the existing home needs is to be strengthened.
2. The women protective homes and rehabilitation of the inmates should be under one jurisdiction and the officers should be women.
3. Separate courts with an activist magistracy with social qualms are to be established to bring speedy justice to the victim.
4. A separate procedure like interviews type of in-camera proceedings should be established. An obligation is to be imposed on the Magistrate to enquire about the way in which women become the victims of this evil, about the rescue home, etc. For doing this, the Magistrate must be sensitised and this job can be done better if the Magistrate is a lady.
5. Rescued girls must not be handed over to police custody. The court must remand the women to the State rescue homes only and not to prison.
6. Separate protective homes may be set up in all Districts, particularly in those areas where prostitution is more rampant.
7. Reform requires a longer custodial stay. The IT(P)A allows a maximum detention period of five years. So five years

stay must be made mandatory except where an earlier release will not prejudice the reformative process.

8. Homes should provide with sufficient accommodation and facilities for the treatment.
9. Medical facilities are to be provided in the homes.
10. Sexually transmitted diseases (STD) are a major source of trauma to those women. Most do not have recourse to any proper treatment. A statutory provision be enacted obliging the court to ensure that victims are examined and treated for STD and cleared before they are released on bail. The moment the woman is arrested, she should be examined by a medical practitioner.
11. It is commonly held that sureties are put up by pimps and brokers and other powerful groups exploiting women who move fast into the court and secure the release of the women, often pretending to be parents or relatives. To prevent this, bail should not be granted at any cost or it should be granted after establishing the true identity of the parents or husbands or women, if any.

Mental Health Custody

1. Normal persons suffering from mental stress, depression, etc., must not be detained in institutions meant for the seriously mentally disturbed. Day care centres and out-patient attention may be good substitutes.
2. Families of the mentally ill prisoners must be identified, educated and sensitized, in order to elicit their support and help in the inmates treatment.
3. Special Mental Health Tribunals should be set up which will also be obliged to visit all psychiatric hospitals and nursing homes-public and private-and those run under different labels like jails with wards for criminals and non-criminal lunatics.
4. Mentally disturbed women shall not be detained in prison.
5. Medical and custodial staff in mental houses and hospitals found negligent must be severely dealt with.

6. The supervisory staff should be personally made responsible for maintaining the medical standards.

References

1. 1991 CriLJ 187: AIR 1991 SC 207.
2. Ministry of Home Affairs through his letter No. 9/18/79 Judicial Cell, dated 10th and 14th March, 1980.
3. *Sheela Barse v. State of Maharashtra*, 1983 CriLJ 642: AIR 1983 SC 378: (1983) 2 SCC 96.
4. *State of Maharashtra v. C.C.W. Council of India*, 2004 CriLJ 14.
5. Report of National Expert Committee on Women Prisoners (1986-87) Vol. I, Para 81, p.119.
6. *Sheela Barse v. State of Maharashtra* AIR 1983 SC 378: 1983 CriLJ 642: (1983) 2 SCC 96.
7. *Ibid.*
8. *Rakesh Chand Narain v. State of Bihar* (1986) Scale 739 cited in Report of National Expert Committee on Women Prisoners (1986-87) Vol. II, p.55.
9. Articles 14, 19 and 21 together with Article 39A of the Indian Constitution.

APPENDIX

I. GENERAL OUTLINES ON PRISON CONDITION

Name of the Jail : ....

1. Capacity of prison/ward : ....
2. No. of detainees held : ....
3. How many are there in a cell? : ....
4. How clean is the cell? : ....
5. Whether medical facilities are available in the prison? : ....
6. Details of hospital staff :

   No. : ....

   Cadre : ....

   Residence : ....

   Timing : ....
7. General cleanliness of the prison : ....
8. Sanitary conditions type, method of cleaning : ....

II. PERSONAL DETAILS

1. Name of the jail : ....
2. Name of the criminal : ....
3. Criminal jail number : ....
4. Present age : ....
5. Native place : ....
6. Caste : OC / BC / SC / ST
7. Religion : Hindu / Muslim / Christian / Others
8. Mother tongue : ....
9. Occupation : ....
10. Marital status : Married / Unmarried / Divorced / Deserted / Separated / Widowed
11. Do you have children? : Yes / No
12. Educational qualification : Literate / Illiterate
13. Family particulars : ....
    a) Parental : ....
    b) Marital : ....

III. CRIME DETAILS

1. Name of the offence/Section : ....
2. Motive behind committing the offence : ....
3. Punishment term : ....
4. Date of entry into the jail : ....

5. Whether any rule of prison violated? : Yes / No

6. Any prison offence committed? : Yes / No

7. If yes, what is the punishment given : ....

IV. IN THE POLICE CUSTODY

1. At the time of arrest:

(a) Time & date of arrest : ....

(b) Mode of arrest : ....

(c) Who arrested you? : Men / Women police

(d) Have you signed arrest memo? : Yes / No

(e) Whether any one used force in arresting? : Yes / No
If yes, nature of force used?

(f) Are you informed of grounds of arrest? : Yes / No

(g) Whether your relatives are informed of your arrest? : Yes / No

(h) Were you searched after arrest? : Yes/No

(i) If yes, who searched you? : Male / Female police

(j) How was the search? : Decent / Indecent

2. In the police lock-up:

(a) Whether kept in separate female lock-up? : Yes/No
If not, where were you kept?

(b) Whether produced before court within 24 hours? : Yes/No
If not, for how many days illegally detained?

(c) What was the treatment given in lock-up? : ....

(d) Who interrogated you? : Male/Female officer

(e) Who guarded you? : Male/Female Constable

(f) Whether your relative was allowed into the premises of police station? : Yes/No

If yes, whether that relative is within your view : Yes/No

(g) Whether your male relative is allowed to accompany from court to police station? : Yes/No

(h) Were you subjected to medical examination? : Yes/No

(i) Whether there is a complaint-box in police station? : Yes/No

(j) Whether bail was offered by the police? : Yes/No

(k) Were you out on bail? : Yes/No
If not, reasons for not getting bail.

V. IN THE JUDICIAL CUSTODY

(a) Whether Magistrate enquired about police treatment in custody? : Yes / No

(b) Was an enquiry made regarding your children? : Yes / No

(c) Whether the Magistrate offered facility of medical check-up? : Yes / No

(d) Whether the Magistrate offered you bail? : Yes / No

(e) Whether legal-aid offer is made by Magistrate? : Yes / No

(f) Are you produced in the court at the end of each remand period? : Yes / No

VI. IN THE PRISON CUSTODY

1. Separation of female prisoners:

a) Is there a separate female wing in prison? : Ward / Building / Annexure

b) Whether convicted and unconvicted prisoners are kept separately? : Yes / No

c) Whether adolescents are kept separately from old prisoners? : Yes / No

d) Whether habitual female prisoners are separated from non-habitual prisoners? : Yes / No

e) Whether prostitutes and procuresses are kept separately from respectable women prisoners? : Yes / No

2. On admission:

a. Were you searched on admission into jail? : Yes / No

b. Whether you are searched by matron?
If not, by whom? : Yes / No

c. Whether search was by done under the orders of Medical Officer? : Yes / No

d. Whether list of articles seized are maintained? : Yes / No

e. List of articles retained : ....

f. Whether prisoner is deprived of any article? : ....

g. Reasons for depriving the article : ....

h. Period of depriving article : ....

i. Whether search is conducted with due regard to decency and privacy? : Yes / No

j. Whether search is conducted in the absence of other prisoners? : Yes / No

k. Are you washing yourself and your clothes? : Yes / No

l. Place of washing. : ....

m. Are you medically examined? : Yes / No

n. Whether any format was used for medical examination? : Yes / No

o. Whether entries such as age, height, weight, health and class of labour promptly made in the medical sheet? : Yes / No

p. Whether tested for T.B.? : Yes / No

If yes, whether the appropriate remedial steps are taken? : Yes / No

What are the steps? : ....

q. Whether there is follow-up with periodical checks? : Yes / No

3. Restrictions on female prisoners:

a. Whether the prisoner is allowed to leave enclosures? : Yes / No

If yes, for what reason : a) Release

b) Transfer

c) Attendance at court

d) Any other legitimate purpose

b. Whether Assistant Matron / Female Warden accompanied? : Yes / No

4. Restriction on female enclosure:

a. Whether any adult male prisoner was allowed into the ward? : Yes / No

If yes, mention the purpose : ....

b. Whether he is accompanied by the Assistant : Yes / No

Matron/female Warden?

c. Whether he is entering in night time? : Yes / No

If yes, give reasons : ....

d. Whether his entry is recorded with reason and time in report book? : Yes / No

e. Whether male wardens are staying outside the enclosure? : Yes / No

If no, for what purpose they are entering into the female enclosure? : ....

f. Whether the female enclosures are locked? : Yes / No

If yes, with whom are the keys kept? : a) Jailer

b) Assistant Matron

c) Any other person

5. Diet:

a. How many times meals are served in a day? : ....

b. What you eat in the main meals?

Main meal – I : ....

Main meal – II : ....

c. Do they provide anything for breakfast? : Yes / No

If yes, give details. : ....

d. Whether they provide any special diet on some occasions? : Yes / No

If yes, give details. : ....

Occasions	Food items
Festival	
Pregnant women	
Nursing mothers	
Sick persons	
Aged prisoners	

6. Clothing:

a. Whether clothing and bedding is provided? : Yes / No

If yes, list them in detail : ....

b. Whether extra clothing is supplied? : Yes / No

If yes, are they providing on the recommendation of the Medical Officer? : Yes / No

List them in the following:

Climate condition	
Sick person	
Aged person	
Inform person	
Any other reason	

c. Whether hospital clothing and bedding are supplied to the female prisoner on admission to the hospital? : Yes / No

If yes, list them in detail : ....

7. Personal hygiene, health, cleanliness:

a. Are they providing the following items?

a) Coconut oil (8 gms) : Yes / No

b) Soap nut (10 gms), twice a week : Yes / No

c) Comb : Yes / No

d) Looking glass : Yes / No

b. Are you suffering with vermin / dirt? : Yes / No

If yes, what precautions are taken by authorities? : ....

c. Whether hair is cut? : Yes / No

If yes,

a) is it with your consent? : ....

b) on advice of Medical Officer : ....

8. Amenities:

a. Are you married? : Yes / No

If yes, are you wearing bangles? : Yes / No

If no, give reasons : ....

b. If the bangles are broken; are they supplying? : Yes / No

If yes, with whose cost : a) Government

b) Self

c. Are you wearing red mark on forehead? : Yes / No

d. Are they supplying "*Kumkum*"? : Yes / No

If yes.

a) quantity : ....

b) with whose cost : a) Government b) Self

e. Are you wearing "*Mangalasutra*" and "Nose ring"? : Yes / No

If no, give reasons : ....

f. How do you handle your menses? : ....

g. Did you have any problems? : Yes / No

h. If you had any problems, what remedial measures were adopted? : ....

i. Is the Medical Officer giving any treatment for the problem? : Yes / No

j. Is the Assistant Matron maintaining a register for this purpose? : Yes / No

9. Sanitation:

a. What type of latrines? : Dry Latrines / Others

b. Is there practice of manual scavenging? : Yes / No

10. Education:

a. Are there any educational facilities? : Yes / No

b. Is there any elementary school? : Yes / No

c. Are you attending prisons school? : Yes / No

d. Is there any qualified teacher? : Yes / No

e. How many hours do you spend in learning? : ....

f. Are you supplied with slate-pencil or other writing materials? : Yes / No

If yes, who is meeting the expenses : a) Government b) Self

g. Is the prison having a library? : Yes / No

If yes, are they providing books, newspapers etc. : Yes / No

11. Recreations:

a. Do you have any free time? : Yes / No

If yes, how do you spend? : ....

b. Are you allowed any entertainment? : Yes / No
If yes, tick in the relevant box

Modes of Entertainment & Recreation	Accessibility (Yes/ No)	Frequency indicate whether regularly / some times / rarely / never
T.V.		
Radio		
Cinema		
Playing outdoor games		
Playing indoor games		
Others		

12. Vocational training/ Labour:

a. How are you employed? :

Type of Labour	Severity of Punishment
Hard	
Medium	
Light	

b. As you employed outside the female enclosure? : Yes / No

If yes, mention the nature of the employment: ....

If no, what is the nature of the employment inside the female enclosure. : ....

c. As a punishment, are you employed in any work like grinding or other type? : ....

If it is other type, explain the nature of work : ....

d. Are you undergoing any vocational training? : Yes/ No

If yes, give the nature of the training : ....

e. Do you think that this helps you after release? : Yes / No

If no, give reasons. : ....

f. Do you recommend any other vocational training which is useful particularly to female prisoners after release? : ....

g. Are you paid in cash or kind or no payment for the labour? : Cash / Kind / No payment

If paid in cash, how much are you able to earn in a month? : ....

h. What is the periodicity of payment? : Daily/Weekly/ Fortnightly/Monthly

i. How do you use your money? :..................................

j. Are you facing any problem at work? : Yes / No

Uncongenial working conditions	
Bias in relation to nature of work	
Sexual harassment	
Health hazard	
Others	

13. Female prisoners and their children:

a. Do you have children? : Yes / No

If yes, give details:

No. of Children	Sex	Age	Details

b. If the child is below 5 years of age, are you keeping the child with you in prison? : Yes / No

If no, why? : ....

If yes, are they providing sufficient diet? : Yes / No

Give details : ....

c. Are they providing clothing for children? : Yes / No

If yes, give details : ....

d. How frequently do you meet your children? : ....

e. How much time do you spend with them? : ....

f. Do you have any suggestion in this regard? : Yes / No

If yes, give your suggestions : ....

14. Release:

a. When any female prisoner is being released, are the jail authorities sending timely notice to her relatives / friends? : Yes / No

b. Are they sending them to their home along with the female warden in the absence of a relative? : Yes / No

c. Are they providing conveyances? : Yes / No

If yes, tick in the relevant box.

Exceeding 16 kms distance	
On health ground	
Customs	
For children	
Other valid reason	

15. Transfer:

a. Are they examined by the Medical Officer before they are transferred? : Yes / No

b. Are they providing conveyance? : Yes / No

If yes, tick in the relevant box.

Exceeding 1.6 kms distance	
On health ground	
Customs	
For children	
Other valid reason	

c. Whether a female warden accompanied her? : Yes / No

d. During transit, whether female prisoners are separated from male prisoners? : Yes / No

16. Safety measures:

a. What are the safety measures adopted in prisons? : ....

17. Interviews and communications with persons:

a. Are you free in writing letters/petitions? : Yes / No

If no, give reasons.

b. Are you allowed to meet your relatives/friends? : Yes / No

If yes, are you given reasonable facilities and privacy for communications? : Yes / No

c. Place of interview : ....

d. Time allowed for interview : a) Half an hour

b) Hour

c) Discretion of the Superintendent

d) Not so particular

18. For pregnant prisoners only:

a. Do you undergo regular checkups during the pregnancy? : Yes / No

If yes, how often? : ....

b. Health problems related to pregnancy, If any, give details : ....

c. Was there any specific reason for health problem? : Yes / No

If yes, what was the reason? : ....

d. What remedial measures did the Medical Officer adopt? : ....

e. Do you take any special diet during pregnancy? : Yes / No

If yes, what are the food items: : ....

19. Abuse / Atrocity:

Nature of abuse/ atrocity	Frequency (if the abuse/ atrocity is of repetitive nature)	By whom	Place	If a regular feature, indicate the period	If happens/ happened in the presence of others, who all are/ were present at the time of abuse/ atrocity	Extent of injury, if any
Severe beating						
Starving						
Burning						
Mental cruelty						
Molestation						
Attempted rape						
Rape						
Fetters / handcuffs						
Others (specify)						

20. If injured:

a) Natural treatment, if any? : ....

b) Prisoners reaction : ....

c) Reaction of fellow prisoners : ....

d) Reaction of other authorities : ....

e) How did you cope with the situation? : ....

f) Nature of support received : ....

g) Whether any action is taken by the authority? : Yes / No

If yes, give details. : ....

21. Visitors to jail:

a. Other than relatives / friends who visited you? : Yes / No

If yes, do you know who is coming? : ....

How frequently they are visiting? : ....

What is the purpose of their visit? : ....

*****

Bibliography

BOOKS

Advani, L.K., "Prisoners Scrap Book", Arnold Associates, New Delhi, 1978.

Anwarul Yaqin and Badar Anwar, "Protection of Women under the Law – An Annotated Bibliography", Deep and Deep Publications, New Delhi, 1982.

Awasthi, Dr., "Law of Bails and Remand", Ashoka Law House, New Delhi, 2002.

Bansal, B.L., "The Law Relating to Human Rights - The Protection of Human Rights Act, 1993", Capital Law House, Delhi, 2000.

Bhatnagar, J.P., "Law Relating to Women and their Rights", Revised Ejaz Ahmed, 2nd Ed., Ashoka Law House, New Delhi, 1998.

Bholeshwarnath, "Mental Health Act, 1987", Eastern Book Company, Lucknow, 1990.

Basu, D.D., "Criminal Procedure Code, 1973", Dum Dum Park, Calcutta, 1979.

Basu, N.D., "Basu's Code of Criminal Procedure", Ashok Law House, New Delhi, 2002.

Ian Brownlie and Guy, S., "Basic Documents on Human Rights", Indian Goodwin-Gill (eds.) Edn., Oxford, 2003.

Justice Palok Basu, "Law Relating to Protection of Human Rights under the Indian Constitution and Allied Laws", Modern Law Publications, Allahabad, 2002.

Kathuria, R.P., "Law of Crimes and Criminology", Vinod Publications Pvt. Ltd., Delhi, 2001.

Kelkar, R.V. , "Outlines of Criminal Procedure", Eastern Book Company, Lucknow, 1984.

Kuldip Nair , "Judgement", Vikas Publishing House Pvt. Ltd., New Delhi, 1977.

Leelamma Devasia, "Female Criminals and Female Victims : An V.V. Devania (eds.) Indian Perspective", Dattsons Publications, Nagpur.

Nagla, B.K., "Women, Crime and Law", Rawat Publications, New Delhi, 1991.

Pillai, P.S.A. , "Criminal Law", Butterworths, New Delhi, 2000.

Rani, M.B., "Female Criminality – An Empirical Study in Andhra Pradesh", Eastern Book Company, Lucknow, 1987.

Sarkar, S.C. , "Sarkar on Criminal Procedure", Indian Law House, New Delhi, 2004.

Tripathi, S.C. and Vibha Arora, "Law Relating to Women and Children", Central Law Publications, Allahabad, 2004.

Vimal Balasubrahmanyan, "In Search of Justice", Women, Law, Landmark Judgements and Media, Shubhada Saraswat Prakashan, Pune, 1990.

2. ARTICLES

Bharathchandra, A Brief Note on "Status of Women Prisoners in Andhra Pradesh", Principal Secretary, Home Department, Government of Andhra Pradesh.

Ahmed, M.R., "Community Service, a new initiative in Penal Reform", D.I.G. of Prisons, Government of Andhra Pradesh.

S.R. Sukumara, I.P.S., "New Initiatives in Penal Reform – Andhra Pradesh", D.G. of Prisons and Correctional Services, Government of Andhra Pradesh, Hyderabad.

Sita Ram Singh. "Human Rights and Policing in India", 1997, Criminal Law Journal, pp.125-128.

3. ACTS

The Constitution of India, 1950.

The Indian Penal Code, 1860.

The Indian Evidence Act, 1872.

The Prisons Act, 1894.

The Prisoners Act, 1900.

The Identification of Prisoners Act, 1920.

The Transfer of Prisoners Act, 1950.

The Prisoners (Attendance in Courts) Act, 1955.

Immoral Traffic (Prevention) Act, 1956.

The Probation of Offenders Act, 1958.

The Code of Criminal Procedure, 1973.

The Criminal Law (Amendment) Act, 1983

The Mental Health Act, 1987.

The Juvenile Justice (Care and Protection of Children) Act, 2000.

Andhra Pradesh Prison Development Board Act, 2001.

The Code of Criminal Procedure (Andhra Pradesh Amendment) Act, 2001.

4. RULES

Andhra Pradesh Prisons Rules, 1979.

5. BILLS

The Prison Administration and Treatment of Prisoners Bill, 1998.

The Indian Prisoners Bill, 1996.

The Prison Management Bill, 1998.

6. REPORTS

Report of All India Jails Reform Committee (1980-83).

Report of Law Commission of India on "Rape and Allied Offences": (Some Questions of Substantive Law, Procedure and Evidence), 84th Report, 1980.

Report of National Expert Committee on Women Prisoners, Vol. I, 1986-87.

Report of National Expert Committee on Women Prisoners, Vol. II, 1986-87.

Report of Law Commission of India on "Women in Custody", 135th Report, 1989.

Report of National Commission for Women on "Custodial Justice for Women", Seminar held in 1993.

Report of National Commission for Women on Second Orientation Course on "Custodial Justice for Women and Children", Conference held in 1994.

Annual Report of National Human Rights Commission, 1997-98.

Annual Report of National Human Rights Commission, 1998-99.

Report of National Commission for Women on "Women in Detention", Seminar held in 2001.

7. LETTERS

Ministry of Home Affairs through Letter No. 9-18-1979, Judicial Cell, dated 10th & 14th March, 1980.

8. MANUALS

Human Rights and Law Enforcement, A Manual on the Human Rights Training for the Police, Series No.5, U.N. 1997.

Women Development and Child Welfare, Department Manual – WD & CD 082, Dr. M.C.R. Human Resource Development Institute of Andhra Pradesh.

9. GOVERNMENT ORDERS (G.Os.)

G.O. Ms. No. 132, Home (Prisons) Department, dated 20-2-1984.

G.O. Ms. No.38, Education (Prog.I) Department, dated 16-4-2002.

Index

❑❑❑